24.95

DATE			

BINDING TORN 3/23/02
KM

© THE BAKER & TAYLOR CO.

International Affairs
1890–1939

At the end of the nineteenth century the European great powers dominated world affairs. The clearest expression of this remarkable fact is the extent of their overseas possessions. The British Empire alone included one quarter of the world's land surface and population, that of France one eighth, while Germany, Portugal, Holland and Belgium were also important colonial powers. A few thousand British officials ruled the entire subcontinent of India, along with its 300 million inhabitants. Even the phrase 'the civilised world' meant Europe and those countries which had inherited European values and customs.

When in 1914, and again in 1939, the mutual antagonisms of the European nation states erupted into explosions of violence which eventually engulfed every major state, no part of the world was to escape some involvement in the wars. The problems caused by the First World War, the collapse of four great empires – the Russian, Turkish, Austro-Hungarian, and the German – during it, and the emergence afterwards in a number of countries of totalitarian governments which regarded war as an extension of diplomacy rather than the result of its failure, provide a backcloth to the events which led to the outbreak of the Second World War. This ensured that Europe's supremacy, which at the beginning of the period covered by this volume was about to be challenged by Japan and the United States of America, would not long survive it.

HM

HOLMES & MEIER PUBLISHERS, INC.
NEW YORK

International Affairs
1890–1939

R N RUNDLE

The cover illustration, from a painting of Lenin addressing the Second All-Russian Congress of Soviets, is reproduced by courtesy of the Society for Cultural Relations with the USSR.

First published in the United States of America 1979 by
HOLMES & MEIER PUBLISHERS, INC.
30 Irving Place, New York, N.Y. 10003

Library of Congress Cataloging in Publication Data

Rundle, Raymond Norman.
    International affairs, 1890–1939.
    Includes index.
    1. World politics – 19th century. 2. World politics –
1900–1945. 3. Europe – Politics and government –
1871–1918. 4. Europe – Politics and government –
1918–1945.
    I. Title.
    D397.R78   1979   327'.09'04   79–12170
R00462 08428
ISBN 0–8419–0516–9 Hardback
ISBN 0–8419–0601–7 Paperback

PRINTED IN GREAT BRITAIN

Acknowledgements
The author and publishers wish to thank the following for granting permission to include copyright material in this book: Prentice-Hall, Inc., for an extract from *Why Hitler Came Into Power* by Theodore Abel; Oxford University Press for two passages from *The German Delegation at the Paris Peace Conference* (1941) by Alma Luckau; Eyre & Spottiswoode (Publishers) Ltd, for an extract from *Life of Mussolini* by Margherita G. Sarfatti (translated by Frederic Whyte and originally published by Thornton and Butterworth); William Heinemann Ltd for a short extract from *Through Two Decades* by Theodor Wolff; Hutchinson and Company for a passage from *An Ambassador's Memoirs* by Maurice Paleologue (translated by F. A. Holt); HMSO for two extracts from *Report of the Royal Commission on Palestine,* Cmd. 5479 (1937).

Thanks are also due to the following for permission to reproduce the illustrations in this book: the Radio Times Hulton Picture Library, pages 3, 4, 10, 15, 17, 43, 44, 58, 59, 61, 65, 68, 71, 74, 84, 87, 96, 112, 113, 116, 123, 127, 133, 145, 153, 154; Mary Evans Picture Library, pages 7, 78, 150; Popperfoto, pages 21, 83, 95, 101, 122; The Illustrated London News, pages 9, 14, 26, 31, 92, 102; the Imperial War Museum, title-page and page 39; Anne Horton, page 151; Sovfoto, New York, page 105; Culver Pictures Inc., New York, page 138; Ford Archives, Henry Ford Museum, Dearborn, Michigan, page 143.

CONTENTS

MAPS

PROLOGUE:
Germany's Ascendancy in Europe

The creation of the German Empire in 1871, after Prussia's victories over Austria (1866), and France (1870–1), had a decisive influence upon European history. The collection of states, for whose leadership Austria and Prussia had competed, was transformed into a German Empire dominated by Prussia, from which Austria was excluded. After 1871 Germany was no longer a geographical term, but a great military power which overshadowed Europe until its defeat in 1918. Unfortunately for the peace of Europe, the French did not forget their national humiliation by Prussia, nor did they become reconciled to the surrender of two French provinces, Alsace and Lorraine. Consequently Bismarck, Chancellor of Germany from 1871 to 1890, had no choice but to keep France isolated, lest the French government should try to recover the 'lost provinces' by a war of revenge.

Bismarck had not demanded any Austrian territory in 1866. Firstly, he had no wish to drive Austria into an alliance with France. Secondly, he anticipated the need to cultivate its friendship. Germany's goodwill was welcomed by the Austrian government, which was having difficulty in preventing the break-up of the empire, as it contained many different nationalities, who wanted to rule themselves. In 1867 the Habsburg Emperor Franz Josef, who reigned from 1848 to 1916, granted the Magyars (Hungarians) equal status with the Austrians, in order to win their support against Slav nationalism. Austria became Austria-Hungary, or the Dual Monarchy, since Franz Josef became King of Hungary as well as Emperor of Austria.

Bismarck's prudent policy of seeking to reconcile Austria-Hungary with Germany soon paid dividends. Austria-Hungary did not take sides in the Franco-Prussian War, whereby the unification of Germany was accomplished. Soon afterwards, in 1873, Bismarck formed the League of Three Emperors, or *Dreikaiserbund*, when he persuaded the three emperors of Germany, Austria-Hungary, and Russia to cooperate with each other in checking the spread of socialism in their lands. When the *Dreikaiserbund* broke up as a result of the quarrels between Austria-Hungary and Russia for territorial influence in the Balkans (see Chapter 3), Bismarck chose Austria-Hungary to be Germany's ally. The Dual Alliance of Germany and Austria-Hungary, signed in 1879, was a prominent feature of European diplomacy until it collapsed at the end of the First World War. Germany and Austria-Hungary became known as the Central Powers, because they were situated in the middle of Europe.

In 1882 the Dual Alliance became the Triple Alliance when it was joined by Italy. The Italians felt cheated in 1881 when the French occupied Tunisia, which had long been coveted by Italy. Bismarck exploited the opportunity to deprive France of a possible ally by persuading Italy to make an alliance with Germany and Austria-Hungary.

Bismarck achieved his most brilliant success in foreign affairs when the Reinsurance Treaty was signed in 1887, making Germany and Russia allies. Since Britain was not on friendly terms with France the latter was completely isolated, and, lacking an ally, powerless to undertake a war against Germany. This apparent stability in Europe, however, was soon to be disturbed by a change in the direction of Germany's foreign policy.

Miles
0   200   400
0   400
Kms

- Triple Alliance
- Dual Alliance
- Alsace-Lorraine
- Ottoman Empire

1   *Europe in 1894*

Germany's 'New Course'

In March 1888 the 91-year-old German Emperor, William I, died. He was succeeded by his son, Frederick II, who was dying of cancer of the throat. Frederick reigned for only three months. His son, William II (1888–1918), the last of the Hohenzollern emperors and the eldest grandson of Queen Victoria, was a brilliant talker, charming, impulsive, intelligent, and unstable. His admiration for Britain was tinged with envy of her empire and power. Often unfairly criticised for

indulging in personal rule, and for helping to bring about the war in 1914, he was nevertheless largely responsible for promoting the growth of the German navy, which embittered Anglo-German relations. In 1890 the clash of personalities between the aged Chancellor and the young Kaiser was resolved by Bismarck's resignation.

William II refused to renew the Reinsurance Treaty, whereby Bismarck had contrived to maintain close relations between Germany and Russia, despite his own clear preference for supporting Austria-Hungary in Balkan affairs. Under the terms of the Reinsurance Treaty

Bismarck, the Iron Chancellor, in the Reichstag, surrounded by deputies

Bismarck assured Russia that it had nothing to fear from Germany unless Russia attacked Austria-Hungary first, but the Russian government was unconvinced and its military preparations remained directed against the Dual Alliance. William's decision in 1890 to rely on Germany's alliance with Austria-Hungary, the so-called 'New Course', merely confirmed what the Russian Foreign Office had long believed – that the Russo-German alliance would not long survive Bismarck's departure from office.

These developments had not passed unnoticed by the French government. As a gesture of friendship, the French loaned Russia large sums of money to enable work to begin on the Trans-Siberian Railway in 1892. Military talks between the two countries in 1890 were followed by a courtesy visit of the French fleet to Kronstadt in 1891. A Russian squadron returned the compliment by visiting Cherbourg and Toulon. In 1893 Tsar Alexander II overcame his distaste for a republican form of government, and agreed to a trade treaty between Russia and France. This was immediately followed by a secret treaty of alliance, whose existence was not made public until 1897.

France therefore escaped from a long period of enforced isolation. Nevertheless, it was Britain, not Germany, which was chiefly affected by the Franco-Russian alliance, since Britain's interests in various parts of the world clashed with those of France and Russia. This was especially so in the Far East, where trade rivalries had intensified over the past decade.

The Far East in the nineteenth century

China, with over 3½ million square miles of territory, comprises one-fourteenth of the earth's land surface. Only Russia and Canada are larger. In the nineteenth century, however, China was an unwilling victim of western imperialism, as the European powers, by means of war and diplomacy, exploited China's weakness. By the Treaty of Nanking (1842), which ended the Opium War between China and Britain, Hong Kong became a British possession, and five Chinese ports were opened to foreign merchants. After the second war between Britain and China (1856–60), British merchants extended their privileged position in China.

During the last quarter of the nineteenth century there was a real danger that the Chinese empire, like the continent of Africa, would be carved into European spheres of influence. Already, by 1860, Russia had taken control of a large area of territory on the north bank of the Amur river, where the town of Vladivostok was founded, close to the Korean border. During the 1880s the French seized control of much of Indochina. Britain annexed Burma in 1886, while Nepal and Tibet freed themselves from China's control in all but name only. Russia and Japan were also busy developing their claims to Manchuria and Korea.

Hong Kong Harbour in 1860

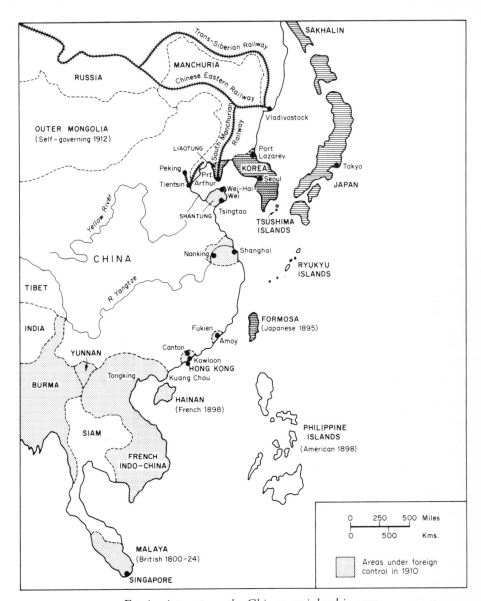

2   *Foreign interests on the Chinese mainland in 1910*

The Chinese resented the forced introduction of Christianity into their country, the exemptions from Chinese laws which foreigners enjoyed, the restrictions placed upon their government (such as its inability to increase customs duties without permission), and the treaty port system, but were unable to resist. They had deliberately rejected the technology which had revolutionised the western world, and were paying the price. Cumbersome sailing junks were no match for ironclad,

steam-driven warships. Poorly armed conscripts could never be the equals of well-organised European forces, equipped with breech-loading rifles and artillery.

Japan, on the other hand, so long the inferior power to China, copied western technology and methods. A parliamentary system based upon the German model was introduced in 1889. Feudalism was abolished. A national army was created, and a modern navy developed. German and British military experts were appointed as advisers. Factories, dock-yards, and arsenals were built. Trade with foreign countries was encouraged. In the forty years following the visit of Commodore Perry's squadron of American warships in 1853, Japan was transformed into a modern industrial nation. In 1894 she was about to join the ranks of the great powers.

The Sino-Japanese War, 1894–5

By 1890 Japan controlled 90 per cent of Korea's trade, so that the Chinese and Russian attempts to extend their influence in Korea were most unwelcome to the Japanese government. After 1885 China tried to reassert its authority over the vassal kingdom of Korea, whose possession by a foreign power would threaten Peking. Li Hung Chang, China's chief minister, modernised the Korean army and navy, and built a railway from Tientsin to the Kaiping coalfield, which was completed in 1889. Russia's intention to extend the planned Trans-Siberian Railway to Port Lazarev, on Korea's east coast, only hastened the outbreak of war, since Japan was anxious to control Korea before Russia became any stronger.

The immediate excuse for the Sino-Japanese War, however, was the Tonghak rebellion. Tonghak, which may be translated as 'Eastern Learning', was a popular religion founded in 1860 by a Korean scholar, Ch'oe Che-u, which grew into a strongly anti-foreign movement. In 1894 Tonghak rebels seized Seoul, the Korean capital.

Under the terms of the 1885 Tientsin Convention both China and Japan had the right to send troops into Korea for the purpose of maintaining law and order. When the Korean government requested China's help in sup-pressing the rebellion, Li Hung Chang responded by sending 2,000 troops. The Japanese government sent a much larger force, and was clearly more intent upon strengthening its influence in Korea's affairs than on dealing with the rebellion, which had been crushed before the Japanese arrived.

War broke out when China refused to cooperate with Japan over introducing reforms in Korea. Japanese forces seized Formosa, and invaded Manchuria, capturing Port Arthur. In April 1895 China agreed to the peace treaty of Shimonoseki.

The great powers had already said that they would not allow Japan to keep Korea. China was forced to recognise its independence, however, and to surrender Formosa and the Liaotung peninsula to Japan. In addition, China paid a heavy fine, and opened four more ports to foreign trade. Unfortunately for the Chinese, the consequences of defeat did not end with the peace terms. The great powers demanded leases of territory and trading rights, which China was soon forced to concede.

The 'Scramble for Concessions'

The European countries had not welcomed the Japanese victory. Russia, supported by France and Germany, forced Japan to return to China the newly won Liaotung peninsula in May 1895. In 1896, however, China paid the price for Russia's diplomatic support when Russia demanded and obtained permission to build the Chinese Eastern Railway across northern Manchuria, thereby shortening the route of the planned Trans-Siberian Railway by several hundred miles. In 1897 the murder of two German missionaries gave Germany an excuse for demanding a 99-year lease of Kiaochow, and permission to build two railways in the Shantung peninsula.

Germany's success in extracting territory from China provoked a scramble among the other great powers to seek compensation, in order to 'restore the disturbed balance of power'. In March 1898 Russia took possession of Port Arthur. Moreover, China agreed that it could be linked by railway with the projected Chinese Eastern Railway. (The Japanese were naturally infuriated.) Britain acquired Wei-hai-wei in order to neutralise Russia's new naval base at Port Arthur, Kowloon on the Chinese mainland opposite

Hong Kong, and recognition that the Yangtze Valley was a British sphere of influence.

The Japanese obtained rights in Fukien province. China leased Kuang Chou Bay to France, and agreed that Tongking and Yunnan province were French spheres of influence. China, on the verge of partition by the great powers, was only saved by their mutual rivalries, and by the diplomatic intervention of the United States of America.

The United States had no desire to obtain Chinese territory, but American businessmen were worried by the recent developments in the Far East, which might restrict their access to the Chinese market. In 1900 America proclaimed an 'Open Door' policy, whereby the great powers would trade freely with China, but would refrain from seizing further territory. This idea was welcomed by Britain, which had come to the brink of war with France over the Sudan in 1898, and was struggling to recover from humiliating defeats in the early stages of the Boer War (1899–1902) (see Chapter 2). Britain joined Germany in persuading Japan and Russia that there should be an end to the partition of China.

The Hundred Days reform movement, 1898

China's defeat strengthened those Chinese who had been urging the government to introduce economic and administrative reforms. The Court was unwillingly and briefly won over to their views. In the hundred days from 10 June to 20 September there was a flurry of reforming activity. The practical results, however, were negligible, since the court officials, whose cooperation was needed to carry out the reforms, insisted that they should be justified by references from the Chinese Classics.

The Boxer Rising, 1900

Foreign interference provoked a violent outburst of nationalism. It was inspired by the *I-ho-ch'uan*, the Society of Righteous and Harmonious Fists, whose members practised a form of unarmed combat. Formed originally during the Taiping Civil War (1851–64), the Boxers, as they were called in the West, were anti-foreign and anti-Christian. The movement was strongest in Shantung, where the German occupation had aroused fierce resentment.

Boxer rebels being executed at Pao-Ting-Fou

The Boxers, encouraged by the Chinese government, attacked foreign consulates in Peking. A European relief force was driven back to Tientsin. A more powerful expedition was hurriedly despatched from Western Europe, with instructions from the German Kaiser to 'act like Huns of old' in suppressing the disturbances. It captured Peking, and the revolt against western influence collapsed.

The Chinese were forced to accept humiliating terms. The forts on the approaches to the capital were dismantled. Garrisons were established on Chinese territory to protect European interests, and China agreed to pay compensation for damage done to foreign property.

The Anglo-Japanese Alliance, 1902

Both Japan and Britain feared Russia's power in the Far East. During the Boxer Rising Nicholas II sent troops into Manchuria, and afterwards showed no sign that he was prepared to withdraw them completely. Japan wished to halt Russia's advance before the Trans-Siberian Railway was completed, but was reluctant to risk war so long as there was a possibility that France, Russia's ally, would come to her aid. The British government was worried in case Japan and Russia should reach an agreement, which would leave Britain isolated in the Far East.

With the growth of international tension towards the end of the nineteenth century, 'Splendid Isolation' was no longer attractive to the British government, which wanted to be on more friendly terms with other countries, particularly when all the European powers belonged to military alliances. Britain's disagreements with France and Russia would take time to resolve, although it is important to realise that none of the difficulties were insurmountable, and that in each country among sections of the ruling classes there was a strong desire to reach an understanding with Britain. Joseph Chamberlain, the Colonial Secretary, therefore tried to form an Anglo-Saxon alliance of Britain, Germany, and the United States in 1899. When this plan failed, an alliance with Japan seemed the easiest solution to Britain's problems.

British public opinion had been impressed by Japan's conduct of the war against China, and admiration had soon developed into a desire for an alliance, which would check Russian ambitions in the Far East. Japan was well-disposed towards Britain, which had taken no part with the other powers in forcing Japan to evacuate the Liaotung peninsula in 1895.

Moreover, there were some similarities between the two countries. Both were island nations, depending upon the strength of their navies for security. Both were adjacent to a continent, in which they were interested in maintaining a balance of power. Just as Britain was ready to go to war in 1914 to defend Belgium's neutrality, so Japan regarded Korea in the possession of a great power as a 'dagger pointed at the heart of Japan'.

Negotiations for an alliance were completed in January 1902. Britain acknowledged Japan's special position in Korea, and each country recognised the other's interests in China. In the event of either becoming involved in a Far Eastern war with a third power, the other would observe a policy of benevolent neutrality. If either should become involved in a war with two or more powers in that region, the other was bound to come to its aid.

This alliance marked Britain's emergence from 'Splendid Isolation', and emphasised Japan's status as a great power. Britain hoped that it would stabilise the Far Eastern situation without increasing her commitments in that part of the world. Undoubtedly, however, Japan gained the greatest benefit from the alliance, since the British navy would deter any country from intervening in a Far East war. Japan was now free either to negotiate an agreement with Russia from a position of strength, or to put her territorial claims to the test of war.

The Russo-Japanese War, 1904–5

When it became clear that the Russian troops would not be withdrawn from Manchuria, the Japanese government adopted a warlike attitude. It demanded that Russia should recognise Japan's exclusive interests in Korea by promising not to interfere in that country's affairs, but it was not prepared to grant similar

The last naval hope of Russia: the Baltic fleet prepares to sail from Kronstadt

recognition to Russia's interests in Manchuria. An agreement was clearly impossible, and both sides made ready for war.

In February 1904 the Japanese navy attacked and destroyed a Russian fleet at Port Arthur. Japanese armies seized the Liaotung peninsula, and invaded southern Manchuria, where a Russian army was decisively defeated in the two-week battle of Mukden. Russia's cause was hopeless after the battle of Tsushima Straits, in May 1905, when the Japanese navy, commanded by Admiral Tojo, annihilated Russia's Baltic fleet, which had sailed half-way round the world in a vain effort to reverse the course of the war.

The Treaty of Portsmouth (USA), 1905

Russia surrendered the southern half of Sakhalin island, transferred to Japan her lease of the Liaotung peninsula, together with the southern branch of the Chinese Eastern Railway, and recognised Japan's paramount position in Korea. Japan's victory confirmed her supremacy in the Far East, and strengthened her influence on the Chinese mainland, for Korea's nominal independence did not last long. In 1907 Japan assumed control over its internal affairs, and in 1910 proclaimed the annexation of Korea.

Events in the Far East proved that the European powers could avoid war with each other and, on occasion, cooperate over colonial problems. In Africa, however, where the colonial powers jostled each other in their bids for what little territory lay unclaimed, there was less room for manoeuvre, and the colonial ambitions of Britain and France led to a crisis over Fashoda in 1898.

Egypt and the Sudan

Anglo-French rivalry was particularly acute over Egypt and the Sudan. French interest in Egypt went back to the time of Napoleon Bonaparte, and the Suez Canal, opened in 1869, had been built by French engineers. Egypt, however, was of great importance to Britain, for the Suez Canal offered the shortest route to India, the jewel of the British Empire. Britain hoped that Egypt would remain under Turkey's nominal control, but by 1875 the Khedive's chronic misrule had reduced the country to the verge of bankruptcy. Egypt's financial difficulties were not even solved when Disraeli, on behalf of the British government, purchased the Khedive's share ($\frac{7}{16}$) of the Suez Canal stock, whereby Britain became the largest shareholder in the Suez Canal Company. In 1876 the Khedive's government went bankrupt, and Britain and France jointly agreed in 1878 to supervise Egypt's affairs, in order to protect their investments in the Suez Canal.

Egyptian resentment against foreign interference led to a nationalist revolt in 1882. When the French declined to cooperate with the British government in restoring order, the system of Dual Control came to an end, and Britain found itself solely responsible for

The battle of Omdurman: the Mahdi's forces advancing to the attack

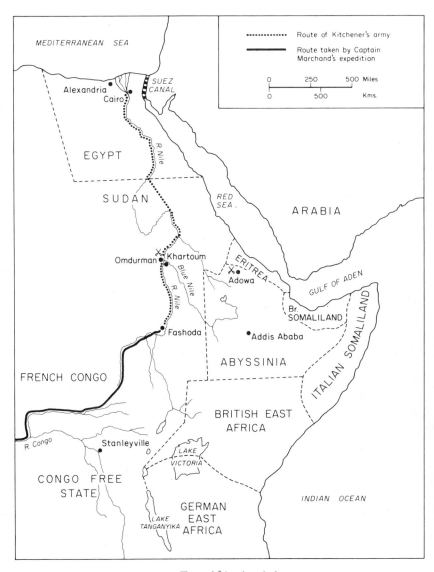

3   *East Africa in 1898*

governing Egypt. Britain intended at first to form a stable administration, whereby Egypt might remain part of the Turkish Empire. But Turkey's weakness, and the development of the Franco-Russian alliance, which threatened the balance of naval power in the Mediterranean Sea, persuaded the British to stay in Egypt.

The French bitterly regretted their exclusion from Egypt, for which they had only them-selves to blame. They argued that Egypt and the Sudan were either under Turkish suzerainty, in which case Britain had no right to them, or 'ownerless', in which case the French had as much right as the British to be there. The logic was indisputable, and both the French and the British realised that the problem could only be resolved by right of possession.

The French sought to establish a protectorate over the disputed Upper Nile region as part of a plan to secure a continuous block of territory stretching from the Atlantic to the Red Sea.

Such a scheme, if successful, would have seriously embarrassed the British in Egypt.

In 1896 a French expedition commanded by Captain Marchand was sent overland from central Africa to claim possession of the Upper Nile. At the same time, in order to frustrate the French plans, a British army under General Kitchener was sent to reconquer the Sudan. In 1898 Kitchener defeated the Sudanese nationalists at the battle of Omdurman. Obeying his secret instructions, Kitchener advanced to Fashoda, where he met the small French force which had arrived a few days earlier, and had claimed the Sudan on behalf of the French government.

Kitchener and Marchand avoided a confrontation which would have caused war between their two countries. Eventually, Delcassé, the French Foreign Minister, gave way, realising that France was powerless to obstruct the British in the Sudan. In March 1899 the French government agreed to surrender its claim to the Nile valley. The Fashoda crisis was the first severe test for Britain's policy of 'Splendid Isolation'. It was soon to be followed by another of even greater dimensions.

The Boer republics

In the 1830s and 1840s the Boers, farmers of Dutch origin, trekked out of the British territories of Cape Colony and Natal, and founded two republics, which they called Transvaal and Orange Free State. The British acknowledged the Boers' right to manage their own affairs by granting independence to the Transvaal in 1852, and to the Orange Free State in 1854.

By 1877 the Transvaal was almost bankrupt and in danger of being overrun by the Zulus. The British tried to prevent an African uprising, which they feared might spread to Cape Colony, by taking the Transvaal under their protection. They promised the Boers self-

government as soon as the danger had passed. But after the Zulu rising had been crushed at Ulundi the British did not keep their promise, and the Boers, who no longer needed protection, proclaimed their independence in 1880. In the brief war which followed, the Boers defeated a tiny British force at the battle of Majuba Hill in 1881, when the British government, despite the loss of prestige, gave the Transvaal its independence by the Convention of Pretoria.

In 1886 the discovery of gold on the Witwatersrand resulted in a gold rush to the Transvaal. Foreigners *(uitlanders)*, including many British, soon outnumbered the Boer population. The newcomers were disliked by the Boers, who feared that they would threaten their independence. The *uitlanders* were heavily taxed, and were denied the right to vote.

In order to strengthen his country's economy, Kruger, President of the Transvaal, decided to build a railway from Johannesburg, through non-British territory, to Delagoa Bay on the Indian Ocean. This would free the Transvaal from its dependence on the Cape Colony railway system, half of whose revenue came from freight charges on goods transported between the interior and the ports of Capetown, Port Elizabeth, and East London.

The Transvaal was becoming the richest state in South Africa, and Kruger's project alarmed Cecil Rhodes, who became Prime Minister of Cape Colony in 1890. Rhodes had founded the British South Africa Company in 1889, whose territory, which later became Rhodesia, hemmed in Transvaal to the north. Rhodes was a fervent imperialist, who planned to create a federation of South Africa under British rule, and dreamed of constructing a wholly British-owned railway from the Cape to Cairo. The Transvaal was the chief obstacle to these schemes, which were also in direct opposition to the hopes of the Boers in Cape Colony. There the Afrikaner Party wanted a Boer federation of South Africa, and an alliance with Germany to protect Boer interests against British imperialism. Such was the background to the Jameson Raid.

The Jameson Raid, 1895

The *uitlanders* in Transvaal plotted a revolt against Kruger's rule. They had the secret support of Rhodes, especially since the completion of the railway to Delagoa Bay in 1895 meant that the Cape Colony railways faced ruin as traffic was diverted on to the cheaper route. A detachment of several hundred South Africa Company Police, commanded by Dr Jameson, was collected on the borders of Transvaal, in readiness to respond to an appeal for help by the *uitlanders*.

The plan to overthrow Kruger's government by force misfired. Groups of Boer militia shadowed Jameson's raiders as soon as they crossed into the Transvaal. Twenty miles from Johannesburg they meekly surrendered. William II's action in sending a telegram to Kruger, congratulating him on preserving his country's independence, aroused a storm of anti-German feeling in Britain, where it was seen as a very unfriendly gesture.

The Boer War

The Boers were convinced that the British government had been implicated in the Raid. Many British, on the other hand, believed that Kruger, with the help of the Dutch living in Cape Colony, wished to destroy British influence in South Africa. Their spokesman was Alfred Milner, Governor of Cape Colony. He was convinced that the Boers would give way before a show of force, and British troops were rushed to South Africa. Kruger demanded that they should be withdrawn, and when this request was refused, war began in October 1899.

The Boers invaded Cape Colony, British Bechuanaland and Natal in November, and laid siege to Mafeking, Kimberley and Ladysmith. Attempts to relieve the towns were driven off with heavy losses. General Buller was defeated at Colenso during the second week of December, a 'Black Week' for the British army, and later in the month at Spion Kop.

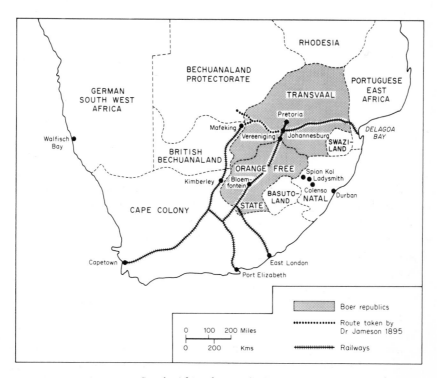

4   *South Africa during the Boer War*

Meanwhile, Kitchener and Roberts were on their way to South Africa with reinforcements. One of the Boer armies, commanded by Cronje, was forced to surrender at Paardeburg, and when Kimberley was relieved the Boers also withdrew from Ladysmith. Bloemfontein, the capital of the Orange Free State, was

to restrict the Boers' movements. These drastic measures, coupled with the presence of over 200,000 British troops, eventually overcame the resistance of the tiny Boer population. In the meantime, as a result of mismanagement, thousands of Boer women and children had died of disease in the

Boer forces, and their supplies, crossing the Tugela river, near Colenso

occupied in March 1900. The news of the relief of Mafeking in May was greeted with wild excitement by the British public.

The Transvaal was annexed in September, but the war continued. Boer commandos led by De Wet conducted guerrilla warfare for almost two years. Jan Christian Smuts invaded Cape Colony and sparked off a second rebellion against British rule. In order to deprive the commandos of their supplies, Kitchener rounded up their families, and herded them into refugee camps, called concentration camps. The farmsteads were burned, and barbed-wire entanglements criss-crossed the Transvaal

concentration camps, and Britain's 'barbaric methods' were savagely condemned in many European countries.

The peace settlement of Vereeniging, 1902

Having defeated the Boers, the British began the process of reconciliation. The Boer farmers were assisted with generous grants of money to set up their farms again, and they reluctantly acknowledged themselves to be British subjects.

Part of the British navy in 1886

In an attempt to placate Afrikaner nationalism, the black population was denied political rights, the Dutch language was preserved, and the Boers were promised self-government. This promise was kept when, in 1910, the Union of South Africa (comprising Cape Colony, Natal, the Transvaal, and the Orange Free State) was created.

Britain's emergence from 'Splendid Isolation'

Although the British were victorious in the Boer War, the dangers of isolation in an envious, largely hostile world convinced them of the need to develop friendships with other countries. Joseph Chamberlain, the Colonial Secretary, was much influenced by the notion of racial solidarity. He wished to develop an alliance of the Anglo-Saxon peoples, which together would dominate world affairs.

For several reasons Germany seemed to be Britain's natural ally. There had been a long period of diplomatic cooperation between the two countries. Both were worried by the implications of the Franco-Russian combination. Although Germany had joined the ranks of the colonial powers in Africa by acquiring Togoland, Cameroon, German East

Africa, and German South West Africa in 1884–5, and was anxious to develop its commercial interests on the Chinese mainland, no insoluble difficulties separated the two countries. Moreover, the idea of an alliance of a great land power with a great sea power attracted many people.

In 1898 Chamberlain proposed an Anglo-German alliance. When William II visited England in November 1900 Chamberlain again raised the subject. But the proposal never passed beyond the stage of vague theoretical discussion. One stumbling-block was Germany's plans to build a large navy. These were not welcomed by a British public, which was sensitive over its problems in South Africa, and keenly aware of Germany as a strong economic rival. Nor was the British government willing to join the Triple Alliance, since this might mean having to defend Austria-Hungary in a war with Russia over the Balkans. Likewise, the German government, which had no quarrel with Russia, saw no reason why it should rescue Britain from its difficulties with Russia and France unless the price was right.

Similarly, an alliance between Britain and the United States was never a practical proposition. Although both were anxious to preserve the 'Open Door' policy towards China, American opinion was against 'entangling alliances'. The only result of talks was the Hay–Pauncefote treaty of 1902, whereby Britain agreed to raise no objection to the construction of the Panama Canal. This treaty removed any possibility of a conflict between Britain and the United States, following the latter's victory in the Spanish-American War of 1898 (see Chapter 17).

Far East dangers

Britain's chief misgivings at the beginning of the twentieth century, however, concerned the Far East, where she could most easily be out-manoeuvred by a combination of powers, especially after the formation of the Franco-Russian alliance. Although Britain's Far East interests were, to a large extent, safeguarded by the Anglo-Japanese alliance (1902), there was a danger that Britain might become involved in a war in that part of the world. This possibility became both real and alarming when Japan attacked Russia in 1904 (see Chapter 1).

The Entente Cordiale

Anglo-French relations during the 1890s had been aggravated by their quarrel over Siam (resolved in 1893), by French attempts to gain control of the Nile valley, and by the Franco-Russian alliance. For France the value of the alliance lay in the protection it offered against a German attack, but Russia, which had no quarrel with Germany, tried to turn it into an alliance against Britain. Russia's requests for French support for her Far Eastern ambitions worried Delcassé, particularly after the signing of the Anglo-Japanese alliance.

An amicable settlement of their colonial differences was clearly in the best interests of Britain and France, for Britain wanted a free hand in Egypt, and France in Morocco. For France the problem was urgent. Not only might the growing political unrest in Morocco spread to the neighbouring French colony of Algeria,

but it might also tempt foreign powers to interfere in Morocco's affairs. Yet with the memory of Fashoda fresh in his mind, Delcassé dared not risk another confrontation with Britain.

Negotiations between the two countries were helped by an exchange of visits by King Edward VII and President Loubet in 1903, which prepared public opinion on both sides of the Channel. After months of hard bargaining an agreement was signed in April 1904. France formally recognised Britain's position in Egypt, in return for British recognition of France's special interests in Morocco. If Morocco ceased to be independent, Spain was to obtain a strip of territory opposite Gibraltar, while France would claim the rest. The long-standing dispute over the Newfoundland fisheries was settled. France surrendered her fishing rights in return for a strip of territory along the frontier of French Gambia. Britain and France also defined their respective spheres of influence in Siam and the New Hebrides.

The *entente cordiale* was not an alliance. It was a limited colonial agreement. It made no provision for any future diplomatic cooperation except over Morocco. Yet it is undeniable that Britain accepted a moral obligation to support France in securing control of Morocco. In this respect it adversely affected Germany's diplomatic position, especially since Italy was proving to be an unreliable ally. Germany's reaction to the *entente* was not long in coming.

The Moroccan crisis, 1905

In 1900, when Sultan Abdul Aziz became ruler, Morocco was the only independent state in North Africa. The Sultan soon lost effective control of most of his country to rebel Berber tribesmen. French merchants and bankers clamoured for intervention to protect their interests in Morocco. The Sultan was required to undertake a programme of reforms put forward by the French government. Delcassé had already secured the approval of Italy,

Spain, and Britain for such a move, but he had neglected to seek the agreement of the United States, and of Germany, which had economic interests in Morocco.

Germany claimed that the *status quo*★ in Morocco should not be altered without her consent. Germany's legal case was beyond dispute, and according to the accepted diplomatic conventions of the late nineteenth century Germany was entitled to concessions in the event of a French occupation of the country. But Von Bülow, the German Chancellor, had more ambitious plans. By exploiting the tension between England and Russia, which had arisen as a result of the Russo-Japanese War, he hoped to revive the alliance between Germany and Russia, and, by exerting pressure upon France, to break the newly formed *entente*.

In March 1905 William II landed at Tangier, where he recognised Morocco's independence and declared that Germany was prepared to protect its legitimate interests in Morocco. William II's provocative speech aroused fears that Germany was planning a preventive war against France whilst her defeated ally, Russia, was helplessly embroiled in revolution (see Chapter 11). Bülow insisted that an international conference should be held to settle the Moroccan question, for he was certain that Germany's case would be supported by other countries. During this war of nerves, Delcassé, who was blamed by the Germans for the crisis, was forced to resign.

In July William II met Tsar Nicholas II on board his royal yacht in the Bay of Björkö, off the Baltic coast. The two Emperors signed a treaty of alliance, promising each other support if either Germany or Russia became involved in a war with another European country. Their initiative, however, met with unfavourable reactions at home, so that the Björkö agreement was quietly allowed to lapse.

When the international conference took place at Algeciras in January 1906 Germany's bargaining position had deteriorated. Only Austria-Hungary supported Germany, and the conference was a resounding failure for German diplomacy. Moreover, since Britain firmly supported France, one important result of the crisis was to widen the scope of the *entente*. Conversations between the military staffs were secretly authorised by the British and French governments. Far from breaking the *entente*, German diplomacy had only succeeded in strengthening it.

The Anglo-Russian entente

Pleased with the success of the new understanding, the French government was anxious that its ally, Russia, and *entente* partner, Britain, should also solve their colonial problems. The moment was opportune. With

William II lands at Tangier

★literally 'the situation as it was'.

Russia no longer a rival in the Far East following Japan's victo. y in 1905, the prospects of an agreement were greatly enhanced so far as Britain was concerned. Russia, having suffered defeat and revolution, was anxious to improve relations with Britain.

The Anglo-Russian *entente* of 1907 settled their differences over Persia, which was partitioned. The northern part was allocated to Russia. The south-eastern area, which bordered Afghanistan, became a British sphere of influence. The two regions were separated by a neutral buffer zone.

By 1907, therefore, two power blocs existed in Europe, the Triple Alliance and the Triple Entente. As yet, however, neither threatened the other, and it would be wrong to think of Europe at this time as being divided into hostile, armed camps. It was only later crises which determined that the Entente Powers would enter the Great War on the same side. One of the most important factors in bringing about this situation in 1914 was the intense naval rivalry between Britain and Germany which developed after 1906. This virtually decided that in 1914 Britain would fight

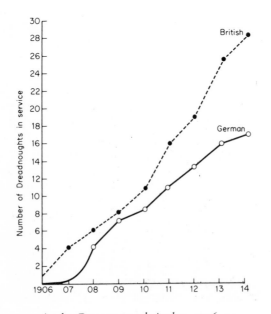

Anglo-German naval rivalry, 1906–14

alongside France and Russia, her chief rivals in 1900, against Germany, with which Britain had no direct quarrel and which in 1900 had been regarded as Britain's chief continental friend.

Anglo-German naval rivalry

During the 1880s the desire for a powerful navy was re-awakened in Britain by the existence of the Triple Alliance. In 1889 the British government declared its intention to maintain a two-power navy standard, meaning that the Royal Navy would be equal to a combination of the next two strongest European navies.

Widespread interest in naval matters was aroused by the publication in 1890 of Mahan's book, *The Influence of Sea Power upon History*. Mahan, an American naval captain, argued convincingly that a country which possessed overseas bases, and the naval strength to dominate the ocean routes, was well placed to become a world power. Mahan's book impressed not only the British Admiralty, but also William II and his naval adviser, Admiral von Tirpitz.

Rapid technological change after 1880 also aroused public interest. Naval strategy was affected by the introduction of wireless, and oil-fired, steam-turbine-driven warships with greater speeds and ranges. More heavily armoured battleships were built to counteract improved shell design and propellants. The development of the torpedo made short-range action dangerous, so that the emphasis shifted to arming battleships with 12-inch guns, with a range of 14,000 yards. Fire power was also increased by the introduction of the gyroscope and director control of gun turrets, which enabled several guns to be aimed accurately and fired simultaneously. The pace of technical progress may be well illustrated by the fact that the loading time for 12-inch guns, four minutes in 1884, was reduced to twenty seconds by 1914.

In 1896 William II announced that Germany should become *weltmacht*, a world power. In accordance with Mahan's accepted theories, this required a strong navy to protect Germany's overseas interests. At the time of the Jameson Raid Britain's mobilisation of a powerful squadron of battleships had enabled her to flout world opinion. This lesson had not been lost upon the German navy planners.

Von Tirpitz was appointed Secretary of State for the Marine in 1897, when the German navy ranked seventh in the league table of navies. Tirpitz, a brilliant propagandist, obtained the backing of the Navy League and the Colonial League, and in 1898 the Reichstag passed the First German Naval Law, whereby a navy of 19 battleships was planned for 1905. Two years later, violent anti-British feeling aroused by the conduct of the Boer War was the background to the passage of a Second Naval Law which envisaged the construction of 34 battleships and 45 cruisers by 1917.

Tirpitz's strategy was based upon his famous 'risk theory'. This involved building a navy sufficiently strong for an attack on it to involve a grave risk for the aggressor. Tirpitz himself made no secret of the fact that the German fleet should be capable of inflicting grievous damage upon the British navy.

At this stage Britain was not unduly alarmed by the German plans. The German navy existed on paper only, and Britain was rapidly expanding an already large navy. The government was more concerned about the strength of the Franco-Russian naval combination in the Mediterranean, and Russia's expansionist policies in the Far East. The Anglo-Japanese Alliance (1902), and the annihilation of Russia's fleets in the Russo-Japanese War allayed these anxieties.

It was the launching of HMS *Dreadnought* in 1906 which profoundly altered the naval balance of power. HMS *Dreadnought* was a revolutionary battleship, so superior in speed and armaments that it immediately outclassed all existing battleships. It was calculated that pre-Dreadnought battleships could survive for only five minutes the salvoes from its ten 12-inch guns. But in making obsolete all existing battleships it meant that the naval race

could start afresh. Germany seized what appeared to be a golden opportunity to achieve naval equality with Britain.

Efforts to slacken the pace of naval construction had little success. In 1909 fear that Germany might catch up led the British public to demand, 'We want eight, and we won't wait'. Rosyth was developed as a base for the Home Fleet. As Anglo-French relations became stronger, so responsibility for the Mediterranean was increasingly left to the French navy, while the British navy concentrated its strength in the North Sea. Inevitably, the German and British navies came to regard each other as their natural enemies.

The Agadir crisis, 1911

Abdul Aziz abdicated in 1908, but the new Sultan of Morocco had no more success in quelling the rebellious tribesmen than he had had. In 1911, with his capital, Fez, under virtual siege, the Sultan appealed to the French government for aid. It sent 20,000 troops, and a French take-over in Morocco seemed imminent.

The German government demanded that its economic interests in Morocco should be taken into consideration, and it despatched the gunboat *Panther* to the port of Agadir which, it was thought, was sufficiently far south of Gibraltar to avoid antagonising Britain. Nevertheless, Germany's gunboat diplomacy alarmed the British, who feared that Germany was about to secure a naval base on the Atlantic coast of North Africa. Lloyd George, an advocate of Anglo-German friendship, in a speech at the Mansion House in July, bluntly warned Germany that if Great Britain, where its vital interests were at stake, was treated 'as if she were of no account in the cabinet of nations, then peace at that price would be intolerable for a great country like ours to endure'.

The navy was alerted. Newspapers in both Britain and Germany openly discussed the possibility of war. The crisis ended in

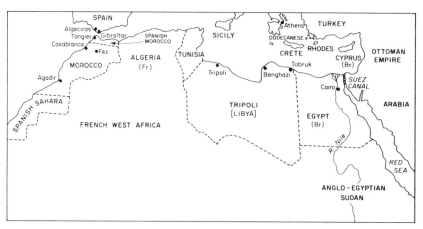

5   *North Africa in 1912*

November, when Germany recognised that a French protectorate over Morocco was inevitable. In return for a free hand in Morocco, the French government ceded to Germany 100,000 square miles of the French Congo.

The Agadir crisis was symptomatic of the growing tensions in Europe. Many Germans suspected that Britain was subtly planning to encircle Germany by a network of colonial agreements and understandings, reinforced by command of the seas. British public opinion was more than ever convinced that Germany was seeking to dominate Europe.

The conquest of Tripoli, 1912

Italian interest in a forward colonial policy had declined following the failure of an attempt to annex Abyssinia,★ when an Italian

★Abyssinia, the oldest state in Africa, reverted to its original name of Ethiopia, following its liberation by British forces in 1941, during the Second World War, after six years of Italian rule.

army had been routed at Adowa in 1896. But Tripoli, an outlying province of the Ottoman Empire, had long been regarded as an area which would eventually become an Italian possession, and in 1911 its conquest seemed a simple operation.

Confident that the French government would have no objections now that its control over Morocco had been secured, Italy declared war on Turkey in September. Italian troops seized the coastal towns of Tripoli, Tobruk and Benghazi, but encountered opposition as they advanced inland. The Arabs were persuaded by their Turkish overlords to resist European colonialism.

Meanwhile, the Balkan states had taken advantage of Turkey's difficulties in North Africa to form a Balkan League, which declared war in October 1912. Turkey was therefore forced to recognise Italy's conquest of Tripoli, and to surrender Rhodes and the Dodecanese Islands, which had been occupied during the fighting. Once again the attention of the great powers of Europe was unwillingly drawn to the Balkan peninsula.

CHAPTER THREE
The Balkan Wars and their Aftermath, 1912–14

The decline of the Turkish Empire had constantly threatened the peace of Europe, for the Ottomans ruled territories in three continents – Africa, Europe, and Asia – which were of great strategic value to other countries. It was in the Balkan peninsula, however, that the greatest danger of conflict always lay.

Austro-Hungarian plans for territorial and economic expansion in the Balkans clashed with Russia's desire to gain influence in this region, and to secure the opening of the Straits (the narrow stretches of sea called the Bosphorus and the Dardanelles, which connected the Black Sea with the Mediterranean) to Russian warships. By the Treaty of Unkiar Skelessi (1833) the Russians had extracted a promise from the Turks that they would close the Straits to the warships of any country at war with Russia. This agreement was reversed by the London Straits Convention (1841), which declared that Turkey should close the Straits to foreign warships in peacetime, and open them to the warships of its allies in a war, thus exposing the Russian Black Sea fleet to an attack by its enemies. The Straits Convention remained in force until 1923.

While Russia had no desire either to see Turkey become strong again, or to be destroyed, it exploited the gradual decline of Turkish power by claiming the right to protect the interests of the Christians in the Balkans, so that the Slavs under Turkish rule naturally

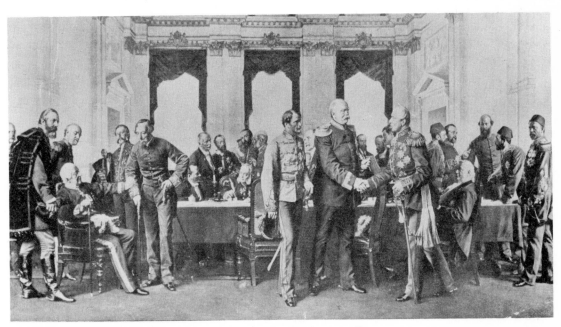

Berlin Congress 1878: the European Powers meet to resettle the Balkans after the Russo-Turkish War. Among the personalities shown are Lord Beaconsfield (Disraeli), sixth from the left, and Bismarck (centre)

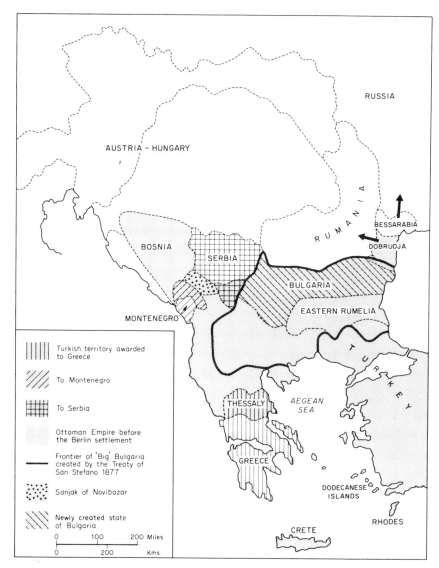

6   *Balkan changes in 1878*

looked to Russia for assistance in their struggles to achieve independence.

Britain opposed the advance of Russian power towards Constantinople and the Straits, and its traditional policy was to support the Ottoman government. Germany, during the long period of Bismarck's chancellorship (1871–90), tried to maintain good neighbourly relations with both Austria-Hungary and Russia. Although William II discontinued

Bismarck's diplomacy, the risk of a confrontation between Austria-Hungary and Russia was small so long as the latter was busy developing its interests in the Far East. The revival of Russia's interest in the Balkans after the defeat by Japan in 1905 heralded disaster.

The Balkan situation was further complicated by the mutual hostility of the Balkan states towards each other. Their only bond of unity was hatred of Turkish rule. Once Ottoman power in the Balkans had been destroyed, the rivalries between Greeks, Bulgars, Serbs, Albanians, Montenegrins, Macedonians, and Rumanians would be intensified. By involving the great powers in their feuds and aggressive schemes of expansion the Balkan peoples increased the chances of a general European war breaking out.

Balkan nationalism, the military weakness and decay of the Ottoman Empire, and the competing interests of the great powers in the Balkans throughout the nineteenth century were collectively known as the Eastern Question. No easy, peaceful solution to this problem existed. In this sense, therefore, it is true to say that the Balkans were 'the powder keg of Europe'.

The Balkan revolt, 1875–8

Balkan nationalism was greatly encouraged by the unification of Italy and Germany. In 1875 a revolt of the Bosnian Serbs against Turkish misrule quickly spread. Turkey's savage reprisals, the so-called 'Bulgarian Horrors', resulted in the Russo-Turkish War (1877).

Turkey was defeated by Russia, and, by the peace agreement of San Stefano, a 'Big Bulgaria', with an Aegean coastline, was formed. Britain, however, fearing that Bulgaria would be dominated by Russia, insisted that it should be greatly reduced in size, and a conference of the great powers was called to settle the issue.

By the Treaty of Berlin (1878) Bulgaria was trisected. The southern part was returned to Turkey. The central part became a special province of the Ottoman Empire, called Eastern Rumelia, under a Christian governor. The northern third was granted self-government. The independence of Serbia, Montenegro, and Rumania, all of which gained small increases of territory, was recognised. At the same time Austria-Hungary was given permission to occupy and administer Bosnia.

The Serbo-Bulgarian War, 1885

The Bulgarians soon proved surprisingly independent of Russian control, so that Tsar Alexander III withdrew all military aid from Bulgaria and made up his mind to secure the expulsion of its ruler, Prince Alexander of Battenberg.

In 1885 the Bulgarian population of Eastern Rumelia revolted against Turkey, and proclaimed their union with Bulgaria. The long-standing enmity between the Serbs and the Bulgars now erupted into war. The Serbs, believing Bulgaria to be militarily weak, attacked in the hope of seizing territory. To their surprise and dismay, they were completely defeated at the battle of Slivnitza.

By 1886 the British government had reversed its policy towards Bulgaria, and it agreed to the union of Eastern Rumelia with Bulgaria. Alexander of Battenberg, however, did not long remain its ruler. He was kidnapped by Russian agents and forced to abdicate. In his place the Bulgarians chose another German prince, Ferdinand of Saxe-Coburg, who ruled Bulgaria from 1886 to 1918.

The Cretan revolt, 1897

A further stage in the decline of Ottoman power was marked by events in Crete in 1897, following murders of Christians and Muslims living on the island. The Cretans, who wanted union with Greece *(Enosis)*, revolted against their Turkish masters, and appealed to the Greek government to annex the island. The Greeks declared war on Turkey, only to be soundly defeated within two weeks.

The Greeks were saved by the intervention of the great powers. With the exception of Germany, which was developing friendly relations with the Ottoman Empire, they forced the Sultan to return all the mainland territory his army had conquered. Greece was required to pay Turkey an indemnity, but Prince George of Greece was made Governor of Crete, which became self-governing. Thus the Turks, who had won the war, were not allowed to enjoy the fruits of their victory, for it was clear that the union of Crete with Greece was only a matter of time.

Meanwhile, Austria-Hungary and Russia agreed to maintain the *status quo* in the Near East. Austria-Hungary had no wish to seek the enlargement of the Balkan states, while Russia was preoccupied with events in the Far East. This apparent stability in Balkan affairs, however, was to be shattered in 1908 following widespread unrest in Macedonia, and the Young Turk Revolution.

The Macedonian problem

After 1878 Macedonia became a focal point of Balkan rivalries. It was coveted by its neighbours, Bulgaria, Serbia, and Greece, for its fertile plains contrasted favourably with the mountainous areas which made up the greater part of the Balkan peninsula, while Salonika was an important outlet to the Aegean Sea. The Austro-Hungarian government also had plans to build a railway through the Sanjak of Novibazar to Salonika.

Even apart from its economic and strategic importance, Macedonia's racial and religious mixture was bound to make it an area of strife and dispute. Many of the inhabitants were Christians, belonging to the rival Greek and Bulgarian Orthodox churches, but the Albanians and Turks were important Muslim minorities. Moreover, the Macedonians themselves, by the late nineteenth century, were developing their own brand of nationalism, symbolised by the formation of the Internal Macedonian Revolutionary Organisation in 1903, with its slogan of 'Macedonia for the Macedonians'.

Turkish government in Macedonia was weak and ineffective, and Macedonia was a prey to marauding bands of Greeks and Bulgars. Both sides attempted to win the allegiance of villages by terrorising their inhabitants. The activities and propaganda of the Greeks and Bulgars angered the Serbs, who wanted to include all the South Slavs in an enlarged Serbia. In this aim they were encouraged by the Austrians in order to distract their attention from Bosnia, and by the Turks, in the hope that by dividing their enemies they might prolong their rule in Macedonia.

In 1903 a rebellion in Macedonia was brutally suppressed by the Turks. Keeping to their agreement of 1897, Russia and Austria-Hungary proposed a programme of reforms which, since it was approved by the other powers, Sultan Abdul Hamid II was forced to accept. It did little, however, to restore peaceful conditions in Macedonia, where the Greeks and Bulgars continued their raids. Such was the state of Balkan affairs for five years before events in Turkey itself suddenly transformed the situation.

The Young Turk revolution, 1908–9

The Young Turks were Turk patriots who were angered by their country's decline, for which they blamed the Sultan's corrupt and inefficient rule. Far from introducing the constitutional reforms he had promised, Abdul Hamid II, who had come to the throne in 1876, dismissed parliament in 1877, and it did not meet again until 1908. Although the Sultan accepted western technology such as railways and the telegraph, he stubbornly refused to modernise the administration of his sprawling empire.

The Young Turk revolt was sparked off by a suggestion of the British government that the Macedonian problem might be solved by the creation of a self-governing state. The great powers were clearly contemplating intervention in Macedonia and the Young Turks, led by an army officer, Enver Bey, feared that unless they acted at once, events would lead to the partition of Turkey's remaining possessions in Europe.

The Young Turks demanded the restoration of the 1876 constitution, and the Sultan gave way to threats that unless he did so the army would occupy Constantinople. The Young Turk ministers wanted more efficient, centralised government of the provinces from Constantinople. They rightly believed that the different racial groups would not long remain content with self-government within the Ottoman Empire, but would immediately press for complete independence. They were prepared to grant religious freedom and political rights to all the inhabitants of the Empire, whether Arabs, Slavs, Jews, Greeks, Armenians or Rumanians, but only on condition that they forgot their separate national identities, and became Ottomans in their outlook. This policy was known as Ottomanisation.

The Young Turks soon aroused hostility. Devout Muslims objected to the introduction of western ideas and customs, which were contrary to the sacred teachings of the Koran. The Arabs of the Yemen revolted, and the Armenians in Asia Minor staged a counter-revolution in Constantinople in 1909. They were supported by Abdul Hamid II, who paid the penalty for its failure by being deposed. Thereafter, the Young Turks ruthlessly eliminated opposition to their policies, so that by 1914 Enver Bey had become a virtual dictator. In the meantime, the troubled events of the Young Turk revolution precipitated the Bosnian crisis and the formation of the Balkan League, which led directly to the Balkan Wars of 1912–13.

The Bosnian crisis

The possibility that the Young Turk measures might strengthen Turkey prompted Austria-Hungary and Russia to secure their positions in the Balkans while Turkey was in turmoil. Aerenthal, the Austrian Foreign Minister, was convinced of the need to annex Bosnia. Without Bosnia, the Dalmatian coastline was virtually isolated from the rest of the empire, and difficult to defend. Secondly, Aerenthal thought that the seizure of Bosnia would remedy the problem of growing Slav unrest on the frontiers of the Habsburg monarchy. Although the annexation would increase the number of Slavs under Austro-Hungarian rule,

it would destroy any lingering hopes in the province that it would one day be united with Serbia.

Izvolski, the Russian Foreign Minister, wished to recover some of the prestige lost as a result of Russia's defeat in the Far East by securing changes at the Straits of Constantinople, which would allow Russia's Black Sea fleet free access to the Mediterranean. Izvolski was optimistic that, in the wake of the recent Anglo-Russian *entente*, Britain would raise no objections.

When the Young Turks summoned representatives from Bosnia to a Turkish parliament, this implied that Turkey would seek to recover full sovereignty over the province. Consequently, Aerenthal and Izvolski met to coordinate their policies. Unfortunately, misunderstanding arose over the timing of their moves.

The Austrians encouraged King Ferdinand of Bulgaria to proclaim his country's independence of Turkey, much to Russia's annoyance, for Bulgaria was Serbia's bitter rival. On the next day the Austro-Hungarian government announced the annexation of Bosnia, before Russia had had an opportunity to obtain Britain's approval for the proposed alterations regarding the Straits. A major European crisis now developed.

The British government refused to agree to any changes at the Straits, since it did not wish to see Turkey weakened any further, and Izvolski felt that he had been tricked by Aerenthal. The Serbian government was enraged by the annexation, and it ordered mobilisation. Turkey threatened to mobilise against Bulgaria unless it was compensated for the loss of annual tribute.

War was only avoided with difficulty. Russia loaned money to Bulgaria so that Turkey could be compensated, and warned Serbia not to act rashly, for no Russian help against Austria could be expected. Eventually Serbia agreed to drop its opposition to the Bosnian annexation, and the danger of war receded.

The Bosnian crisis had grave consequences. The understanding between Austria-Hungary and Russia over Balkan affairs was destroyed.

*A Bulgarian and a Greek soldier humiliate a
Turk by marking the sign of the Christian cross
on his fez, thereby insulting the Muslim faith*

Russia felt humiliated by Germany's threat of
mobilisation, which had forced her to abandon
Serbia. Russo-German relations, which had
been friendly until the crisis, became hostile,
so that William II believed that Russia was
deliberately planning war. Britain and France
were conscious that they had given little
support to Russia, in contrast to Germany's
support of her ally. Meanwhile, Serbian
opinion was inflamed over the annexation of
Bosnia, and the feeling grew in both Austria
and Serbia that sooner or later war between
them was inevitable.

The Balkan League, 1912

In 1912 Turkey's difficulties in the war against
Italy gave the Balkan states an opportunity to
attack her. Serbia, Bulgaria, Greece, and
Montenegro formed the Balkan League, whose
aim was to expel the Turks from the Balkan
peninsula, which was to be divided between
them. Serbia was to have northern Macedonia,
including the port of Durazzo on the Adriatic
coast. Bulgaria hoped to expand her territory

to the Aegean, and to obtain Salonika and
Constantinople. Greece also wanted southern
Macedonia and Salonika. Events were soon to
prove that this unlikely alliance was only made
possible by hatred of Turkish rule, and that it
would last only so long as Turkey remained a
threat.

The Balkan Wars, 1912–13

In October 1912 the Balkan League attacked
Turkey. The Montenegrins laid siege to the
port of Scutari. The Bulgars invaded Thrace
and advanced towards Constantinople and
Salonika. The Serbs defeated the Turks at the
battle of Monastir, captured Durazzo, and
joined the Bulgars in the attempt to capture
Adrianople. Meanwhile, the Greeks had seized
parts of southern Macedonia, and had won the
race with the Bulgars for possession of Salonika.

The great powers were anxious to end the
Balkan war as soon as possible. Austria–
Hungary did not welcome Serbia's success,
and was determined to prevent Serbia acquiring
an Adriatic coastline. Russia did not relish the
idea of Constantinople falling into Bulgaria's
hands. Germany and Britain were concerned
to prove that cooperation between the powers
was possible. A truce was therefore arranged
in December, and the great powers met in
London to agree on a peace settlement.

In February 1913, while negotiations were
still taking place, fighting broke out again.
The Serbs and Bulgars captured Adrianople,
and the Greeks extended their hold on the
Aegean coast. The Montenegrins finally
captured Scutari, which the powers had already
decided should belong to a newly created,
independent Albania.

By the terms of the peace treaty of London
(May 1913), Turkey lost all its European
territories with the exception of a strip of
mainland territory protecting Constantinople.
Northern and central Macedonia were awarded
to Serbia. Greece obtained southern Macedonia,
including Salonika. Bulgaria acquired Thrace
and an Aegean coastline, Montenegro part of
the Sanjak of Novibazar. An independent

7   *The Balkan League, 1912*

Albania was set up, making Serbia a land-locked state.

The Treaty of London satisfied none of the Balkan states. The Greeks and Serbs refused to surrender Macedonian villages which their troops had captured. The Bulgars, who had suffered the heaviest casualities in the fighting, felt cheated. Montenegro was forced to evacuate Scutari, while the Serbs bitterly resented Austria-Hungary's action in denying

them an outlet to the sea. Rumania, which had taken no part in the first Balkan war, was alarmed at the growth of Bulgaria, and demanded compensation in the form of territory south of the river Danube.

The second Balkan war broke out in June 1913, when Bulgaria attacked Serbia and Greece. This was a complete disaster for the Bulgars, whose armies were flung back across their frontiers. Rumania declared war on

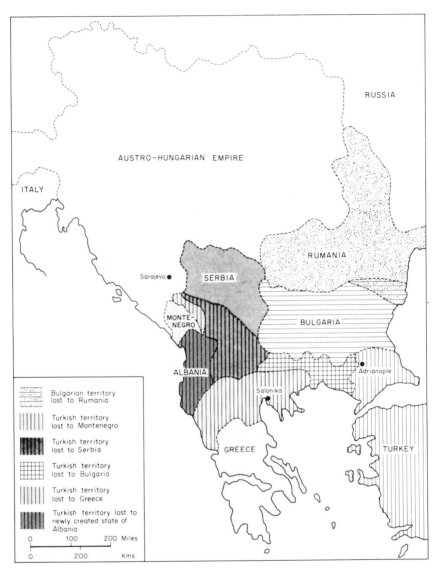

8   Territorial changes in the Balkans, 1912–13

Bulgaria, as did Turkey, which recaptured Adrianople. By the end of July the Bulgars were forced to sue for peace.

The Treaty of Bucharest, August 1913

The Treaty of Bucharest merely created an uneasy truce in the Balkans, 'where national rivalries were stimulated by the gains and losses resulting from the two Balkan wars. Turkey, Greece, and Serbia kept the areas their forces had won during the course of the second Balkan war. Rumania acquired part of southern Dobrudja from Bulgaria. Bitterly resentful of its defeat, Bulgaria was ready to associate itself with the Central Powers in its desire for revenge against Serbia. The latter, despite having nearly doubled its territory, was already contemplating the next stage of its national development – war with Austria-Hungary and the conquest of Bosnia. Greece, which had several potential enemies, was divided in its allegiances. King Constantine was pro-German, but his powerful Prime Minister, Venizelos, who dreamed of extending the frontiers of Greek rule into Asia Minor, was impressed by the strength of the Entente Powers.

The assassination at Sarajevo and its aftermath

The fragile peace in the Balkans lasted less than a year. On 28 June 1914 a young Serb nationalist, Gavrilo Princip, assassinated the Archduke Francis Ferdinand, heir to the Habsburg throne, and his wife, during a state visit to Sarajevo, the capital of Bosnia. Responsibility for the murders lay with the Black Hand, a terrorist organisation founded in 1911, whose members were sworn to achieve the union of all Serbs. Few people at that time could have foreseen the terrible consequences of the shots fired by Princip.

Austria-Hungary had become greatly alarmed by Serbia's championship of Slav aspirations, which were an unsettling influence within the multi-racial Habsburg Empire. The assassination seemed an ideal opportunity to crush or humiliate Serbia so completely that the Bosnian Serbs would be forced to reconcile themselves to Austrian rule. The Austrian government therefore accused the Serbian government of complicity in the murders. An ultimatum demanding unconditional acceptance of Austria's terms within forty-eight hours was sent to Belgrade. Despite the severity of the conditions, Serbia rejected outright only one, which it asked to be referred to international arbitration. Austria, however, was not interested in a compromise settlement, a fact which the Serbian government itself recognised by ordering general mobilisation of its forces the day before it replied to the Austrian ultimatum.

In the developing crisis the German government promised its full military support to Austria-Hungary. This famous 'blank cheque' not only reflected the Kaiser's view that Germany had no choice but to stand by its only reliable ally, but also the German High Command's assessment that if war was inevitable sooner or later, then the circumstances of 1914 favoured the Central Powers. France's military preparations were geared to a war in 1915, Russia's to 1917. In Russia, moreover, tsardom was threatened by social unrest, while Britain was deeply divided by civil strife in Ulster, where civil war appeared almost certain. Furthermore, the Sarajevo murders were a terrible crime, repugnant to the vast majority of people in every country, and strong measures by the Austro-Hungarian government had been expected.

In any consideration of the outbreak of war in 1914 it is important to realise that the German government did not deliberately seek war. On the contrary, it tried to ensure that if war did break out it would remain a localised Austro-Serbian war. It believed that any delay in resolving the crisis only increased the chances of the conflict spreading to other countries. Germany's decision to mobilise in support of Austria-Hungary was intended to deter Russia from intervening.

Russia, however, had yielded to German pressure in 1908–9 over the annexation of Bosnia. It could not abandon Serbia again without great loss of prestige and damage to its interests in the Balkans. The Tsar ordered mobilisation on 30 July. The German government demanded immediate cancellation of this order, and when this was refused declared war on Russia on 1 August. Two days later Germany declared war on France.

Britain declared war on Germany on 4 August, when German armies violated Belgium's neutrality, which had been guaranteed by the Treaty of London in 1839 (the 'scrap of paper' referred to by German propagandists). It was not until 6 August, however, that Austria-Hungary declared war on Russia, and only on 12 August that Britain and France declared war on Austria-Hungary.

Summary of the causes of the First World War

There is no straightforward answer to the question, 'Why did war break out in 1914?' Any study of its origins must take into account the events described in this and the previous chapter which form, as it were, a background to the war. No other war has had such an intensive study made of its causes, yet generations of historians have failed to agree on them. It has been equally fashionable at one time or another to blame the Kaiser, Austro-Hungarian diplomacy, nationalism, colonial rivalry, capitalism, military alliances – to name only some of the chief causes.

Certainly the desire of subject peoples with a strongly developed sense of national identity to become self-governing was an important cause, for it could only be achieved at the expense of existing states. Thus Slav nationalism threatened the destruction of the Austro-Hungarian and Turkish empires. The disputed ownership of Alsace-Lorraine was an ever-present potential cause of conflict between France and Germany.

A second important cause was imperialism. All the great powers, and many of the lesser European states, had empires, which they wished to preserve or expand. The concept of 'empire', with its overtones of a nation's glorious achievements, and its promise of future wealth and prestige, was a highly emotive one. The Germans, late starters in the race for colonies, bitterly accused the British of begrudging them their 'place in the sun'. Such was the strength of British imperialism that in 1914 Britain, without properly consulting its Empire, was able to commit it to a war against the Central Powers, in which it had no direct interest.

Imperialism engendered economic rivalry and militarism. Colonies were important sources of raw materials and foodstuffs, markets for manufacturers, and outlets for surplus capital. Railways financed by European bankers were built in many parts of the world, so that their natural resources could be more fully exploited. Investors demanded that their governments take steps to protect their interests, even if this meant offending other governments.

As nations competed fiercely with each other for economic and political influence, so they were driven into forming military alliances. Their existence increased international tensions, and complicated the task of diplomats in their efforts to reach peaceful solutions to problems. Moreover, continental empires required large armies to defend them, and overseas empires needed powerful fleets and naval bases to guarantee their security. From the 1890s onwards an arms race developed, as the great powers became preoccupied with defending their world-wide interests.

It may be an over-simplification to state that by 1914 Europe was divided into two armed camps. Britain tried to avoid commitments to France and Russia, and in 1914 was on better terms with Germany than at any time in the previous twenty years. Neither Rumania nor Italy, both members of the Triple Alliance, entered the war in 1914, and even when they eventually did so, they fought on the side of the Entente Powers. Nevertheless, the arms race and the existence of military alliances were important contributory factors in bringing about the war.

In the final analysis war was made inevitable by excessive patriotism, and by the military preparations which each European great power made in order to achieve victory in a war. For most people the prospect of defeat was worse than war itself. The military staffs of both sides were convinced that victory would go to those countries that mobilised first. This assumption dominated their minds, with fearful consequences, since they dared not allow their enemies time to gain the initiative. When Austria-Hungary attacked Serbia the war quickly gained a momentum of its own, which overpowered the efforts of statesmen on both sides who sought to preserve peace. In this sense civilian governments were trapped by their war plans. It was the decision of the German government to declare war on France, in order to accomplish its rapid defeat, which ensured that the Austro-Serbian war became a world war.

Few people expected the war to last very long, even though warning voices had pointed out the lessons of the American Civil War (1861–5) and the Russo-Japanese War. In both conflicts machine-guns and artillery had given most of the advantages to the defenders. Nor was it fully appreciated that any war between industrial nations, efficiently organised, and with civilian populations behind the war effort, was certain to be prolonged and costly.

The Schlieffen Plan

The geographical position of the Central Powers gave them the advantages of centralised communications, but exposed Germany to the threat of having to wage war simultaneously on two fronts. This fact, together with Austria-Hungary's known military weakness, conditioned the strategic planning of the German High Command long before war broke out. Between 1891 and 1906 the German Chief-of-Staff, Count von Schlieffen, evolved his famous plan.

In any war against France and Russia it was assumed that Russia would be slow to mobilise, while France would be the chief military threat. Since the vast hinterland of Russia ruled out any hope of achieving a rapid victory in the east, the immediate need was to defeat France decisively within weeks of the outbreak of war. Germany could then deal with Russia in a more leisurely fashion.

Schlieffen's strategy was to concentrate Germany's armies against France, leaving the Austrians to contain the Russians. France's defeat was to be brought about by a lightning invasion of Belgium and Luxemburg by several

German armies. Striking through into weakly defended northern France, they would seize the Channel ports en route to the encirclement of Paris. The German troops in Alsace-Lorraine would merely contain the anticipated French advance into the 'lost provinces'. Once Paris had been captured, the French armies would be trapped between opposing German armies and forced to choose between annihilation and surrender. Violation of Belgium's neutrality would almost certainly bring Britain into the war, but this fact was discounted by the

The Cossacks were dreaded Russian cavalry. This picture of forced marching shows Cossacks on the way to the front line, each with two infantrymen standing in his stirrups

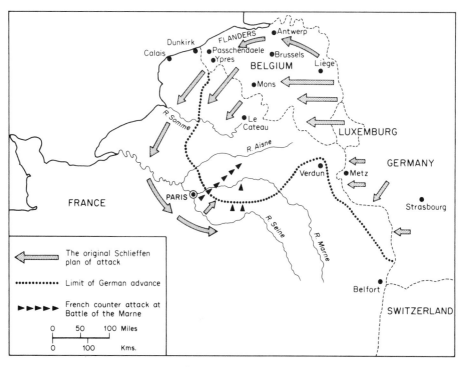

9   *The Western Front, 1914*

German High Command. Britain's tiny professional army could have no decisive influence during the first few months of the war, by which time the German generals expected the war to be over. Furthermore, the Royal Navy would be ineffectual in a short war, since a blockade of Germany's ports would have to be prolonged to harm German production or morale.

German armies crossed the Belgian frontier on 4 August and soon captured the great fortress of Liège. The speed of the German advance threatened to engulf the French and Belgian armies. They were saved by the unexpectedly swift arrival of the British Expeditionary Force, which went into action on 21 August. The BEF, though small in numbers, delayed the German advance at the battles of Mons and Le Cateau. The French and British armies managed to conduct an orderly retreat towards good defensive positions well served with road and rail communications.

Before the end of August the Schlieffen Plan was breaking down. Moltke, the German

commander, modified it by detaching six divisions from the armies in northern France and sending them to East Prussia to check the advancing Russian armies. Meanwhile, the German field commanders in northern France were alarmed by the widening gap between their two armies. One of them, General Kluck, lost his nerve and ordered his army to veer southwards in order to maintain contact with the other army, commanded by Bülow. Moltke did not overrule this order, and thereby abandoned what was left of the Schlieffen Plan, for Kluck's line of advance would fall short of the French capital. Paris was saved when General Joffre counter-attacked at the battle of the river Marne in early September, and pushed the German armies back to the river Aisne.

Falkenhayn, the Prussian Minister for War, replaced Moltke, and tried to revive the Schlieffen Plan. After the capture of Antwerp, Falkenhayn attempted to outflank the French armies in northern France. The result was four weeks' bitter fighting around Ypres, at the end of which the German advance had been halted. During the fighting, as both sides desperately tried to outflank each other in the so-called 'race to the sea', a trench system was constructed which only ended when the coast was reached. Thereafter fighting on the western front never moved outside a strip of land ten miles wide, adjoining the network of trenches, until the German offensive of March 1918.

At the end of 1914, 10 per cent of France, containing important coal and steel industries, lay in enemy hands. Yet the battles of the Marne and Ypres were in one respect decisive: they shattered Germany's hopes of achieving victory in a short war, and they ensured that Germany would have to wage war on two fronts.

balanced by the collapse of the Austro-Hungarian offensives against the Serbs and the Russians. Although Belgrade, the Serbian capital, was captured on 2 December, the battered remnants of the Serbian army fiercely attacked the over-confident Austro-Hungarian troops, and routed them. By 15 December the Serbian government was able to declare that not one free enemy soldier remained on Serbian territory.

Meanwhile, the Russians had invaded Poland and in the battle for Lemberg had inflicted enormous casualties upon the Austrians. When the Russian offensive eventually came to a standstill at the end of the year, quiet descended upon the eastern front, with both Russia and Austria-Hungary temporarily exhausted.

The eastern front to the end of 1914

In the meantime, 800 miles to the east, the Russians had mobilised far more quickly than either their friends or their foes had expected. Russian armies commanded by Rennenkampf and Samsonov threatened to invade East Prussia at the end of August. Thereby the Russians made an invaluable contribution to the Allied war effort. The two army corps, under Hindenburg and Ludendorff, despatched by Moltke to defend the German homeland, could have made the difference between the success and failure of the Schlieffen Plan.

The Russians failed to exploit their initial advantage in numbers, and on 26 August Samsonov's army marched into a trap. In the three-day battle of Tannenberg the Russians lost over 100,000 prisoners, and Samsonov committed suicide when he realised the full extent of the disaster. Rennenkampf's army was now doomed. At the battle of the Masurian Lakes in early September it was destroyed as an effective fighting force. In these two battles the Russians suffered more than a quarter of a million casualties, and lost huge quantities of equipment.

Germany's successes, however, were counter-

The war at sea in 1914

The expected fleet action between the British and German navies did not take place. Admiral Jellicoe dared not risk the loss of the Grand Fleet, even though the Royal Navy considerably outnumbered its German counterpart. Apart from its tasks of defending the coastline against invasion, and safeguarding the ocean routes for British merchant ships, the navy's wartime role was to blockade the enemy. Thus Jellicoe followed the cautious policy of 'keeping the fleet in being', while waiting for a favourable opportunity to engage enemy battleships. The German response was also cautious. Mines and submarines were used in the hope of whittling down Britain's supremacy in capital ships, and a submarine blockade of the sea approaches to the British Isles was begun.

The first successes at sea went to Germany. The cruisers *Goeben* and *Breslau*, at large in the Mediterranean when war broke out, reached Constantinople, where their arrival was a blow to Britain's naval prestige. The Turkish government had been irritated by the seizure of two dreadnoughts being built in British shipyards for the Turkish navy, and the Kaiser

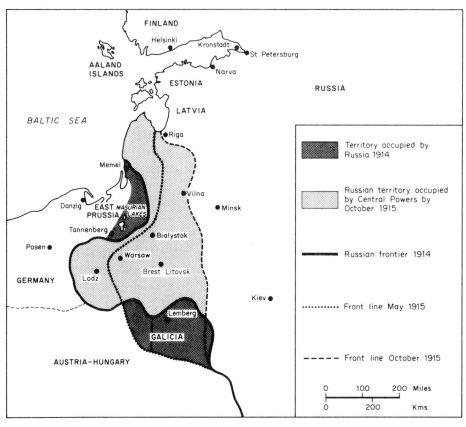

10   *The Eastern Front, 1914–15*

promptly offered the two warships to Turkey as compensation. The fact that they had eluded the British navy greatly assisted German diplomacy in persuading Turkey to ally herself with the Central Powers in November 1914.

In the Pacific the German cruiser *Emden* preyed upon merchant shipping until she was destroyed by the Australian cruiser *Sydney* in November. The German cruisers *Scharnhorst* and *Gneisenau*, commanded by Admiral von Spee, defeated a British squadron at Coronel, off the coast of Chile. This provoked the British Admiralty to send the battleships *Inflexible* and *Invincible* into the South Atlantic to eliminate them, and on 8 December the German cruisers were sunk at the battle of the Falkland Islands.

In Far Eastern waters the Japanese navy cleared the seas of German merchant ships,

which either sailed for neutral ports, where they were interned for the duration of the war, or were captured or sunk.

The capture of Germany's colonies

The only decisive results achieved in 1914 were in the colonial sideshow, which had no significant bearing on the course of the war. Japanese troops captured the German naval base of Tsingtao on the Shantung peninsula in November. A New Zealand expeditionary force seized Samoa, and Australian troops captured New Guinea. In South Africa Germany lost all her possessions by the end of 1914, with the exception of the Cameroons, which held out until 1916, and German East Africa, which resisted until the end of 1917.

The Gallipoli campaign, April to December 1915

The stalemate on the western front forced both sides to consider ways of breaking the deadlock. Turkey's entry into the war had severed communications between Russia and her allies, Britain and France. Russia, after her disastrous defeats in East Prussia, appealed to her allies for help against the Turks, who had invaded the Caucasus. Ever since the Turkish declaration of war Winston Churchill, First Lord of the Admiralty, had been attracted by the prospect of an amphibious attack on the Dardanelles, the classical way for a sea power to exploit its superiority. He persuaded the British and French cabinets in January 1915 to agree to a hastily planned assault upon the Dardanelles. Churchill's imaginative but controversial proposal would enable Britain and France to honour their debt to Russia for her prompt assistance in August 1914. The defeat of Turkey would create the opportunity for a flanking attack in the Balkans on the Central Powers, while Russia, which had been promised possession of Constantinople and the

Dardanelles, would be kept in the war. Such were the assumptions which lay behind the Gallipoli campaign.

In March the navy attempted to clear the minefield in the Straits and to silence the Turkish artillery on the coast. Three warships had been blown up when Admiral Robeck cancelled the operation just as the Turkish shore batteries were running out of ammunition. The departure of the British warships was viewed by the Turks with a mixture of astonishment and relief.

After this failure, plans were drawn up for landing troops on the Gallipoli peninsula. The Allies, however, had squandered the vital element of surprise by proclaiming their intentions to the Turks. The six-week delay before the landings took place on 25 April 1915 proved fatal to the expedition's chances of success. General Liman von Sanders took command of the Turkish army and re-organised the Turkish defences. Although the landings were successful, the Allied troops (mainly Australians and New Zealanders) were confined to their narrow bridgeheads. Over 200,000 of them became casualties,

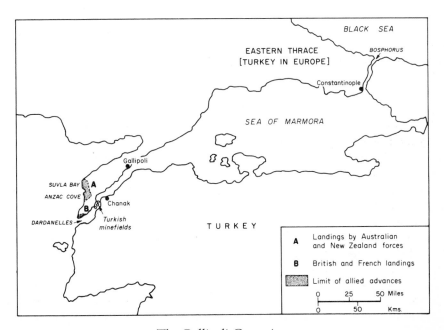

11   *The Gallipoli Campaign, 1915*

either in battle or through disease, before it was decided to abandon the expedition and evacuate the troops. This perilously difficult operation was carried out under cover of darkness without the loss of a single soldier – the only redeeming feature of an ill-conceived and most unfortunate campaign.

The Gallipoli campaign, which had promised so much, accomplished nothing. The dream of an alliance of Balkan states against the Central Powers faded. In October 1915 Bulgaria joined the Central Powers, and helped the Austro-German army in overrunning Serbia. The fiasco tarnished the reputations of Asquith, the British Prime Minister, and Churchill. Perhaps most depressing of all, it seemed to confirm the view of those who argued that the decisive theatre of war was the western front, where all available resources should be concentrated. In Britain the realisation that there was no short cut to victory prepared the way for conscription, which had been unacceptable in 1914. In January 1916 widowers without children and single men between the ages of 18 and 41 were liable for compulsory military service. In May 1916 conscription was applied to married men as well.

Italy's entry into the war, April 1915

When war broke out, Italy had formed part of the Triple Alliance with Germany and Austria-Hungary for over thirty years. For ten months the Italian government was torn by indecision. Many Italians wished to fight alongside Austria-Hungary, the great Catholic state, and the bulwark against Slav nationalism which threatened to engulf the Dalmatian coastline, long coveted by Italy. On the other hand, Italy had much to gain from a successful war against Austria-Hungary, which ruled *Italia Irredenta*, the 'unredeemed Italy', consisting of the Trentino and Trieste. Moreover, Italy's long coastline, and few natural resources, made her very vulnerable to blockade by a naval power.

These arguments finally persuaded the Italian government to sign the Treaty of London (April 1915), whereby Italy allied herself with Britain and France in return for the promise of the Trentino, Trieste, Istria, and much of Dalmatia. Many Italians, believing that the war was almost over, welcomed the decision, whereby Italy would share the spoils of a victorious war.

But the army was unprepared and Italy proved a doubtful asset to the Allies. The Italian troops suffered appalling casualties at the hands of the Austrians, while Italy's intervention came too late to prevent an Austrian offensive which resulted in the capture of Warsaw in August 1915, and the expulsion of Russian troops from Poland.

The eastern front in 1915

The Allies gained no comfort from events on the eastern front in 1915. Falkenhayn, who had succeeded Moltke in September 1914, reluctantly agreed with Hindenburg and Ludendorff that Germany's military effort should be concentrated on the eastern front, where a war of movement and great territorial gains was possible, while generally remaining on the defensive on the western front. In May von Mackenson launched a combined Austro-German offensive in Galicia. In July Ludendorff's army emerged from its defensive positions in East Prussia, and captured the vital rail junction of Bialystock. The badly mauled Russian armies retreated to a line running from Riga on the Baltic coast to the Rumanian frontier. Russian losses during the campaign amounted to two million men, of whom over one million were killed or wounded.

The war at sea, 1915–17

During 1915 Germany and Britain tightened their blockade of each other. The German government declared the western approaches to the British Isles a war zone in February, which neutral vessels entered at their own risk, and began a campaign of unrestricted submarine warfare. The British government retaliated by issuing orders-in-council, stating that all goods destined for Germany were contraband of war, and liable to seizure by ships of the Royal Navy.

Although Britain's action brought protests from neutral countries, and angered the United States, Germany lost any sympathy she gained by sinking the *Lusitania*, a passenger liner on its way to Liverpool from America. Twelve hundred passengers, including 128 Americans, were drowned. The loss of innocent lives shocked American opinion, and President Wilson warned Germany that its U-boat campaign could bring an end to America's neutrality. Germany abandoned unrestricted submarine warfare for the next two years, until it was re-introduced in 1917 in a desperate effort to starve Britain into submission.

The battle of Jutland

In May 1916 the German High Seas Fleet under Admiral Scheer ventured from Kiel into the North Sea in an attempt to lure the British Grand Fleet into a trap. On 31 May Hipper's force met a squadron of British warships commanded by Admiral Beatty. The battle was fought cautiously and at long range, while the rest of the two rival fleets rushed to the scene. When night fell the German fleet retired to harbour, having sunk 3 battle cruisers and 3 heavy cruisers, for the loss of 1 battleship, 1 battle cruiser, and 4 light cruisers; 6,000 British sailors lost their lives, compared with 2,500 Germans. Both sides claimed a victory.

Germany's resumption of unrestricted submarine warfare

In January 1917 Germany resumed unrestricted submarine warfare. The German government believed that the United States would

eventually declare war on the Central Powers. On this assumption the renewal of unrestricted submarine warfare was a calculated risk. Almost certainly it would mean America's entry into the war on the side of the Entente Powers, but the German Admiralty was optimistic that Britain could be starved into surrender in six months, before American intervention could become effective. How close to success the German plan came is borne out by the fact that at the height of the U-boat campaign Britain had only six weeks' supply of foodstuffs left.

U-boat sinkings in the first four months of the year were so severe that Admiral Jellicoe was forced to admit that 'it is impossible for us to go on with the war if losses like this [875,000 tons sunk in April alone] continue'. Fortunately for Britain, the development of anti-submarine devices, such as depth charges and hydrophones, and the organisation of a convoy system, greatly reduced losses from U-boat attacks. After April 1917 America's shipbuilding resources were added to Britain's, and by the end of the year the German U-boat menace had been overcome. Even so, U-boats sank 15 million tons of shipping during the war, or one quarter of the world's shipping in 1914.

The western front, 1915–16

Throughout 1915 French forces commanded by General Joffre continued their set-piece offensives in Artois and Champagne. Attacks were preceded by artillery bombardments calculated to destroy the enemy trench system and barbed wire entanglements. But as soon as the barrage lifted, the defenders emerged from their dug-outs and dragged their machine-guns into position. The infantry, advancing in orderly lines, were mown down in their hundreds and thousands.

By the end of 1915 the deadlock which had developed on all fronts convinced both Joffre and Falkenhayn that victory could only be achieved on the western front. Joffre planned a combined summer offensive in the Somme area, where the British and French armies could cooperate. His plans, however, were upset by the German onslaught at Verdun.

Verdun

Falkenhayn believed that the French army could be destroyed, if it was forced to fight in circumstances favourable to the Germans. His strategy was to lure the French army into the defence of Verdun, the last of the great French strongholds to fall in the Franco-Prussian War (1870–1). Verdun was exposed on three sides to German artillery, but Falkenhayn correctly calculated that it would be recklessly defended by the French for sentimental reasons. French reserves would be steadily committed to its defence, and could be systematically annihilated by artillery and ground attacks. German losses would be heavy, but as the Germans outnumbered the French, the latter would be bled white first. These were the crude tactics of a war of attrition.

By the end of January 1916 Falkenhayn had transferred over half a million troops from the eastern front, and had massed 1,300 heavy guns covering a front only eight miles wide. Joffre ignored the warning signs of an impending German attack, confident that his own offensive would force the enemy to abandon their plans.

The attack upon Verdun opened with a nine-hour bombardment. General Pétain was ordered to defend Verdun whatever the cost. Reinforcements were rushed to the scene and by July Nivelle, who replaced Pétain in May, had forced Falkenhayn on to the defensive. During the seven-month battle the French casualties were 370,000 men, while the German losses amounted to 330,000.

The French pleaded with their allies to put forward the timing of their offensives in order to relieve the pressure at Verdun. Brusilov prematurely attacked the Austrians along a 300-mile front in Galicia. The Austrians were taken by surprise, but Brusilov had no reserves to exploit initial gains, and his offensive came to a halt when German troops were rushed to the assistance of the Austrians.

Meanwhile, Britain's conscript army had launched its first offensive at the battle of the Somme, which lasted from 1 July to 18 November. On the first day's fighting the British suffered 57,000 casualties, of whom 19,000 were killed. In September tanks were used for the first time. They took the German troops by surprise, but the break in the German lines could not be exploited. Thus the weapon which might conceivably have brought about a decisive victory was squandered in an ill-prepared attack in a campaign which had already failed. When rain and mud halted the battle a mere seven miles had been gained in return for over 600,000 casualties.

The western front in 1917

In December 1916 Joffre was replaced by Nivelle, who had made his reputation at Verdun. Nivelle persuaded the French and British cabinets that one more offensive would bring about the collapse of the German army. But his plans were disrupted when the German troops abandoned their front-line trenches in the spring and occupied a newly-constructed, immensely strong fortified position ten miles to the rear, known as the Hindenburg Line. Nivelle's offensive gained only four miles of ground for heavy losses. Thoroughly weary of apparently pointless fighting and heavy casualties, whole sections of the French army mutinied. Nivelle was dismissed. Pétain, his successor, suppressed the mutinies firmly, but insisted that the French armies should remain strictly on the defensive until their morale had recovered.

The British now had to bear the brunt of the fighting on the western front, in order to prevent the enemy from discovering the full extent of the demoralisation of the French army. In an optimistic effort to capture the Channel ports, Haig launched costly offensives at Ypres and Passchendaele. Like Nivelle, Haig was convinced that the German army was close to collapse, but when winter rains turned

Mud was one of the appalling conditions with which both sides had to contend. Here British soldiers manhandle artillery along a railway track

low-lying Flanders into a water-logged countryside, and swamp-like conditions halted the British attacks, little ground had been gained.

The collapse of Russia, 1917

By 1917 Russia was on the verge of defeat. On the home front widespread political discontent forced Tsar Nicholas II to abdicate in March. A provisional government under Kerensky tried to continue the war. When the Germans captured Riga in September, however, the Russian army collapsed, and thousands of soldiers deserted, voting with their feet against a continuation of the war. Soon afterwards, in November, the Bolsheviks led by Lenin and Trotsky seized power, and immediately sued for peace. This enabled the German High Command to speed up the transfer of German troops from the eastern front to the western front.

The peace treaty of Brest Litovsk, signed in March 1918, stripped Russia of one third of her population, and all the European territories she had acquired over the past three hundred years. It was a bitter settlement, made necessary by Lenin's determination to purchase peace at any price in order to consolidate the Revolution (see Chapter 11). But by breaking their promise not to conclude a separate peace with the Central Powers, the Russians forfeited Allied goodwill, as well as the right to take part in the peace settlement which followed the defeat of Germany and her allies.

The United States enters the war, April 1917

During the early stages of the war American public opinion had been strongly isolationist. Many Americans were recent immigrants from Central Europe, and their sympathies were with the Central Powers. But the German government mis-handled its diplomatic relations with the United States. In January 1917 British intelligence intercepted a coded message from the German government to its ambassador in Mexico – the Zimmerman Telegram, which stated that in the event of the United States entering the war, Germany should ally with Mexico, which would be promised Texas, Arizona, and New Mexico. The publication of this document in American newspapers seriously damaged Germany's cause.

It was Germany's resumption of unrestricted submarine warfare in January 1917, however, which, more than any other factor, pushed the United States into a declaration of war. Germany's decision outraged the feelings of many American citizens. President Wilson broke off diplomatic relations with Germany, and ordered American merchant ships to be armed and to open fire upon submarines if they were attacked. From this it was but a short step to war. The abdication of Nicholas II and the advent of a liberal, parliamentary regime in Russia removed any qualms Americans might have felt about entering a war in support of an autocratic tsardom. On 2 April Congress declared war on Germany, to protect 'democracy, the rights and liberties of small nations, to bring peace and safety to all nations, and to make the world itself at last free'.

Germany poised for victory

The military situation for the Allies at the beginning of 1918 was grim. Russia had deserted them. The United States could not bring its immense resources of manpower and materials to bear for several months. The German army for the first time had a numerical superiority on the western front. On the Italian front the Austrians had gained a spectacular victory at Caporetto, in the previous October. In a headlong retreat which only ended outside Venice, 250,000 Italian soldiers deserted or were taken prisoners-of-war. The only Allied success was general Allenby's

capture of Jerusalem in December, but this victory could not influence events on the western front, where the initiative now lay with the Central Powers.

The German spring offensive

In March 1918 German armies commanded by Ludendorff and Hindenburg attacked the junction of the British and French armies on a fifty-mile front. It was a desperate effort to win the war before American intervention became effective. The German armies drove forty miles towards Paris, and brought the Allies to the brink of defeat, before the offensive lost momentum in June. In August, Foch, who had been made commander-in-chief of all Allied forces in Europe, began a series of sharp counter-attacks upon the extended German line. With American troops now pouring into France at the rate of over 200,000 per month, Germany's lack of reserves was a fatal weakness.

The collapse of the Central Powers

On 8 August, which Ludendorff called 'the black day of the German army', the Germans suffered a major reverse at the Somme. By late September the German armies had been driven back across the Hindenburg Line. Ludendorff informed the Kaiser that the war was lost, and he demanded that a civilian government should be formed, with the aim of seeking an immediate armistice.

While the German armies were retreating before incessant attacks by superior forces, Germany's allies were collapsing one by one. Bulgaria surrendered on 30 September, and Turkey on 30 October, after General Allenby had captured Damascus, together with an entire Turkish army. The Austro-Hungarian Empire was disintegrating as the Czechs and Poles deserted the Habsburg monarchy in order

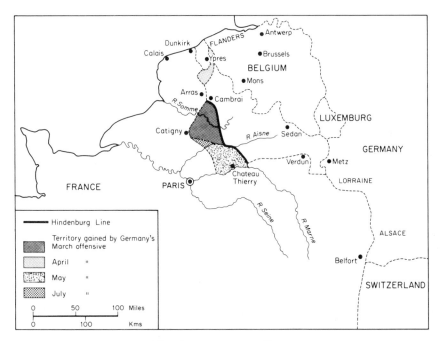

12   *The German spring offensive, 1918*

to fight for their national independence. At the battle of Vittorio Veneto in October the Italians gained revenge for the humiliation of Caporetto, and Austria-Hungary signed a ceasefire agreement on 4 November.

Germany's military situation was now hopeless. American forces reached Sedan by the end of October, and British troops broke through the German lines into open country. On 11 November 1918, two days after the Kaiser bowed to the inevitable by fleeing to Holland, Germany accepted the armistice terms offered by the Allies at Compiègne, and the Great War came to an end.

In January 1918 President Wilson of the United States of America outlined to Congress the text of his Fourteen Points. These were intended to be the basis of the peace settlement at the end of the war. Wilson stated America's aim of making the world 'fit and safe to live in, particularly for every peace-loving nation which, like our own, wishes to live its own life, determine its own institutions, and be assured of justice and fair dealing by the other peoples of the world against force and selfish aggression'. The Fourteen Points may be summarised as:

1. *Open covenants of peace openly arrived at – no private international understandings.*

2. *Freedom of navigation upon the seas in peace and war.*

3. *The removal, so far as possible, of all economic barriers to world trade.*

4. *The reduction of national armaments to the lowest point consistent with domestic safety.*

5. *Colonial claims to be dealt with according to the principle that the interests of the populations concerned must have equal weight with the claims of the colonial power.*

6. *The evacuation of all Russian territory. Russia to be welcomed into the society of free nations under institutions of her own choice, and to be given assistance of every kind that she might need and desire.*

7. *Belgium to be evacuated and restored.*

8. *All French territory to be freed and the invaded portions retored. Alsace-Lorraine should be returned to France, thus righting the wrong done to France by Germany in 1871.*

9. *Italy's frontiers should be adjusted along clearly recognisable lines of nationality.*

10. *The peoples of Austria-Hungary to be given the freest opportunity for self-government.*

11. *Rumania, Serbia and Montenegro to be evacuated and guaranteed their political and economic independence. Serbia to be given a coastline.*

12. *The Turkish parts of the Ottoman Empire should form a separate state, but the other peoples ruled by the Turks should be given their independence. The Dardanelles should be open at all times to the ships of all nations.*

13. *An independent Polish state should be set up and given access to the sea.*

14. *A general association of nations should be formed to preserve future peace.*

At 11 o'clock on the morning of 11 November 1918 the guns on the western front stopped firing, and silence descended upon the battlefields where many hundreds of thousands of men had lost their lives during four years of terrible warfare. By the Armistice of Compiègne Germany agreed to evacuate all occupied territory, and to withdraw beyond the right bank of the Rhine. The peace treaties of Brest Litovsk and Bucharest were cancelled. Germany surrendered its navy, and large quantities of military equipment, including aeroplanes, lorries, locomotives and railway wagons, while the Allied blockade of Germany was to be maintained until peace had been signed. The Allies were determined to ensure that although the German armies had not surrendered they would not be able to resume the fighting.

The Allies were agreed that to insist upon unconditional surrender would be an unnecessary humiliation of Germany. Thus German troops were allowed to march back in good order to their homeland, while along the eastern front some German armies were left in position, in order to stop the spread of communism. In these arrangements lay the origin of the belief, held by many Germans after the war, that they had been deceived by Allied promises. They never fully appreciated that the German High Command had told the government in November 1918 that further resistance was useless, leaving the civilian authorities with no choice but to agree to an armistice.

Nine weeks passed before delegates from thirty-two states assembled at Paris to begin drafting the peace treaties. This delay enabled a general election to be held in Britain where, because of the war, eight years had passed since the previous one. In the famous 'Khaki Election' of December 1918 anti-German feeling ran very high, and no candidate who showed any signs of sympathy for Germany stood any chance of being elected to Parliament. Lloyd George became Prime Minister with a large majority, and he went to Paris with a mandate to 'Make Germany Pay'.

The French Prime Minister, Clemenceau, also received an overwhelming vote of confidence in the French Chamber of Deputies. The 78-year-old Frenchman, nicknamed 'The Tiger' for his unrelenting hatred of Germany, was made Chairman at the Conference, out of

Delegates of the four victorious great powers at the Versailles Peace Conference: (left to right) Lloyd George, Orlando, Clemenceau, Wilson

courtesy since France was the host nation.

President Wilson was the only head of state at the Conference. An idealist and a deeply religious man, Wilson believed that his mission was to formulate a just and lasting peace settlement. Aloof and sensitive to criticism, he did not try to cultivate good relations with the press and public. He soon disagreed strongly with Clemenceau, who was determined to inflict a harsh settlement upon the Central Powers. Wilson also knew that American public opinion was becoming increasingly hostile to any further involvement in Europe's affairs. Even before he arrived in Paris, Wilson's party, the Democrats, had lost its majorities in both the Senate and the House of Representatives to the Republicans in the Congressional elections of November 1918. This weakened Wilson's position in Paris, and later resulted in Congress refusing to ratify the Versailles Treaty.

These three statesmen, Wilson, Clemenceau, and Lloyd George, were the 'Big Three'. Most of the major decisions at the Conference were taken by them. Neither Italy nor Japan, the other two great powers represented at Paris, played very important parts. Italy was preoccupied with obtaining favourable frontier adjustments, while Japan was chiefly concerned with claiming German territories in the Pacific and consolidating its influence in China.

After six months of deliberations the final details of the peace settlement with Germany were decided. Although the actual terms had been kept secret, the German government was aware that they were savage. Speaking at the Trianon Palace Hotel at Versailles in May 1919, Count Brockdorff-Rantzau, head of the German delegation, said:

We are under no illusions as to the extent of our defeat and the degree of our powerlessness. We know that the strength of the German army is broken. We know the intensity of the hatred which meets us, and we have heard the victors' passionate demand that as the vanquished we shall be made to pay, and as the guilty we shall be punished.

The demand is made that we shall acknowledge that we alone are guilty of having caused the war. Such a confession would be a lie. . . . We deny that the people of Germany, who were convinced that they were waging a war of defence, should be burdened with the sole guilt of that war.

The treaty was presented to the German delegation on 16 June 1919. They were given

expired, the German delegation indicated their readiness to sign. This ceremony took place in the Hall of Mirrors at Versailles on 28 June, the fifth anniversary of the assassination of the Archduke Ferdinand.

By the terms of the treaty Germany lost 28,000 square miles, or 14 per cent, of her

Allied officers watching the handing over of the Versailles peace treaty to the German delegation

seven days to consider it, but they knew that thirty-nine Allied divisions were poised on the Rhine ready to advance into a defenceless Germany should they reject it. On 22 June the delegates said they would sign if the War Guilt clauses were deleted. The Allies refused this request outright, for the clauses were the legal justification for reparations. Moreover, they had been angered by the scuttling of the German Fleet lying at Scapa Flow, in Scotland. At 5 p.m., two hours before the deadline

territory. Alsace-Lorraine was returned to France. Germany's request that the inhabitants should vote on this matter was refused. The coal mines of the Saar were handed over to France as compensation for the ruin of France's northern coalfields. An International Commission was to administer the Saar territory for fifteen years, when its future would be decided by a plebiscite. (In 1935 the Saar opted for reunion with Germany, which repurchased the mines.)

Belgium was awarded three areas: Moresnet, Eupen, and Malmedy. A plebiscite determined the Danish-German frontier. The largely Danish-speaking northern half of Slesvig chose to join Denmark, while the southern part voted to remain German.

In Eastern Europe Germany renounced the gains it had made by the treaties of Brest part of West Prussia, which voted to stay German (see map 13). Danzig became a Free City, administered by the League of Nations but with Poland enjoying special rights, such as control over its foreign affairs. Germany also lost the port of Memel. In 1920 the League agreed to its seizure by Lithuania.

The union of Germany and Austria

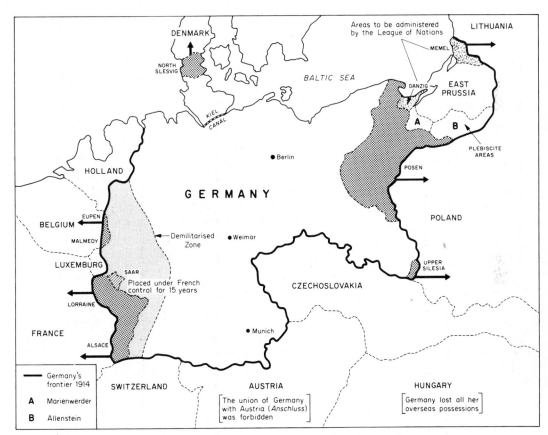

13   *Territorial changes made by the Treaty of Versailles, 1919*

Litovsk and Bucharest. Posen, West Prussia and part of Upper Silesia were transferred to Poland. The acquisition of West Prussia gave Poland access to the sea, thus fulfilling one of the Fourteen Points, but separated East Prussia from the rest of Germany. German protests succeeded in winning Allied agreement for plebiscites to be held in the districts of Allenstein and Marienwerder in the southern (*Anschluss*) was forbidden unless it was authorised by the unanimous consent of the League's Council. Since France was a Permanent Member of the Council it was assumed that such a move would always be vetoed.

Germany lost all its overseas territories, amounting to one million square miles. A strip of German East Africa was given to Belgium; the remainder became the British colony of

Tanganyika. Britain and France shared Togoland and the Cameroons, while German South West Africa was given to the Union of South Africa. Germany's possessions in the Pacific Ocean south of the Equator were divided between Britain, Australia and New Zealand. Those north of the Equator were awarded to Japan, to the anger of China, which subsequently refused to sign the Treaty of Versailles.

German territory on the west bank of the Rhine, and three bridgeheads on the east bank (Cologne, Coblenz and Mainz), were to be occupied by Allied troops. Provided Germany fulfilled its treaty obligations, the zones would be successively evacuated at five-year intervals. German territory west of the Rhine, and a strip of territory 50 km wide adjoining the right bank of the Rhine, were to be permanently demilitarised. No armed forces, military installations, or army manoeuvres were to be allowed in these areas. Any violation of these provisions was to be regarded as a 'hostile act calculated to disturb the peace of the world'. As a guarantee of good faith over the cancellation of the Treaty of Brest Litovsk, Germany agreed to withdraw all her troops from the Baltic states immediately the Allies decided that stability had returned to Eastern Europe.

Germany was made virtually defenceless by severe restrictions placed upon its armed forces. The army was limited to 100,000 men. To prevent the development of a conscript army, officers were required to serve for twenty-five years, and all other ranks for twelve years. Tanks, heavy artillery and military aircraft were prohibited. The General Staff was disbanded. Germany's navy was limited to twelve destroyers, six light cruisers, and six 'pocket' battleships with a maximum of 10,000 tons displacement. Submarines were banned. To ensure that these provisions were observed, the German armaments industry was to be strictly controlled and inspected, but in the event this proved to be an impossible task.

Germany unwillingly accepted legal responsibility for the war. Article 231, the War Guilt clause, stated: 'The Allied and Associated Governments affirm and Germany accepts the responsibility of Germany and her allies for causing all the loss and damage to which their nationals have been subjected as a consequence of the war imposed upon them by the aggression of Germany and her allies.'

Under the armistice terms Germany agreed to pay for damage done to Allied civilian property. Subsequently the principle of reparations was extended to cover the full cost of the war, so that pensions and war debts were included. In the opinion of Lloyd George, naming the figure the Allies had in mind would frighten the Germans into refusing to sign the treaty, while any figure which did not frighten them would not be acceptable to the French and British electorates. Accordingly, a

The transfer of German minorities

Territory transferred	Ruled by	Population	German-speaking
EUPEN-MALMEDY	BELGIUM	60,000	47,000
NORTH SLESVIG	DENMARK	160,000	40,000
SUDETENLAND	CZECHOSLOVAKIA	3,255,000	2,775,000
MEMEL	LITHUANIA	141,000	72,000
DANZIG	LEAGUE	336,000	328,000
POLISH CORRIDOR	POLAND	939,000	185,000
POSEN	POLAND	1,974,000	346,000
SILESIA	POLAND	919,000	272,000
ALSACE	FRANCE	1,219,000	1,153,000
LORRAINE	FRANCE	655,000	481,000

Based on *Geographic Aspects of International Relations*, by Charles C. Colby

Reparations Commission was set up to decide the amount Germany should pay. The figure eventually decided was £6,600,000,000 plus interest. This compared with the £2,000 million which the British Treasury calculated Germany could reasonably be expected to pay, and the so-called 'businessman's estimate' of £24,000 million.

Criticisms of the treaty

Reparations were the most controversial aspect of the Versailles Treaty. They were intended to serve two purposes. Apart from paying for wartime losses, they would, if paid in full, destroy any chance of Germany re-emerging as a great power for the next fifty years. In the event reparations benefited no country.

J. M. Keynes, the famous economist, in his book *The Economic Consequences of the Peace*, argued that reparations were vindictive, impractical and completely beyond Germany's capacity to pay. If Germany paid in gold the cash could only be earned by massive exports of manufactures, which would cause unemployment in the receiving countries. Payment in goods was unacceptable for the same reason. No sensible financial settlement was possible unless the Allies were prepared to cancel their war debts, but so long as the American government demanded the repayment of wartime loans (amounting to £2,000 million), Britain and France were determined to collect the money from Germany in the form of reparations. Reparations were ended in 1932, but in the meantime they embittered relations between the victors and defeated.

The French were dissatisfied with the treaty, for, having won the war at a grievous cost, they lost the security to which they felt they were entitled. At the Paris Conference Clemenceau had demanded the creation of a buffer state on the west bank of the Rhine to safeguard France in any future war with Germany. Lloyd George and Wilson had refused. All that Clemenceau obtained was a temporary military occupation of the Rhineland, its demilitarisation, and a Treaty of Guarantee, whereby the United States and Britain promised to come to the assistance of France if she was the victim of an unprovoked attack by Germany. When the United States Senate refused to ratify the treaty, this promised security vanished, since the British government claimed that its guarantee was dependent upon America fulfilling her obligations.

Significant German minorities were transferred to other states, particularly Poland and Czechoslovakia, as shown opposite.

The German government declared: 'We shall never forget those who are to be severed from us. They are flesh of our flesh. Wherever it can be done, we shall take their part as if it were our own. They will be torn from the Reich, but they will not be torn from our hearts.' Minorities remained a constant source of irritation to the governments concerned, especially after the advent to power of the Nazis in 1934.

It was unwise not to have involved Germany in the peace negotiations. The Germans always bitterly resented the fact that the treaty had been signed under duress, and the *Diktat* of Versailles was a favourable propaganda topic with the Nazis.

Finally, the very harshness of the treaty discredited the Weimar government in Germany, which was responsible for signing the armistice and the peace treaty. Had the peace settlement been less savage in its treatment of Germany, the Weimar Republic would have stood a greater chance of winning the loyalty of the German people, and if the Republic had not been destroyed by Hitler in 1934, the course of international history would have been very different.

CHAPTER SIX
The Reconstruction of Eastern Europe

In 1914 the greater part of Eastern Europe, the area roughly encompassed by the Baltic, Adriatic and Black seas, lay within three great empires – the German, Austro-Hungarian and Russian. By 1919 each had been destroyed by war, defeat and revolution. The bulk of their populations, Poles, Czechs, Serbs and Croats, even Austrians and Hungarians (Magyars), had declared their separate existence within new nation states. Their recognition or establishment by the peacemakers at Paris owed much to a general acceptance of President Wilson's principle of national self-determination, but they reflected other important if sometimes incompatible aims. These were the isolation of communist Russia and the containment of Germany, now every much reduced in power. Furthermore, the mixture of races in this part of Europe made it impossible to create new states without including significant minorities in each.

The Treaty of St-Germain with Austria, September 1919

The Austro-Hungarian Empire paid dearly for its alliance with Germany and for its expansionist policy in the Balkans. A major Allied war aim was national self-determination for the subject peoples of the Dual Monarchy. Furthermore, both Italy and Rumania had been enticed into declaring war on the Central Powers by promises of Austro-Hungarian territories.

Bohemia, Moravia, Austrian Silesia and parts of Lower Austria were transferred to the new state of Czechoslovakia. Galicia was awarded to Poland and the Bukovina was given to Rumania. With few exceptions frontiers were drawn, and populations placed under new governments, without regard to the wishes of the inhabitants concerned, and often without accurate detailed knowledge of geography and topography. Austria's union with Germany (*Anschluss*) was forbidden, and Austria was expressly warned not to consider policies which might compromise her separate existence.

The South Tyrol, containing 235,000 Austrians, was transferred to Italy, which thereby secured the Brenner Pass, as promised by the Treaty of London of April 1915. Italy also acquired Trieste and Istria.

Austria was forced to accept its share of the blame for the war, and agreed to pay reparations for a period of thirty years. Its army was limited to 30,000 men. As a result of the treaty 4 million German-speaking inhabitants became the subjects of foreign governments. Austria lost over two-thirds of its territory, and over three-quarters of its population, which in 1920 was reduced from 30 to $6\frac{1}{2}$ million. Of these, over 2 million lived in Vienna. Austria was likened to a head without a body, and as an economic unit could be expected to survive only with great difficulty.

Bela Kun and the communist revolution in Hungary

The Magyars hoped to escape the most serious consequences of the war by claiming that since they had formed part of the Austro-Hungarian Empire, they had had no alternative but to accept Austria's decision to declare war

POLAND

GALICIA

CZECHOSLOVAKIA

GERMANY

BUKOVINA

AUSTRIA

SOUTH
TYROL

TRENTINO

HUNGARY

TRANSYLVANIA

CROATIA

Trieste

ISTRIA Fiume

BANAT

SLOVENIA

ITALY

RUMANIA

DALMATIA

BOSNIA

YUGOSLAVIA

BULGARIA

HERZE-
GOVINA

	Post war Austria and Hungary			Awarded to Rumania
	Newly created state of Czechoslavakia			Awarded to Serbia to become part of new state of Yugoslavia
	Territory allocated to re-created Poland			Awarded to Italy
	Boundary of Austro-Hungarian Empire in 1914			

0   50   100   150 Miles

0   150   Kms.

14   *The break-up of the Austro-Hungarian Empire*

on Serbia in 1914. When the peacemakers eventually presented their bill, the Magyars realised that Hungary was to be the chief loser as a result of the war. In the meantime, however, between the signing of the armistice and the ratification of the Treaty of Trianon, Hungary was torn by political dissension and civil disturbances.

In October 1918, after the government had recalled its troops from the front lines, a bloodless revolution placed a Hungarian nobleman, Count Karolyi, in power, and Hungary became a republic. Karolyi was an idealist who lacked the necessary determination and ruthlessness to force others to comply with his wishes. He gave many of his estates to the peasants but failed to persuade other nobles to do likewise. He hoped to reconcile the Slav population of historic Hungary with the Magyars, but was not allowed time to accomplish his aim. He introduced an electoral law giving the vote to all adults who could read, but refused to hold elections until 'all Allied troops had left – by which time he had fallen from power.

His successor was Bela Kun, a dedicated communist, who established the first communist government outside Russia. Bela Kun had been one of half a million Hungarian prisoners-of-war in Russian camps. Many of them witnessed the events of the 1917 Revolution and were converted to communism. In November 1918 Bela Kun founded the Hungarian Communist party at a meeting in Moscow. Several hundred Hungarian communists were sent to agitate against Karolyi's government and bring about its downfall. Communist propaganda proved attractive to raw recruits and idle, undisciplined troops returned home from the trenches. Soon Bela Kun had built up an organised party of several thousands in Hungary. With money given him by the Russian communist government he bought thousands of rifles left behind by disarmed German troops, and inspired a communist uprising in Budapest.

Karolyi arrested Bela Kun and other communist leaders, but was persuaded to release them when Lenin seized a Hungarian Red Cross mission in Moscow and held them hostages. In Hungary itself there was considerable popular support for Kun, who had refused to go into hiding when he learned that he was to be arrested. Furthermore, Karolyi appeared unwilling to resist the Czechs, Yugoslavs and Rumanians who were intent upon seizing Hungarian territory. The socialist party, Karolyi's chief support, deserted him and joined the communists. Karolyi fled, and Bela Kun took his place.

Communism was ruthlessly imposed upon the Hungarian people. All ranks and titles were abolished. Transport, banking and private houses were taken over by the state. All industrial and business firms with more than twenty employees were nationalised. All land not personally cultivated by its owner was seized by the government. Ex-convicts were sent into the countryside to terrorise the population into submission. Yet resistance steadily grew. The peasants proved unwilling to exchange their produce for a worthless currency, when they knew that with industry in a state of chaos few goods were available to be bought. Moreover, because Bela Kun was convinced that peasant farmers were inefficient, the nobility's lands were not shared out among the peasants. Instead, the nationalised landed estates were formed into collective farms, managed by the previous owners. The peasant saw little difference between the new system and the old one of private ownership.

Bela Kun deflected mounting criticism of his rule by suddenly attacking the Czechs in Slovakia. In June 1919 Magyar forces recaptured most of the territory occupied by the Czechs, but were withdrawn when the French government threatened to intervene. Bela Kun next attacked Rumanian troops who had not retired as promised when the Magyars evacuated Slovakia. The war-weary Hungarian army, however, failed to press home its attack.

A fierce reaction set in against Bela Kun's policies and methods, and at the beginning of August he sought refuge in Austria. A right-wing regime was set up under Count Karolyi, a cousin of the Karolyi ousted by Bela Kun, with Count Teleki as Foreign Minister and Admiral Horthy as War Minister. The new administration exacted revenge for communist excesses. Thousands of Bela Kun's supporters were beaten, tortured, and imprisoned. More than 5,000 were killed. In March 1920 Admiral Horthy was appointed Regent, with considerable powers, for he could veto proposed legislation and appoint and dismiss prime ministers. Since he was also commander-in-chief of the armed forces he became virtually dictator.

The Treaty of Trianon, June 1920

With the communist administration destroyed, the peace treaty was presented to

Horthy's government for ratification. Its terms were savage. The Hungarian army was restricted to 35,000 volunteers and, like the German, was forbidden to possess military aircraft, tanks or heavy artillery. Hungary lost two-thirds of its territory, more than half its road and rail network, and most of its timber and iron-ore resources. Rumania, Yugoslavia and Czechoslovakia gained most from Hungary's dismemberment. Rumania alone obtained an area of land larger than post-war Hungary itself. Hungary's population was reduced from 18 million to a little over 7 million. Hungarian resentment over the treatment meted out to her was bitter and long-lasting. Alongside Germany and Italy, Hungary sought to overthrow the Versailles settlement.

The Treaty of Neuilly with Bulgaria, November 1919

Bulgaria was firmly punished by the peace-makers for her involvement in the war, which had nearly resulted in the destruction of Serbia, and had embarrassed the Entente Powers by bringing the influence of the Central Powers down to the Straits of Constantinople. Since Turkey had also entered the war in November 1914 on the side of Germany and Austria-Hungary, the Allies were prevented from supplying Russia with war materials via the Straits as an entry to the Black Sea.

Greece acquired Western Thrace, so that Bulgaria lost the access to the Aegean Sea gained as a result of its victories in the Balkan Wars of 1912–13. Bulgaria also surrendered the Southern Dobrudja to Rumania. Its army was limited to 20,000 men, and reparations were demanded. Having lost 8 per cent of its territory, Bulgaria associated itself with other revisionist states, and in September 1940, during the Second World War, recovered the Dobrudja.

Rumania and Yugoslavia

By the secret Treaty of Bucharest (August 1916) Rumania had declared war on Austria-Hungary in return for promises of territory, which included the Bukovina, Banat and Transylvania. Although Rumania forfeited its claims by signing a separate peace agreement with the Central Powers one year later, it was nevertheless handsomely rewarded after the war by additional territory. Rumania obtained Transylvania, Bukovina and part of the Banat from Hungary, the Southern Dobrudja from Bulgaria, and Bessarabia from Russia, where the communist government was so deeply involved in civil war that it was unable to prevent this loss of territory. As a result of these gains Rumania contained over one million Magyars, nearly one million Russians and Ukrainians, over 700,000 Germans, a similar number of Jews, and 350,000 Bulgarians.

Yugoslavia, on the other hand, was an entirely new state, created partly in recognition of Serbia's claim that it should unite all the Slav peoples of the Balkans, and partly as compensation for Serbia's sufferings during the war. The new Kingdom of Serbs, Croats and Slovenes as it was first named, was the most complicated state created by the Versailles settlement. Built around the two formerly independent states of Serbia and Montenegro, it inherited Slovenia and Dalmatia from the Austrian half of the Habsburg Empire, and Croatia from the Hungarian half. In addition the new state gained Bosnia and Herzegovina, annexed by Austria-Hungary in 1908, and Macedonia, which had belonged to Turkey up to the Balkan Wars of 1912–13.

Yugoslavia, Rumania and Czechoslovakia, another new state created by the peace settlement, formed a Little Entente, or military understanding, with one another, in order to deter Hungary, the chief loser, from trying to recover its lands. Yugoslavia also became involved in a long dispute with Italy over possession of Fiume, which was not finally resolved until 1924 (see Chapter 9).

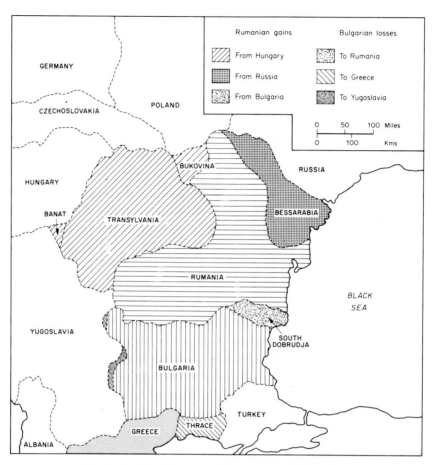

15   *The territorial settlement of Rumania and Bulgaria, 1919–20*

Czechoslovakia

In October 1918, during the final stages of the First World War, Czech nationalists, inspired by two professors of Prague University, Thomas Masaryk and Eduard Benes, proclaimed their independence of Austro-Hungarian rule. Masaryk became President of the Czechoslovak Republic from 1918 to 1935, when he was succeeded by Benes, who had been Foreign Minister since 1918. Although 6 million Czechs warmly welcomed the new state, Czechoslovakia was largely an artificial creation which owed much to France's preoccupation with restraining Germany, and Western European governments' fear of Bolshevik Russia.

Unlike the defeated nations, the Czechs were allowed to send a delegation to the Paris Peace Conference to present their case. Benes argued that the Czechs and Slovaks were branches of the same race, which was debatable, but the Slovaks had nowhere else to go, and in the new state they were placed on equal terms with the Czechs. Some 600,000 Ruthenians were included, chiefly because they were opposed to union with Poland or Rumania, along with 700,000 Magyars. The $3\frac{1}{4}$ million Germans who lived in the Sudetenland, however, were the most resentful minority.

Very conscious of having constituted the ruling class in the old Austro-Hungarian Empire, the Sudetens had declared themselves part of Austria in October 1918. When Czech troops occupied the Sudetenland to lay

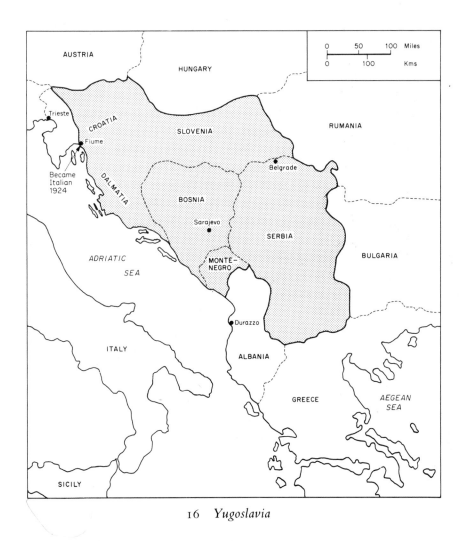

16　*Yugoslavia*

claim to the territory, Austria was in no position to help, while Germany itself showed very little concern, feeling that the Sudeten Germans were part of the Austro-Hungarian Empire. The Sudetens themselves offered little resistance to the Czechs, for they were convinced that a plebiscite would confirm their desire to join Austria. But the Sudetenland was awarded to Czechoslovakia in order to give the new state a strategic frontier.

Relations between the German minority and the Czech government were never harmonious. When Hitler became dictator the Sudetens were encouraged by the Nazis to agitate for reunion with the German Fatherland. When Germany occupied the Sudetenland in 1938

Hitler claimed that he was coming to the defence of a cruelly persecuted minority (see Chapter 20).

Poland

In the early seventeenth century Poland had been a major European power, second to France only in size of population, and to Russia in territory. Unfortunately, once its military power waned, Poland, lacking defensible frontiers, became a prey to aggressive, more efficiently organised neighbouring states. By the end of the eighteenth century Poland had been successively par-

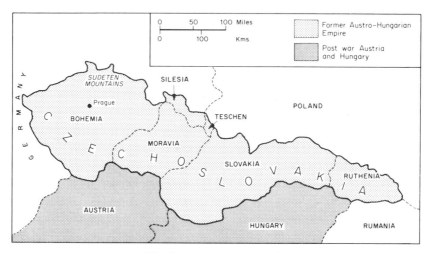

17   *The formation of Czechoslovakia*

titioned by Austria, Prussia and Russia, and its separate existence ended. It was only after Russia withdrew from the First World War that the creation of Polish state with access to the sea became a major war aim of the United States, Britain and France.

During the war two rival Polish patriots worked for the liberation of their people. Roman Dmowski hoped for an Allied victory, while Joseph Pilsudski campaigned for the Central Powers. He expected a Polish state to be set up after the defeat of Russia. In January 1919 Ignacy Paderewski, an astute statesman, healed the rift between them and persuaded them both to join a Government of National Union, in which Pilsudski was made President and Dmowski headed Poland's delegation at the Peace Conference. In the meantime, Poland embarked upon a series of military adventures against Russia, Germany, Lithuania and Czechoslovakia, when she laid claim to large tracts of territory on the basis that possession amounted to nine-tenths of the law. By the time the so-called Curzon Line, defining the proposed frontier between Poland and Russia, was announced, Poland had already won possession of a large area of land to the east of the line, and the final frontier was fixed much further to the east than had been originally intended.

Much controversy centred over the town of Vilna. Formerly the capital of Lithuania, Vilna

had been part of the Russian Empire for 150 years. When Lithuania declared itself independent it was unable to occupy the town, which changed hands several times during the Russo-Polish War (1920–21). When Russian troops recaptured Vilna the Bolshevik government awarded the district of Vilna to Lithuania (July 1920).

Almost immediately a Polish general, Zeligowski, captured the town. The Lithuanian government which had been installed there fled to safety, while the Poles denied that Zeligowski had official support. Back home, however, Zeligowski was looked upon as a national hero, and the government took no action to secure his removal from Vilna. By the Treaty of Riga (March 1921), which ended the Russo-Polish War, Russia declared that the Polish-Lithuanian frontier was a matter for the two countries concerned to resolve.

The League of Nations suggested that a plebiscite should determine the fate of Vilna. Poland agreed, but Lithuania refused, on the grounds that Poland's occupation of the town had given ample opportunities to ensure that the outcome of the plebiscite would be favourable to Poland. Furthermore, Russia objected to the presence of a League of Nations force to supervise the plebiscite. The League was reluctant to become involved in a dispute with Russia, and took no action. Eventually, in 1923, the Conference of Ambassadors,

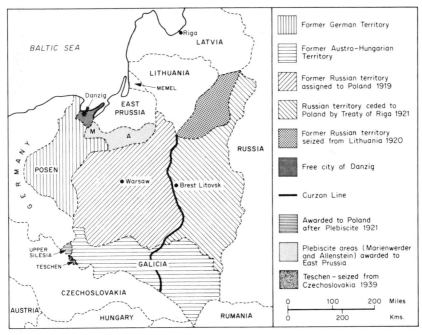

18   *Poland, 1919–39*

strongly influenced by French support for its Polish ally, awarded Vilna to Poland.

Poland's frontiers in 1921 included lands taken from Russia by the Treaty of Brest Litovsk, part of Galicia, and German lands. West Prussia gave Poland access to the sea (the Polish Corridor). The German port of Danzig became a Free City administered by the League of Nations, but with Poland enjoying considerable rights there. Poland also acquired part of East Prussia, though it was denied the districts of Marienwerder and Allenstein, where plebiscites in 1920 confirmed

the inhabitants' wish to be ruled by Germany.

Post-war Poland faced huge problems. Lacking large-scale industry, Poland had an agrarian economy. Its population of 27 million contained 6 million Russians and 700,000 Germans. Neither the Soviet Union nor Germany gave up hope of recovering their former lands. Germany in particular never forgave Poland for the separation of East Prussia from the rest of Germany. After twenty years' existence the Polish state was destroyed in 1939 by a simultaneous attack by Nazi Germany and the Soviet Union.

The German revolution, 1918

In September 1918 the German High Command realised that Germany's defeat was inevitable. This grim news was concealed from the Reichstag, and from the public, which believed that Germany was winning the war. The supreme commander, General Ludendorff, advised the Kaiser to make his government more representative of the people, in the hope that it would be in a more favourable position to negotiate with the Allies. On 1 October Prince Max of Baden, who had sufficient prestige to command the support of the army, formed a coalition government.

This meant that leading politicians had to be informed of Germany's desperate military situation. They were shocked to learn that total disaster on the western front was only a matter of weeks away. Many Social Democrats were utterly dismayed by the prospect of forming a government. They realised they would carry a heavy responsibility for Germany's humiliation.

This was precisely Ludendorff's intention. He was determined that the prestige of the German army should be preserved intact. Moreover, he blamed the Social Democrats for Germany's defeat. The Social Democrats, the largest political party in 1914, had opposed the war. Most had loyally supported the war effort once war had been declared, but in April 1917 the party had split into three factions. The largest group was the Majority Social Democrats. The Independent Social Democrats wanted a swift end to the war and radical social reform. An extreme socialist group, the Spartakists, led by Rosa Luxemburg and Karl Liebknecht, was openly revolutionary in

its aims. 'These gentlemen [Socialists],' Ludendorff told the Kaiser, 'whom we have to thank for bringing us to this pass, must now eat the dish which they have prepared.'

By late October a bitter mood of pessimism gripped the German people. Germany's spring offensive had clearly failed. Each day thousands of fresh American troops arrived on the battlefields of the western front. The war was lost. Many politicians now believed that the only course left was to negotiate quickly the best terms that could be obtained.

The Allies would only agree to an armistice after the Kaiser had abdicated. The Americans considered the Kaiser, as head of the government which had declared war, responsible for destroying world peace, and President Wilson insisted that the German people should disown him. Eventually, on 9 November, William II abdicated, and fled to Holland.

Meanwhile, revolution had broken out. On 28 October German naval units at Kiel and Wilhelmshaven mutinied when they were ordered to put to sea against the British fleet. The German Admiralty wanted the navy to make a final contribution to the fighting, but the German sailors, their morale sapped by two years of harsh discipline and enforced idleness, refused to undertake a pointless, suicidal mission.

Soldiers ordered to suppress the mutiny refused to fire upon fellow countrymen simply in order to prolong a war that was already lost. Soldiers and sailors fraternised with the civilian population. The government was powerless, and the disturbances spread to the towns and cities of north-west Germany. Mass meetings were held, when soviets, or councils of workers, soldiers, and sailors, were elected to take over the functions of local government. The Bavarian monarchy collapsed on 7 November, when Ludwig III, the last of the Wittelsbach kings, fled, and Kurt Eisner, an Independent Social Democrat, became Chancellor of a Bavarian republic. The atmosphere of the revolution is captured in this extract from an eye-witness account of events in Berlin on 9 November.

Endless processions of soldiers and sailors marched past. Most of the workers were of middle age, with grave bearded faces. They had not had the army training in fatigues, but they had the trade unionists' corporate spirit, and marched conscientiously in order. Some of them were shouldering rifles which had been handed to them from some store. Everybody had a red badge. Alongside the processions, the motor cars of the revolution rushed past, evidently on important business.

Later, when darkness fell, the trams stopped running, and the few pedestrians on peaceful business scuttled apprehensively homewards, against a background of spasmodic rifle shots, which continued throughout the night, and all next day.

On that day the German republic was proclaimed. The next day a mass meeting of the Berlin soviets elected six People's Commissioners to form a Council for ruling Germany. They included Friedrich Ebert, as chairman, and Philip Scheidemann, both Social Democrats.

The Social Democrats wanted a parliamentary democracy, for they detested the idea of social revolution. Ebert considered that his chief task was to maintain law and order, otherwise revolutionary violence would erupt in Germany. Unless he succeeded, the Allies would feel compelled to occupy Germany to stop the spread of communism.

The support of the army was essential if the provisional government was to survive. For its part, the High Command was anxious to preserve its privileged position in German society, and wished to prevent the spread of communist doctrines among the armed forces.

Ebert therefore made a deal with General Groener. The government agreed to be responsible for maintaining discipline in the armed services, provided that the army cooperated with the republican government, which it disliked, in fighting Bolshevism.

Secondly, Ebert wished to convene a National Assembly, which would draft a new constitution for Germany. The Spartakists (so called after Spartacus, the slave who led a revolt against Imperial Rome), demanded immediate political reforms. They wished to establish a communist state, as the Bolsheviks in Russia were doing. But their proposals were rejected by a congress of workers and soldiers' councils, dominated by Social Democrats. At the end of December 1918 the Spartakist Leagues broke their links with the Independent Socialists, and formed themselves into the German Communist party.

The Spartakist revolt

On 6 January 1919 the Spartakists organised a general strike and armed insurrection in Berlin, and occupied government buildings in a bid to overthrow the republic and establish a socialist state. After several days of bitter street fighting, government troops stormed their headquarters on 15 January. Three days later Karl Liebknecht and Rosa Luxemburg were captured and murdered. A further outbreak of left-wing violence took place in March, when more than 1,000 people were killed before the army brutally restored order.

Civil war in Bavaria

Violence also swept through Bavaria after Kurt Eisner was assassinated on his way to announce his resignation as head of the coalition government, following his party's defeat at the polls. A general strike was called, which developed into civil war. The Bavarian government called in the help of the army, which ruthlessly crushed the revolt in May. The bloodshed in Munich, and earlier in Berlin,

Armed Spartakists organise a road block in the centre of Berlin, January 1919

together with the Social Democrats' reliance on the army, were unfavourable omens for the Weimar Republic.

The Weimar constitution

In the January elections the Social Democrats received 38 per cent of the votes. The new National Assembly met in February 1919, in the small town of Weimar, since Berlin was still considered unsafe. Ebert was chosen as President. Scheidemann was appointed Chancellor, and formed a coalition government of Social Democrats, Democrats, and members of the Centre Party.

A constitution was drawn up by July, establishing a federal system of government. Germany was divided into seventeen states, or *Länder*. These ranged in size from Prussia, with a population of 35 million, to the tiny state of Lippe, with 45,000. Under the German Empire (1871–1918) the states had had their own parliaments and governments. Although Prussia had dominated Germany, important states such as Bavaria and Saxony were fiercely independent. The states lost their separate

assemblies under the new constitution. Instead they were represented in the Reichsrat, or Upper Chamber, which could delay, but not prevent, legislation passed by the Reichstag.

The Reichstag, or Lower Chamber, was elected for four years by universal suffrage, with both men and women over the age of twenty having the vote, and proportional representation. Germany was divided into thirty-eight electoral districts. In each one the parties published lists of candidates. The number of votes each party received decided the number of candidates from its list returned to the Reichstag. (This system was later modified, so that 60,000 votes were needed to return a candidate.) The German electoral system had two chief disadvantages. Firstly, it encouraged a multiplicity of parties, which in the later years of the Weimar Republic was to make effective government virtually impossible. Secondly, voters could not support individual candidates, only their party's list.

The constitution also guaranteed fundamental human rights, such as equality before the law, freedom of religious belief, of association, and personal liberty. In theory, at least, Germany appeared to have a perfect system of parliamentary democracy.

The Kapp *putsch*, March 1920

The Versailles Treaty, which reduced Germany's status from that of a world power to a defenceless European country, outraged most Germans. Moreover, the circumstances of Germany's defeat, together with the fact that no high-ranking officer had signed the armistice, created the myth that the army had been 'stabbed in the back' by civilians, who had proceeded to overthrow the monarchy and establish a republic. Right-wing extremists viciously branded the Weimar politicians as the 'November Criminals'.

There were many other discontents. Fear of communism, and its threat to social order, was combined with nostalgia for the good old days of the Hohenzollern Empire, when strong government was allied with compassion for the working classes. Pre-war prosperity was contrasted with post-war food shortages, high prices, and inflation. Anti-semitism was rife. Jews were blamed for many of Germany's misfortunes, and were made out to be racketeers who profited from other people's troubles.

Various nationalist plots threatened the existence of the infant republic. The most notorious was that headed by Dr Kapp, leader of the Fatherland's Party. He was supported by General von Lüttwitz, who won over many influential officers who believed that an alliance of the army and the working classes, whose patriotism had been proved during the war, could overthrow the government and replace it by a right-wing, authoritarian regime.

The immediate occasion for the *putsch* was the Inter-Allied Military Control Commission's demand for the disbandment of two marine brigades commanded by Captain Ehrhardt, a well-known *Freikorps* leader. *Freikorps* (Free Corps), semi-legal organisations, had been created at the end of the war, chiefly to guard Germany's eastern frontiers against the spread of communism. They were composed of ex-servicemen, and were strongly nationalist in their outlook. Though not officially part of the regular army, they were regarded by it as a useful para-military addition, and as a means of evading the Versailles Treaty, which restricted the army to 100,000 officers and men. The central government had welcomed *Freikorps* help in combating left-wing disturbances, and also had no wish to disband them. At the same time the government's reliance on these organisations was unfortunate, for political opponents regarded it as a major weakness, which could be exploited to bring about the Republic's downfall.

On the night of 11 March, 5,000 marines occupied government buildings in Berlin.

Failure of the Kapp Putsch 1920: a detachment of German soldiers, supported by a tank, help to restore order in Berlin

Ebert's government was declared deposed, and a provisional government led by Dr Kapp and General von Lüttwitz was proclaimed. The cabinet fled to the safety of Stuttgart, having first called for a general strike in the capital. Lacking open support from the army, which waited to see what would happen, and faced with a general strike which made Berlin a lifeless city, Kapp and Lüttwitz were powerless. After a few days they recognised that their attempted coup had failed ignominiously, and fled abroad.

An unfortunate sequel to the Kapp *putsch* was a communist-inspired uprising in the Ruhr, which the *Reichswehr* (Army) crushed ruthlessly. Meanwhile, sympathetic courts passed light sentences on those involved in Kapp's conspiracy. By these actions the government permanently alienated a section of the working class, whose resistance to the *putsch* had saved the Republic.

Reparations and inflation, 1921–32

Insidious, yet far more dangerous, threats to the stability of the Weimar Republic were reparations and rapid inflation. In 1921 the Reparations Commission fixed the amount Germany should pay at 132,000,000,000 gold marks, the equivalent of £6,600,000,000. Reparations were intended by the Allies to serve different purposes. The first was to make Germany pay for the cost of the war, and thereby atone for her War Guilt. The second was to prevent Germany becoming powerful again, by making heavy demands upon her economy. A third was to enable the Allies themselves to repay their war debts to the United States, which amounted to 11,000 million dollars.

Payment of reparations proved an impossibility. The tremendous burden of debt was an overwhelming strain on Germany's currency reserves. Restraints had been placed upon Germany's trade, so that payments could not be made out of export earnings. Germany's budget could only be balanced by adopting dangerous measures, such as heavy borrowings

from foreign countries, and by printing more paper money to cover the deficit.

These measures were self-defeating. They increased Germany's indebtedness, and accelerated the inflationary spiral. Foreign bankers became unwilling to lend money to Germany when they realised they would not recover their loans. The value of the German mark fell catastrophically. At the beginning of 1922 the rate (which in 1914 was just over 4 marks to the dollar) had dropped to 162; by the end of the year it had plummeted to 7,000 marks to the dollar.

In January 1923 the German government defaulted on reparations payments. In an effort to force Germany to pay, French and Belgian troops occupied the industrial area of the Ruhr. Cuno's government called for a campaign of passive resistance to the occupation forces, and banned all reparations deliveries until the troops were withdrawn. The French government retaliated by imposing an economic blockade, which cut off the Ruhr, and most of the Rhineland, from the rest of Germany. German inflation soon reached astronomical proportions. By July 1923, 160,000 marks were required to buy one American dollar; by late late November 4,200,000,000,000 marks were needed, and Germany's currency had become valueless abroad.

At home two thousand presses had difficulty in printing sufficient quantities of banknotes to keep up with the depreciation of the currency. The week's wages of a small firm employing ten people had to be carried in laundry baskets. Workers were paid thrice weekly, and spent the money immediately. Stores closed at noon every day in order to re-price their goods.

The savings of the German middle classes were wiped out, and the plight of people who lived on fixed incomes was desperate. The standard of living of the working classes fell as prices always raced ahead of wages. Hitler accused the government of being responsible for their misery, and declared that the Weimar Republic had become a 'robber's state'.

Not everyone suffered, however. Those people who owed money, such as a mortgage, benefited, because they were able to repay it easily. Speculators bought property and capital goods with borrowed money, making fortunes overnight. Factory owners installed modern machinery in their plant, paid for in devalued currency. The government also benefited, as the National Debt was virtually wiped out.

Cuno's government was unable to cope with the crisis. In August 1923 Gustav Stresemann, leader of the People's Party, became Chancellor in a broadly-based coalition government. Stresemann realised that the alternative to ending the campaign of passive resistance in the Ruhr was the utter ruination of the German economy. In September he yielded to French pressure, despite the fact that Poincaré, the French Prime Minister, offered no concessions in return.

Stresemann's surrender provoked fierce opposition from the nationalists. In Bavaria Gustav von Kahr, who detested the Weimar regime, was appointed Commissioner with special powers. Stresemann announced a state of national emergency. This strong action restrained Kahr from entering into a confrontation with the central government, but it did not deter Hitler from attempting his Beer Hall *putsch* in November (see Chapter 8). Stresemann was forced to resign two weeks later, although he was to remain Foreign Minister until his death in 1929.

The new Cabinet, headed by Wilhelm Marx, stabilised the currency by introducing the Rentenmark. In the absence of sufficient gold reserves the new currency was backed by a mortgage on all land and industry. The Rentenmark was valued at one gold mark, and the old paper marks were gradually redeemed at their current value. In the summer of 1924 the Rentenmark was replaced by the Reichsmark.

The revaluation of the German mark, and the resumption of reparations payments, mollified the French government, and made possible a Franco-German reconciliation. This process was assisted when the stubborn Poincaré was replaced in May 1924 by the more conciliatory Edouard Herriot.

Meanwhile, an international committee under the chairmanship of an American general, Charles Dawes, was devising a new scheme of reparations. The Dawes Plan, agreed in August 1924, involved a system of graded annual payments calculated according to Germany's capacity to pay. An international loan was raised to help Germany establish a stable currency.

The Dawes Plan did not alter the amount of reparations to be paid, and its success depended upon a prosperous Germany. When world trade slumped in 1929 the Young Plan reduced the reparations bill to £2,000 million. Two years later, at President Hoover's suggestion, all international debt repayments were postponed for one year. Finally, at the Lausanne Conference in 1932, reparations were cancelled.

When reparations were imposed by the Allies they were expected to last fifty years,

Gustav Stresemann

but they survived less than a decade. During that time Germany obtained loans in excess of what she paid. Since one of Hitler's first actions when the Nazis won power in 1934 was to repudiate all foreign debts incurred by the Weimar governments, Germany actually made a 'paper profit' from reparations.

Foreign policy, 1921–33

The Weimar Republic's foreign policy, and that of Hitler after it, can only be properly understood when the full extent of Germany's bitterness towards the Versailles Treaty is appreciated. Most Germans believed their country had been tricked into agreeing to a ceasefire by promises the Allies had no intention of keeping. Having been forced to admit War Guilt, Germany was to be crippled by reparations, loss of territory, and restrictions placed upon her armed forces. No leading German politician ever publicly accepted that Germany's eastern frontiers were unalterably fixed, any more than the *Diktat* of Versailles was regarded as a final settlement. Its revision was a constant goal of foreign policy. All parties were agreed upon this. They only differed over the means whereby it could be achieved.

The Allies soon found it impossible to prevent Germany from secretly rearming. Forbidden to develop an air force, Germany became a leading power in civil aviation, with civil air liners designed for easy conversion into bombers. Submarines were built under contract in Holland and Spain. The *Reichswehr* became a training school for officers, so that the armed forces could be rapidly expanded. Hitler's announcement of rearmament in 1935 was only made possible by the efforts of the army, industrialists, and politicians of the Weimar Republic, who connived at evasion of the Versailles Treaty. The available evidence suggests that an army of 35 divisions existed before the Nazis came to power.

The Treaty of Rapallo, 1922

This treaty of Russo-German friendship shocked Germany's former enemies. Yet it was hardly surprising in the light of international developments since 1918. Both the Soviet Union and Germany were outcasts of the European society of nations. Both countries had a tradition of cooperation which went back to the days of Bismarck's Reinsurance Treaty of 1887, designed to protect Germany from the danger of a war on two fronts. Some Germans even attributed their defeat in 1918 to the rejection of the Russo-German alliance.

Three other factors influenced Germany's decision to align itself with the Soviet Union. Neither country had accepted the loss of territory involved in the establishment of Poland in 1919. Furthermore, a plebiscite in Upper Silesia in 1921 had confirmed Poland's possession of this valuable territory. Secondly, Russia as an agrarian country was ideally placed to exchange foodstuffs and raw materials for manufactures. In the third place, the German Communist party welcomed closer ties with the Soviet Union.

Each country surrendered claims to reparations from the other. Diplomatic relations were resumed. Close collaboration between the Red Army and the *Reichswehr* was agreed upon. German troops were able to take part in military exercises on Russian soil, involving the forbidden use of tanks, poison gas and aircraft. Trade between the two countries was to be extended.

As a result of Rapallo, Germany emerged from its brief period of isolation. The value of the alliance from a military point of view, however, can easily be over-estimated; Germany could never successfully challenge one of its neighbours so long as rearmament was secret. Nevertheless, the Russo-German alignment was a useful diplomatic support during the Locarno negotiations three years later.

The Locarno treaties, 1925

The occupation of the Ruhr in 1923 convinced European statesmen of the need for a Franco-German reconciliation. A start was made with the introduction of the Dawes Plan, which modified reparations in Germany's favour. Subsequently, the relationship between Germany and France was greatly improved by the treaties of Locarno in 1925, and Germany's admission to the League of Nations in 1926.

There were five separate treaties signed at Locarno, a Swiss holiday resort. They were largely the achievement of Gustav Stresemann, Aristide Briand, and Austen Chamberlain, the Foreign Secretaries of Germany, France and Britain respectively. Germany promised to make no attempt to alter its frontiers with France and Belgium. Britain and Italy agreed to act as guarantors of the frontiers in Western Europe, as defined by the Treaty of Versailles. These arrangements seemed to offer France the security she wanted.

The demilitarisation of the Rhineland was reaffirmed. Any violation of the Versailles provisions regarding the Rhineland would be regarded as a hostile act. Significantly, however, Britain and Italy promised intervention only if the violation was flagrant, i.e. it was a step leading directly to war. This had important implications for the future, for in 1936 German troops were allowed to occupy the Rhineland unopposed (see Chapter 20).

No mention was made of Germany's eastern frontiers. It was, therefore, clear that Germany had not ruled out the possibility of using force to alter her frontiers with Poland and Czechoslovakia, with whom France had military alliances.

The Locarno agreements weakened the Versailles Settlement by upholding only parts of it. Nevertheless, Germany had freely accepted the loss of Alsace and Lorraine as final, thus removing the most important cause of tension in Europe. In the resulting atmosphere of international goodwill, Allied forces of occupation were withdrawn from the Cologne zone in 1926. Germany was admitted to the League of Nations in the same year, with the status of a Permanent Member of the Council. In 1928 Germany signed the Kellogg–Briand Pact (the Pact of Paris), an exercise in 'moral diplomacy' which outlawed war. In 1929 the Young Plan eased the problem of reparations. Finally, in 1930, foreign troops evacuated the Rhineland, five years ahead of schedule.

By this time the optimism of earlier years had faded. In the next five years German democracy failed to survive the economic crisis which developed after 1929, when Stresemann's death removed from the international scene the only politician who might have saved the Republic. Assaulted by its enemies from all directions, the Weimar Republic faltered from crisis to crisis, until in 1934 the Reichstag surrendered its sovereignty to Hitler.

If the decade between 1919 and 1929 may be categorised as a period when most Germans tried to accept the bitter consequences of defeat, the next decade witnessed the savage triumph of German nationalism. Within six years of coming to power Hitler destroyed the Versailles Treaty, and made Germany the master of continental Europe. Unfortunately, this was the prelude to the catastrophe of the Second World War, in which millions of people died.

CHAPTER EIGHT
Germany's Path to Dictatorship

Completely disconcerted, a bourgeois generation faced the new world of 1918. It had managed during the war, suffering bitter need in the belief that some time, after peace was made, it would be able to continue down the broad, comfortable avenue it had travelled before. Now it found itself confused and frightened. . . .

We soldiers of the front had never known the fabulous, comfortable road. Fighting had become our life purpose and goal. The new state of affairs was a surprise to us. But we could not sit on the side lines, like people in a trance. Somehow we had to take a hand in affairs, one way or the other. . . . In those days our trust in the old leaders, in the old generation, was destroyed, struck dead. We had to take fate into our own hands.

With these words an ex-serviceman described his state of mind when he returned to a defeated Germany after the armistice had been signed. His feelings were typical of many Germans who could not understand how Germany came to be defeated. Many of them joined semi-legal military organisations, or *Freikorps*, to fight communist revolutionaries in different parts of the German Empire.

Among them was an Austrian corporal, who was recovering in a military hospital from the effects of being gassed by British troops. On leaving the hospital he became an instructor in an army camp, where his duty was to indoctrinate the troops against communism. In March 1920 he was discharged from the army and returned to civilian life. This man was Adolf Hitler.

The son of a minor customs official in the Austrian town of Braunau, Adolf Hitler was born in 1889, the third child of his father's third marriage. In 1873 his father, who was

illegitimate, changed his name from Schicklgruber to Hitler, a fact which later pleased his son mightily. Indeed, one can speculate whether his father's original surname would not have posed an insuperable problem for a politician with ambitions of becoming a dictator. 'Heil Schicklgruber' as a form of greeting could never have had for Germans the magic appeal which 'Heil Hitler' possessed.

Hitler attended a variety of schools, for his father found it difficult to settle in one place. On leaving school Hitler moved to Vienna. His ambition was to become an artist, but he failed to pass the entrance examination for the Academy of Fine Arts. In Vienna he eked out a drab existence selling small paintings. It was during his stay in Vienna that Hitler developed a vindictive hatred for Jews, whom he regarded as parasites on German society, and a contemptuous dislike for the Slavs who made up a large part of the Austro-Hungarian Empire. In *Mein Kampf (My Struggle)* Hitler wrote that these feelings caused him to leave the city for Munich in 1913. 'I was repelled by the conglomeration of races which the capital showed me, repelled by this whole mixture of Czechs, Poles, Hungarians, Ruthenians, Serbs and Croats, and everywhere the eternal mushroom of humanity – the Jews, and more Jews. The longer I lived in this city the more my hatred grew for the foreign mixture of peoples which had begun to corrode this old site of German culture.' The more likely reason for Hitler's departure was to avoid compulsory military service.

Nevertheless, when war broke out in 1914, Hitler immediately volunteered for service in a Bavarian regiment. There is little doubt that he was a courageous soldier, for he was twice wounded, and twice decorated for bravery, the second time being awarded the Iron Cross First Class, which was usually reserved for officers.

In September 1919 Hitler became the seventh committee member of a group in Munich which called itself the German Workers Party. The others included General Epp, and one of his staff officers, Ernst Roehm. Epp provided from army *(Reichswehr)* funds the money for the group to purchase its own newspaper, the *Volkischer Beobachter,* in 1920. Roehm, who was later to be eliminated during Hitler's purge of the Nazi party in June 1934, was chiefly responsible for the formation of the SA *(Sturm Abteilung),* brown-shirted Storm Troopers, whose function was to protect party meetings, and to beat up and intimidate political opponents.

Hitler soon dominated his colleagues and, in July 1921, was appointed leader of the now renamed National Socialist German Workers Party. Shortly afterwards he spent a month in prison for breaking up a meeting of the Bavarian League. Undeterred, Hitler continued to defy the civil authorities by encouraging the Brown Shirts to indulge in street fighting, and by an attempt (which went unpunished) to break up the communists' May Day parade of 1923.

The Munich *putsch,* 1923

Hitler wanted to overthrow the Weimar Republic, end reparations, and nullify the Versailles Treaty. To most Germans such aims were foolhardy at a time when the Allies

Hitler addressing an early meeting of the German Workers Party
(an artist's impression)

were in total command of a disarmed Germany. Even in Bavaria the Nazis were by no means the most important political party. Outside Bavaria the Nazi movement was regarded as part of the lunatic fringe of politics. Yet in November 1923 Hitler believed that the crisis resulting from the French occupation of the Ruhr and the total collapse of the German currency provided the opportunity to overthrow first the government of Bavaria, and then the Weimar government itself.

Hitler described the Weimar Republic as a 'robber's state', responsible for the misery of the German people, which would increase because the state had become the biggest swindler and crook. Thus the government, whom he called the 'November Criminals', not France, were the chief enemy. Already, in February 1923, the violence of Nazi propaganda had persuaded several armed patriotic leagues to join the Nazis. In September Hitler became one of the leaders of the German Fighting Union committed to the destruction of the Republic and the Versailles Settlement. At a nationalist rally in that month Hitler attracted attention to himself by contriving to stand next to General Ludendorff, the national hero, on the rostrum. Hitler believed he could unite under his leadership all the nationalist, anti-republican parties in Bavaria. Having won control of Bavaria, he would mount an assault upon Berlin, just as Mussolini had done in Italy in 1922 (see Chapter 9). There is no doubt that Hitler had been deeply impressed by Mussolini's March on Rome, and that he felt he could achieve the same result in Germany.

When Gustav Stresemann, the German Chancellor, announced an end to passive resistance in the Ruhr, and the resumption of reparations payments, the fury of nationalists and communists knew no bounds. Stresemann, however, had foreseen this reaction and had asked President Ebert to declare a state of emergency, entrusting the Minister of Defence, and the Commander-in-Chief of the German army, General von Seeckt, with full governmental powers.

The Bavarian government defied the central government by proclaiming its own state of emergency, and by placing power in the hands of Gustav Kahr, the State Commissioner, General Otto von Lossow, commander of the armed forces in Bavaria, and Colonel von Seisser, head of the state police. Kahr refused to carry out orders from Berlin, and when Seeckt sacked Lossow for refusing to suppress the Nazi newspaper, declared that Lossow remained in command of the army in Bavaria. At this point Seeckt warned the Bavarian government that any rebellion would be crushed by the German army.

Hitler, anxious lest Kahr, Lossow and Seisser should lose their nerve, decided to act. Because the Nazis did not have sufficient strength and popular backing to seize power unaided, he planned to put the Bavarian ministers, who sympathised with him, in a position where they had to support him. In this way he would win over the Bavarian cabinet, army, and police.

Hitler's opportunity came when Kahr, accompanied by Lossow and Seisser, addressed a large meeting of businessmen and industrialists in a Munich Beer Hall on 8 November. Kahr was in the middle of his speech when SA troops surrounded the building, and Hitler pushed his way into the Hall. Hitler stood on a table and fired a revolver shot in the air to attract attention. He shouted to a stunned audience that the National Revolution had begun, and that the Bavarian government had been overthrown. He ordered the three ministers to accompany him to a side room, where he offered them posts in a provisional government of Germany. Kahr would be Regent of Bavaria, Lossow would command the *Reichswehr,* and Seisser the Police. They were silent. Hitler then returned to the Hall, where he announced that a new government had been formed, containing himself, Ludendorff, who had been hastily brought to the Hall, Kahr, Lossow, and Seisser. This announcement was greeted with applause. Back in the side room Ludendorff advised Kahr and his associates to join a great national cause. Hitler now left to attend to other matters, and Ludendorff, who had been placed in charge of the Hall, allowed Hitler's new 'ministers' to return home, where they promptly changed their minds.

Kahr retired to Regensburg, out of Hitler's reach, and issued a proclamation condemning the *putsch*. 'The deception and perfidy of ambitious comrades have converted a demonstration in the interests of national reawakening into a scene of disgusting violence. The declarations extorted from myself, General von Lossow, and Colonel von Seisser at the point of a revolver are null and void. The National Socialist German Workers' Party, as well as the fighting leagues *Oberland* and *Reichskriegsflagge*, are dissolved.'

Events seemed to be slipping from Hitler's grasp. Ludendorff now proposed that a march of Nazis and their supporters, led by himself and Hitler, would still bring success. Ludendorff was convinced that the police would not open fire on him, and that they would join forces with the Nazis.

On the following morning, a column of 3,000 Nazis led by Hitler and Ludendorff headed towards the city centre, where they were confronted by a police cordon. Somebody shouted that Ludendorff was heading the march, and Hitler called upon the police to surrender. A shot rang out, whether fired by the Nazis or by the police is not known. Immediately shots were exchanged. Within seconds the street was littered with Nazis clutching the pavements to save their lives, while sixteen of their number, and three police, lay dead or dying. Only Ludendorff and his aide-de-camp marched through the police line, where they were promptly arrested. Behind them, in the street, Hitler, whose shoulder had been dislocated when the man next to him, with whom he had linked arms, was mortally wounded, picked himself up and was hustled into a waiting car. One by one the other marchers retired from the scene. The attempted revolution had been a fiasco.

Hitler was arrested two days later and, together with Ludendorff, was tried on a charge of high treason. Ludendorff was acquitted and Hitler was sentenced by judges with nationalist sympathies to five years' imprisonment, of which he served less than nine months before he was released from Landsberg Fortress. Hitler used the trial to publicise his political views, for the judges allowed him to make long speeches from the dock attacking the Bavarian government and institutions. He greeted the verdict by declaring: 'You may pronounce us guilty a thousand times over, but the goddess of the eternal court of history will smile and tear to shreds the brief of the State Prosecutor and the sentence of this court. For she acquits us.' In prison Hitler spent much of his time in comfortable surroundings dictating *Mein Kampf,* a rambling account of his life and ideas.

Hitler rebuilds the party

Hitler was released on parole from Landsberg Fortress in December 1924. His party was weak and divided by bitter quarrels over policy and tactics, because Hitler had deliberately encouraged internal feuds in order to reduce the threat to his leadership while he was in prison. In the December election Nazi membership of the Reichstag dropped to fourteen, compared with the thirty-two seats the party had won in the previous May election. Nazism appeared to be on the decline.

Hitler immediately began to rebuild his party. He reassured the Bavarian authorities that he would not use armed force to achieve political power, and was rewarded by the lifting of the ban on the National Socialist Party. Nevertheless, Hitler was forbidden to speak in public until 1927. The party organisation was overhauled. Germany was divided into thirty-four *Gaue*, or districts, corresponding to the electoral districts, each under the charge of a *gauleiter*, or party chief. Each district was subdivided into *kreise*, or circles, which in turn were divided into *ortsgruppe*, or local groups.

In other ways Hitler strengthened his grip on the party's rank and file. He outmanoeuvred rivals such as the North German Nazi leader Gregor Strasser, and emphasised his position as *Fuehrer*, or leader. In 1925 he won over to his side the brilliant intellectual and master of propaganda, Dr Joseph Goebbels, whom he appointed *gauleiter* of Berlin. In the same year he formed the SS *(Shutzstaffel)*, a black-shirted élite force who swore an oath of loyalty to Hitler, and acted as his personal bodyguard. Young people between the ages of fourteen and eighteen years were encouraged to join the Hitler Youth and the League of German Girls. Membership of the Nazi party grew slowly – from 27,000 in 1925, to 49,000 in 1926, 72,000 in 1927, and 109,000 in 1928. During this period Hitler patiently formed the efficient organisation which enabled him to exploit the discontent created in Germany by the Great Depression.

Economic crisis and the collapse of the Weimar Republic

In October 1929 the New York stock market crashed, with disastrous results for Germany, whose prosperity depended upon its exports of manufactures. As shortages of orders forced many factories to close down, so millions were thrown out of work. In January 1930 $2\frac{1}{2}$ million were unemployed. By December 1931 the total had reached $4\frac{1}{2}$ million, and not until a peak of nearly 6 million was reached in 1933 did unemployment slowly decline. By that time production, compared with the figures for 1929, had been halved.

Hitler did not understand how or why this catastrophe had occurred, but he knew how to exploit it. He had something to offer every section of the electorate. He promised businessmen and industrialists that he would destroy communism and build a prosperous Germany. He would create jobs for the unemployed and give farmers higher prices. The army was attracted by prospects of rearmament, expansion, and quicker promotion. Above all else, Hitler appealed to millions of Germans who blamed their misfortunes upon the injustices of the Treaty of Versailles. For although the Allied army of occupation had been finally withdrawn from German soil in 1930, many Germans bitterly resented the assumption that Germany was

Hitler taking the salute at a march past of National Socialist storm troops in the town of Weimar (November 1930)

responsible for the First World War. Until June 1932, when reparations were cancelled by the Lausanne Conference, Germans expected to pay instalments for another fifty years.

While the Great Depression formed a backcloth against which the growth of the Nazi party must be seen, Hitler was assisted into power by the mistakes of his political opponents, and by the disrepute into which the Weimar Republic had fallen. At the Communist International held in Moscow in 1928 the German Communist party was instructed to regard the Social Democrats, not the Nazis, as their chief rivals. The futility of the two largest working-class parties fighting each other, instead of collaborating against the Nazis, their common foe, was only realised when it was too late.

Secondly, with the increase in political violence and extremism in Germany in the early 1930s coalition governments found it impossible to govern without recourse to Article 48 of the Constitution. This enabled the President to issue emergency decrees when the government could not command a majority in the Reichstag. This placed the Social Democrats in a dilemma. On the one hand, to accept the frequent use of Article 48 threatened the survival of democratic government. On the other, to oppose it opened up the fearful prospect of political and economic disorder, and bloodshed, as supporters of the extreme left- and right-wing political parties fought each other in the streets. The moderates desperately hoped that President Hindenburg, with his immense prestige, would be the saviour of the Republic. Their hopes were to be cruelly shattered.

In March 1930 Hermann Müller's coalition government collapsed when it failed to reach agreement on the problem of unemployment relief. Heinrich Bruening formed another coalition government and called for another election in September. The Nazis increased their vote from the 810,000 they had polled in 1928 to an astonishing 6,400,000 votes. With 107 seats in the Reichstag the Nazis became the second largest party, and a force to be reckoned with. The Communists, who

were also intent upon destroying democracy in Germany, emerged as the third largest party, with 4,600,000 votes and 77 seats.

The Nazis' success at the polling booths persuaded Hitler to stand as a candidate in the 1932 presidential election. The Nationalist candidate, Duesterberg, polled $2\frac{1}{2}$ million votes, Thälmann, the Communist, nearly 5 million, and Hitler over 11 million. Hindenburg received $18\frac{1}{2}$ million votes, marginally short of the majority required. In the second ballot Hindenburg polled over 19 million votes, while Hitler won 13 million, picking up most of the votes formerly cast for Duesterberg, who had dropped out of the contest. Hitler had doubled the Nazi vote in two years, but a majority of people had voted in support of the Weimar Republic.

During the presidential election plans drawn up by the SA for a Nazi seizure of power were discovered. Several states led by Bavaria and Prussia demanded that the Reich government ban the organisation. On the advice of the Bruening government Hindenburg issued a decree banning the Nazi military organisations, which were described as private armies whose very existence was a permanent source of trouble to the civilian population. On Hitler's express orders the SA and SS, which now numbered four times the strength of the German army as laid down by the Treaty of Versailles, did not resist. They removed their uniforms, but kept their organisation.

General Schleicher, however, who regarded the SA as a useful addition to the army, stirred up opposition in the army to the ban. He went behind Bruening's back to President Hindenburg, criticising the prohibition on the grounds that it was one-sided, for the Social Democratic *Reichsbanner* had not been affected by it. Schleicher bluntly informed the aged President that the army could no longer be relied upon to support the government against a Nazi bid for power. Hindenburg was persuaded by Schleicher and others that Bruening should be replaced as Chancellor. Bruening made little attempt to remain in office, and Hindenburg appointed in his place von Papen, a wealthy German aristocrat and conservative who, he was assured by Schleicher, would enjoy the confidence and support of the Nazi party in the Reichstag.

Papen formed a right-wing cabinet which included Schleicher as Minister for Defence, but far from achieving a stable majority in the Reichstag, Papen's position was even more hopeless than Bruening's had been. In an effort to curry favour with the National Socialists Papen reversed the ban on the SA and SS. Murder and violence in the streets followed as Nazis and communists fought each other. In July 1932 eighty-six people were killed in street battles. After a particularly serious riot at Altona, near Hamburg, where the Nazis staged a provocative march through the working-class districts of the town, Papen seized the excuse to dismiss the Prussian government by presidential decree, on the flimsy excuse that the Social Democrats, who had remained in office though they no longer commanded a majority in the Prussian Diet, were incapable of maintaining law and order. Papen made himself Reich Commissar of this vital state, which gave him control over three-fifths of Germany. The Social Democrats offered no resistance, for even if they had won a confrontation with the Nazis, who were convinced that Papen's intention was to hand over power to them, they would have faced bitter attacks from the communists. The dismissal of the Prussian ministers further discredited constitutional government in Germany. More and more people became convinced that the choice now lay between the two extremist parties, the Nazis and the Communists.

In the election of July 1932, the fourth in five months, the Nazis doubled their vote, and became the largest party in the Reichstag with 230 seats. The Social Democrats won 133 seats, the Centre and Catholic parties 97, the Communists 89, and the Nationalists 39. Far from improving the situation, the election had only served to make Papen's task even more difficult. Papen offered Hitler the posts of Vice-Chancellor and Reich Commissar for Prussia in return for Nazi support in the Reichstag. Hitler refused, being unwilling to play second fiddle to Papen

when his own party was the largest in the Reichstag.

No sooner had the Reichstag been convened than it passed as overwhelming vote of no confidence in Papen's government. Papen dissolved the Reichstag and called for yet another election in November, when the Nazis lost 34 seats, and appeared to have passed the peak of their success. The Communists, however, increased their vote by 20 per cent, and confidence in Papen's ability to deal with the threat of communism dwindled. Hindenburg therefore accepted Papen's offer to resign. Hitler was once again approached by the President, who offered him the Chancellorship on condition that the Nazi programme and names of candidates for Cabinet office were submitted to the President for approval. Hitler refused, and Hindenburg asked Schleicher to form a government.

Schleicher's tactics were to split the Nazi party by offering Gregor Strasser, the powerful leader of the Nazi left wing, cabinet office, provided he could guarantee the support of a bloc of Nazi votes. Strasser was convinced that Hitler's refusal to accept office except on his own terms amounted to political suicide. Hitler obtained proof of Strasser's negotiations with Schleicher and expelled him from the party.

To many observers it appeared as though Hitler had overplayed his hand. It was at this time that Hitler staked his political reputation on an all-out effort to win a massive majority in the tiny state of Lippe, where a by-election had arisen. The Nazi propaganda machine was applied to the task of persuading the Lippe electorate to vote National Socialist. All the Nazi leaders addressed public meetings there during the election campaign, and the result was a greatly increased vote for the Nazi party. Since Schleicher had by now failed in his efforts to form an alliance with the Social Democrats, both Hindenburg and Schleicher were convinced that no stable government could be formed without Hitler's support.

Papen, who had joined the Nationalists, still had much influence over the aged President. He persuaded Hindenburg to swallow his dislike of Hitler and appoint him Chancellor, with Papen as Vice-Chancellor. On 30 January 1933 Hitler was sworn in as Chancellor of Germany. Since the new government would contain only three Nazis Papen was convinced that he had neatly fenced Hitler in. Hitler would provide the necessary voting power in the Reichstag to keep the coalition government alive, while Papen would provide the policies. Both Papen and Hindenburg, however, had fatally under-

more powerful Germany, and dire warnings of what would happen if the communists increased their representation in the Reichstag. In Prussia Goering, the Prime Minister, drafted 40,000 SA into the police on the excuse of strengthening the forces of law and order. Hundreds of officials and civil servants were replaced by Nazis. Even the Reichstag Fire was adroitly turned by Hitler to his own advantage. When the parliament building was destroyed by fire on the night of 27 February

Hitler meets President Hindenburg in the early 1930s

estimated Hitler's political skills and ruthless determination to make himself master of Germany. Within a year the Weimar Constitution was destroyed, as the Reichstag voted Hitler full powers of dictatorship.

Hitler first insisted that fresh elections were needed for the electorate to affirm its support of the new government. During the interval between the dissolution of the Reichstag and polling day, Nazi propaganda bombarded the voters with promises of a more prosperous,

Hitler immediately blamed the Communist party, though Van der Lubbe, a Dutch communist who confessed to the crime, claimed that he had acted entirely on his own initiative. Nevertheless, the Communist party was outlawed by an emergency decree, and its newspaper premises closed. Four thousand communists were arrested, and the police were given powers to search suspects and confiscate their possessions.

Yet in spite of all their efforts the Nazis

failed to win the majority of seats Hitler needed to be independent of his allies, the Nationalists. The Nazis won 287 seats out of the 608 seats in the Reichstag, polling 44 per cent of the votes cast. Hitler resolved his problem by a delightfully simple solution. He altered the Weimar Constitution. Two days after the opening of the Reichstag in the temporary premises of the Berlin Opera House, he secured the passage of an Enabling Bill. This gave the government power to make laws without the consent of the Reichstag, and to conclude treaties with foreign countries. To obtain the two-thirds majority required for an amendment to the constitution Hitler had the support of the Nationalists, and of the Catholic Centre Party, whose votes were won by promises to support the Church. The eighty-one elected communist deputies had been banned from taking their seats in the Reichstag. Only the Social Democrats voted against the measure. Intended to provide strong government during a period of extreme national difficulty by giving Hitler extraordinary powers, the Bill made it possible for him to establish a dictatorship within a few months. Hitler became Dictator of Germany not by a forcible seizure of power, but legally through the consent of the democratically elected representatives of the German people.

Hitler in power

For the next ten years Hitler enjoyed the support of the great majority of the German people, since the evil sides to National Socialism were at first obscured by its successes, as Hitler fulfilled the pledges he had made before coming to power. By 1937 unemployment had been reduced from 6 million to 1 million. The armed forces were steadily expanded after 1935, and industrial production soared under the stimulus of a massive programme of rearmament. Germany's frontiers were enlarged by the union with Austria in 1938, the absorption of the greater part of Czechoslovakia in 1938–9, and the conquest of Poland after a brief struggle in

1939. The loss of personal freedom seemed a small price to pay for the benefits which Hitler's government provided. By the time the true nature of the Nazi dictatorship was revealed, only very brave and dedicated opponents of the regime dared to criticise or resist.

Germany becomes a police state

In February 1933, immediately after the Reichstag Fire, President Hindenburg signed a decree for the Protection of the People and State, suspending those clauses of the Weimar constitution which guaranteed civil liberties. They were never restored by the Nazi government, and German citizens could be arbitrarily arrested and imprisoned without trial.

Special courts were set up to deal with political offences. Following the acquittal of three of the four defendants accused of setting fire to the Reichstag buildings, a decision which infuriated Hitler, a People's Court was created in April 1934 to try cases of treason. The new court was composed of five selected judges who conducted trials in secret. There was no jury, and no appeal against their sentence.

Enemies of the government were sought out by the Secret State Police *(Geheime Staats-polizei)*, or Gestapo for short. First established in Prussia in April 1934 by Hermann Goering, the Gestapo became a nation-wide organisation after 1936, when the separate state police forces were amalgamated and placed under the control of the SS leader, Heinrich Himmler, who became Chief of the German Police. The Gestapo was not even subject to the ordinary processes of the law; instead, it derived its authority from Hitler, in his capacity as supreme judge of the German people. Aided by the Secret Service, the intelligence organisation of the SS, the Gestapo became an instrument for terrorising people into submission.

Political offenders were sent to concentration camps, which were administered by the SS with ruthless efficiency. The camp guards were known as Death's Head units, so-called because of the skull-and-bones insignia on the lapels of their uniform. During the Second World War the concentration camps, especially those in countries occupied by Germany, became extermination centres in which millions of victims died.

Hitler consolidates his hold on the party and the state

Hitler proceeded rapidly to strengthen his position after 1933. The state parliaments were abolished and their functions taken over by the central government. Germany became a one-party state as all political parties, with the exception of the Nazis, were prohibited. Trade unions were banned, and strikes were made illegal, since under the National Socialist system of government the interests of private individuals and sections of the population were sacrificed for the welfare of the whole community. The electorate was bombarded with Nazi propaganda and promises, and in the plebiscite of November 1933, when Hitler put his measures to the test of public opinion, 96 per cent of the voters approved of all that he had done.

The chief threat to Hitler's authority now came from within the Nazi party itself. Ernst Roehm, the SA leader, wanted his Brownshirts to become the nucleus of an expanded German army, with himself as commander-in-chief. Hitler, who was anxious not to alienate the army, which was strongly opposed to Roehm's ideas, also disliked Roehm's plans for social revolution now that the Nazis had achieved power.

The showdown between the two Nazi leaders occurred on the night of 30 June 1934, the 'Night of the Long Knives', when Roehm and many of his closest associates were murdered by the SS. Prominent victims included General von Schleicher, Gustav von Kahr, and Gregor Strasser. The actual number of people who died is not known for certain, but it was between 100 and 400. Hitler justified the bloodbath by claiming that urgent measures

had been necessary to combat a dangerous plot to overthrow the state.

In August 1934 President Hindenburg died at the age of eighty-seven. Hitler became Head of State and Commander-in-Chief of the armed forces. The office of President was abolished and Hitler took the titles of *Fuehrer* (Leader) and Reich Chancellor. All officers and men in the armed forces were required to swear an oath of personal loyalty to Hitler. Thus the army recognised Hitler as the highest legitimate authority in Germany. In August 1934 in a 95 per cent poll 38 million Germans registered their approval of Hitler's assumption of complete power, while only 4 million disapproved.

Political indoctrination

Hitler always claimed that his power rested on the support of the German people. To a large extent this was certainly true, but it should not be forgotten that as time went by it was not only dangerous to criticise the government openly in any way, but also difficult for ordinary citizens to distinguish between truth and propaganda. Radio broadcasting was controlled by the state. Press censorship was carried out by the Ministry of Propaganda headed by Dr Goebbels, who instructed newspaper editors what news to print, and what news to suppress. During the period 1933-7 over 1,000 newspapers were closed down, and the opposition press was eliminated. In this way the German people were allowed to learn only what the government wanted them to learn.

Effective steps were taken to indoctrinate the young. Teachers had to take an oath of loyalty to Hitler and, as in many other professions, evidence of being a committed supporter of National Socialism was a condition of obtaining a post. Between the ages of six and eighteen boys and girls were expected to belong to various Hitler Youth organisations. Parents could be punished if they tried to prevent their children from joining. At the age of fourteen most boys joined the Hitler Youth of their

The SA headquarters in Nuremberg: the placard says 'By resisting the Jews I fight for the Lord'

own free will, after spending four years in the *Jungvolk* (Young Folk), but after 1939 they were conscripted into it whether they liked it or not. Girls joined the League of German Maidens. At the age of eighteen males went into the Labour Service, while some of the girls worked on the land.

Hitler's theory of race

In *Mein Kampf* Hitler developed the idea that all human progress was the result of man's struggle for existence, in which the strong triumphed over the weak. This principle that 'might' constituted 'right' applied equally to nations and individuals. Hitler believed that mankind could be divided into Aryans, racially pure, superior human beings whose ideal type was tall, blond, and strong in physique and intellect, and non-Aryans, who were inferior beings. The Aryans, as the master race, were destined to rule the earth, subjugating the other peoples to their will. Hitler claimed that the Germans, as Aryans, were a racial elite and that his mission was to unite them and lead them to their rightful place of power in the world.

According to Nazi philosophy, each individual surrendered his interests to the *Volk*

(a German term which has no exact equivalent in the English language, but which may be roughly translated as 'Folk'), which gave meaning and importance to the individual's existence. All the apparatus of the state, its laws, its justice, army, party, administration, was the means of preserving the *Volk*. The will of the *Volk* was expressed by the *Fuehrer*, whose power was rooted in the support of the people.

Anti-semitism

Hitler's views on race were incapable of clear definition, but they help to explain his contempt for liberal ideas, and his hostility to communism. Hitler's special hatred, however, was reserved for the Jews, who were portrayed as the scapegoats for everything that had gone wrong in German society. As well as being made responsible for Germany's defeat in the First World War, and subsequent humiliation by the peace settlement, the Jews were accused of attempting to undermine German society and to destroy its ideals and the nation's honour.

The persecution of Jews under Nazi rule began in 1933 when shops owned by Jews were systematically boycotted. Then by stages Jews were banned from public office, and excluded from the professions, such as the civil service, journalism, law, and medicine. The Nuremburg Laws of September 1935 deprived German Jews of citizenship. Jews became outcasts in society. Many shops and hotels refused to admit them, and their entry into certain towns, where not expressly forbidden, was at their own risk. Many Jews, the fortunate ones, emigrated, but after 1938 those who had stayed behind in the hope that conditions would improve, were unable to leave. Many of them later perished in gas chambers and concentration camps, as a result of Hitler's deliberate policy to exterminate the Jewish race.

Germany prepares for war

Germany's economic recovery by 1937 seemed to foreign observers little short of miraculous. Within five years of the Nazi seizure of power unemployment had been reduced to manageable proportions, while industrial production and national income doubled. The guiding genius behind Germany's prosperity was Dr Hjalmar Schacht, who was appointed Minister for Economics in 1934.

Schacht solved the problem of Germany's lack of currency reserves and credit by a variety of ingenious methods. He manipulated currency rates in order to promote German trade deals, blocked foreign accounts so that they had to be spent in Germany, and arranged to pay for imported raw materials with arms. Armaments manufacturers were guaranteed payment by the introduction of bills of credit printed by the Reichsbank, which were accepted by the other banks as a form of cash. Firms which expanded and employed more workers were given generous tax relief. A public works programme was financed largely by the state to provide employment. Town slums were cleared, and motorways *(autobahnen)* were constructed.

The extravagant use of raw materials by some government departments worried Schacht, and in 1936 he persuaded Hitler to appoint Goering as Commissioner for Raw Materials and Foreign Exchange. Goering's position in the Nazi hierarchy was such that he could override his colleagues, but the appointment soon led to Schacht's downfall. Schacht had always been openly critical of Hitler's plans to make Germany independent of imports. Schacht believed that complete self-sufficiency in raw materials *(Autarky)*, which was the objective of Goering's Four Year Plan introduced in 1936, was an impossibility, and in 1937 he was dismissed by Hitler.

The German economy during the late 1930s was geared to war, for *Autarky* and the production of synthetic *(ersatz)* goods such as rubber and textiles were intended to make Germany independent of foreign countries, and so render any future naval blockade of Germany a useless exercise. It was both the triumph and tragedy of National Socialism that by the end of 1940 Hitler had largely succeeded in making Germany the master of Europe. The conquest of much of Central Europe provided Germany with the foodstuffs and raw materials she needed, and virtually guaranteed Nazi overlordship of Europe. The fatal flaw of Nazism, however, was its insatiable lust for power and domination, which caused Hitler in 1941 to make the mistakes of attacking the Soviet Union and involving Germany in war with the United States of America.

'Revolution is not a surprise packet that can be opened at will. I do not carry it in my pocket. . . . Revolution will be accomplished with the army, not against the army; with arms, not without them; with trained forces, not with indisciplined mobs called together in the streets. It will succeed when it is surrounded by a halo of sympathy by the majority, and if it has not that, it will fail.'

Mussolini

As a blueprint for revolution this forecast proved remarkably accurate. On 22 October 1922 the fascist congress headed by Mussolini issued instructions for an armed uprising, which would frighten the Italian government into handing over power to Mussolini and his Blackshirt party. During the next few days fascists in every part of Italy seized control of public services and administrative buildings in the provincial towns and cities. This was the prelude to a march on Rome by many thousands of armed fascists, who converged on the capital by road and rail. King Victor Emmanuel III, urged by his Prime Minister, Facta, to recruit the help of the army and to proclaim martial law, hesitated until it was too late. The army interpreted the king's silence as approval of Mussolini, and its loyalty to the government became uncertain. The king was left, therefore, with no alternative but to ask Mussolini to form a government. Melodramatically accepting office, Mussolini said to the king, 'Your Majesty will forgive my attire. I have come from the battlefield.' Without realising it, Victor Emmanuel had virtually signed the death warrant of Italian democracy. Mussolini was its chief executioner.

Benito Mussolini was born on 29 July 1883. His mother was a village schoolmistress. His father was the local blacksmith, an atheist, and a socialist agitator whose movements were closely watched by the police. Mussolini was encouraged by his father to look after his own interests without the help of others. He was often involved in fights, early evidence of the need for action which Mussolini displayed as an adult. At the age of nine Mussolini was sent to a boarding school run by catholic priests. He was not a model pupil. The boarders were divided into three grades according to parental income, and Mussolini was in the lowest grade, a fact which he bitterly resented. Argumentative, a compulsive attention-seeker, the youthful Mussolini was expelled from the school two years later for wounding another pupil.

This experience did not deter Mussolini from eventually becoming an apprentice teacher, but after one year his contract was not renewed and in 1902, possibly to escape military service, he scraped up the fare to Switzerland. Here he found work as a bricklayer. He soon impressed a group of socialists with the violent sincerity of his political views, and was given a job as a trade union official. He showed considerable skill and provocation in handling strike meetings and demonstrations, and was elected secretary of the bricklayers' union.

Mussolini's gift for political agitation and writing not only brought him police surveillance but also, in 1909, the editorship of a local newspaper in the Austrian town of Trento. His vigorous pronouncements led to the banning of the newspaper and to Mussolini's imprisonment on charges of inciting others to violence. Undaunted, he continued his campaign by starting a socialist weekly, *La Lotta di Classe (The Class Struggle)*, and often walked thirty miles in a day to harangue workers on the evils of the capitalist system.

When the First World War broke out Mussolini was editor of the socialist newspaper *Avanti (Forward)*. To the fury of his socialist colleagues, Mussolini published an editorial calling for an Italian declaration of war upon Austria. This was in sharp contrast to his action three years earlier, when Italy had declared war on Turkey and seized Tripoli. Then he had organised a strike in protest against the war. Railway lines were torn up to stop the transport of troops by rail, the army was called in to crush the strike, and Mussolini spent five months in gaol for his part in the affray.

Since then Mussolini had become a nationalist, anxious for Italy to acquire Austrian territories largely or partly inhabited by Italians. Mussolini's attempt to defend his views before a large gathering of socialists was drowned in a torrent of catcalls and hostile chanting, and he was banished from the party. When Italy entered the war in 1915 Mussolini joined up and served in the front line against Austrian troops. In February 1917 he was seriously wounded when the howitzer he was helping to load exploded. After spending six months in a military hospital Mussolini was invalided back into civilian life in an Italy now bitterly divided by the war. Even final victory at Vittoria Veneto did not avenge the disastrous defeat at Caporetto when 250,000 Italians were taken prisoner during a humiliating sixty-mile retreat.

The growth of fascism

Fascism had its origins in the disillusionment and feelings of wounded national pride which characterised the mood of the Italian people in 1919. Most Italians felt cheated when President Wilson refused to recognise the provisions of the secret Treaty of London (1915), whereby Italy had been promised Adriatic ports, the Trentino and Trieste, and a zone of influence in Asia Minor, in return for her entry into the war. Instead, at the peace settlement, Italy was awarded Trieste and the Trentino only, which was considered a poor return for 600,000 soldiers killed and over one million wounded.

Nor did victory bring a magic solution to Italy's economic ills. Rapid inflation affected everyone. Demobilised soldiers found it hard to find jobs. Even those who were successful often had difficulty in adjusting to humdrum civilian life. Southerners had become more aware of the greater wealth of northern Italy, and resented the marked contrast in their standard of living compared with northerners. Emigration, which hitherto had been a safety valve for Italy's unemployed, was now restricted by the United States of America and by European countries mindful of their refugee problems and racial minorities. Yet the government seemed either reluctant, or powerless, to remedy these ills. At the same time the socialist party, although the largest and best organised, was content to leave those it considered responsible for involving Italy in the war to clear up the debris.

Mussolini through his newspaper *Popolo d'Italia* called for the moral and national regeneration of Italian life. Then in March 1919, with a few blackshirted *arditi*, or commandos, he formed the Fascist party. Its name was derived from the party's emblem, the *fasces*, or elm rods which, coupled with an axe, had in ancient Rome symbolised the consul's power of life and death. *Squadristi*, or uniformed combat groups, were formed to break up socialist meetings, and to smash strikes. Many employers sought the aid of fascist squads to destroy troublesome trade unions. Petty criminals and alcoholics were roughly dealt with. The favourite punishment meted out was to dose the victim with a pint of castor oil. Crime in the major cities noticeably decreased!

Fascism attracted Italians who wanted a strong government, respected at home and abroad. When D'Annunzio seized Fiume in September 1919 he was applauded by Mussolini, who justified this action by referring to the 'rights of victory'. Yet Mussolini was careful not to associate himself too closely with the affair, so that when D'Annunzio's forces were eventually expelled from the city on Christmas Eve 1920 by the Italian navy he did not lose face. When socialists seized industrial premises and factories in many northern towns and cities in the summer of 1920 they were opposed by the *fasci di combattimento*. Eventually the occupation came to an end when the government agreed to minor concessions. But Giolitti, the Prime Minister, a moderate with a distaste for energetic measures, and a preference for

could bring order into public affairs and create a moral climate of opinion in the country. Thus in the elections of May 1921 fascists won 35 seats, in sharp contrast to the elections held eighteen months previously, when fascists had failed to win a single seat.

When a socialist-inspired general strike occurred in 1922, fascists broke it by operating the vital public services in the major cities and towns. At this point Mussolini became

Mussolini and his blackshirts

'wait and see' methods, was discredited by abandoning to an ex-servicemen's organisation responsibility for fighting socialism. More dangerous still, democracy was seriously undermined by the spectacle of extremist political groups indulging in street-fighting, and by the illegal occupation of public buildings and private properties.

By this time many workers, small businessmen, and industrialists, though they disliked the strong-arm tactics of the *fascisti*, were beginning to see in fascism a movement which

convinced that fascism had sufficient strength and popularity to seize power. On 22 October the March on Rome was ordained. Placards appealed to the army not to take part in the struggle, for 'fascism does not march on the agents of public administration, but against that class of imbecile politicians who, during four long years, have not known how to give a government to the nation'. Eight days later Mussolini became, at the age of thirty-nine, Italy's youngest premier. In November an overawed Chamber of Deputies gave him full powers by 275 votes to 90. Those who had intended to use Mussolini as a temporary expedient to infuse order into Italian political life before resuming normal democratic procedures had fatally miscalculated.

Fascism in action

Now Fascism throws the harmful theories of Liberalism upon the rubbish heap. When a group or a party is in power it is its duty to fortify and defend itself against all. The truth is that men are perhaps tired of liberty. . . . For the youths of today, who envisage the dawn of a new era, there are other words which exercise a more potent fascination : Order, Organisation, Discipline.

Fascism knows no idols, worships no fetishes. It has already stepped on and, if need be, will quietly turn round to step once more, over the more or less putrid body of the Goddess Liberty.

Mussolini, 1923

Mussolini's contempt for the niceties of parliamentary government was soon translated into action, and within four years democracy in Italy had ceased to exist. In January 1923 the *squadrismo* received legal recognition as the Militia for National Safety, so that an armed force of over 300,000 men was committed to the support of the fascist government. In November 1923 the electoral law was altered to favour fascist candidates, and in the elections of April 1924 fascists received 65 per cent of the vote and won 374 seats.

When the new parliament met, only Matteotti had the courage to criticise the new regime. Shortly afterwards he was kidnapped and murdered by fascist thugs. The government disclaimed all knowledge of, and responsibility for, this foul crime, and the murderers, who were caught and tried, received light sentences. A number of opposition deputies, in a vain attempt to bring about the government's fall, refused to sit in the chamber any longer. In the so-called Aventino Secession they boycotted parliament, only to discover in December 1925, when they tried to resume their places in the chamber, that Mussolini had made sure they could not do so.

Meanwhile all opposition to fascist rule was gradually stifled. A special tribunal was established to try crimes against the state. These were very loosely interpreted, while there was no appeal against the sentences, which were usually very heavy. The press was censored, and many political opponents were driven into exile. As a result of constitutional changes between 1925 and 1928 the remnants of democracy were swept away, and a one-party state was created.

In 1925 Mussolini became the Head of Government and ceased to be responsible to parliament. Instead he was appointed by the king and could only be dismissed by him. Likewise ministers were appointed and dismissed by the king on the recommendation of the Head of Government. A Fascist Grand Council was formed. The Council nominated the Head of Government and ministers. This effectively deprived the king of any constitutional power, for as Mussolini was the leader of the Fascist party the Fascist Grand Council had to oppose him before the king could be asked to dismiss him.

With the passage of a law in 1926 enabling the government to issue orders-in-council, parliament lost its law-making function, and became a rubber stamp for the decisions of the Fascist Grand Council. Under Article VI of the new constitution the consent of the Head of Government was needed before any matter could be placed on the parliamentary agenda, and freedom of debate disappeared.

The development of the corporative state

Mussolini realised that a strong political party was essential. Efficient government and the regulation of the nation's economic life depended upon it. But Mussolini believed that conventional political parties representing the interests of classes, or religious or racial groups, divided rather than united society. He believed that people involved in the same economic fields of activity had more in common with each other than those who belonged to a particular class or group in society.

In 1926 thirteen great corporations, or associations, were created. Six corporations represented workers in commerce, finance, agriculture, industry, sea and air transport, and land transport. Six more represented the employers in these economic areas. The thirteenth was composed of professional people and intellectuals. The corporations replaced trade unions, and regulated the economic and cultural life of the national. Strikes and lock-outs were made illegal.

By a law of 1928 the corporations could put forward the names of 800 candidates for the Chamber of Deputies. From these the Fascist Grand Council would select 400 to be sub-mitted to the electorate for approval. Thus elections based on a system of returning candidates for individual constituencies were abolished, and the electorate lost virtually all its power to influence the composition of parliament. The corporative state, Mussolini's most original achievement, meant the end of democracy in Italy, which now became a totalitarian state.

In 1934 the Law on Corporations increased the number of corporations from thirteen to twenty-two. In 1938 the Chamber of Deputies was renamed the Chamber of Fasces and Corporations.

Fascist achievements at home

Many measures introduced by Mussolini, however, benefited the Italian people, and were widely approved. Changes were made in the legal code and practice, so that the system has survived with few alterations to this day. Taxation was reformed and the trade deficit reduced. With economic improvement in the 1920s the Italian currency became stronger and the lira was revalued. Farmers were encouraged with subsidies to produce more wheat. In 1928 work began on draining the Pontine Marshes, near Rome, whereby a large tract of malaria-infested land was converted into fertile farmland.

Mussolini's most notable domestic achieve-ment, however, was the Concordat of 1929. By the terms of this agreement the Pope recognised the Kingdom of Italy, while Mussolini acknowledged the Pope as head of an independent Vatican State and declared Roman Catholicism to be the official state religion. This pact healed the rift between Church and State which had existed ever since the Papacy had been robbed of its territories in 1871, when the Kingdom of Italy had been created. The Pope's recognition of the fascist regime bestowed upon it an air of respectability, and enabled devout Catholics to take part fully in public life.

During the world slump in trade in the 1930s Mussolini tried to reduce Italy's dependence upon imported raw materials, especially coal and oil. Hydro-electric power stations were built, harnessing the energy of mountain streams, and the main railway lines were electrified. He sought to reduce un-employment by an ambitious programme of public works. Motorways, or *autostrada*, were constructed to improve the road network. Blocks of flats to rehouse the poor, and impressive railway stations, were built in some of the major cities. New industries were developed under state protection. Nevertheless, in spite of all his efforts, Mussolini was unable to cure Italy's chief weakness, its shortage of raw materials, which involvement in the Second World War was to expose.

Mussolini's foreign policy

Unfortunately for the Italian people, Mussolini's foreign policy flattered mainly to deceive. In the 1920s it owed much to the support of Italy's wartime allies, France and Britain. In the 1930s its successes were due largely to the unwillingness of the French and British governments to annoy Mussolini, lest he allied Italy with Nazi Germany, and to their reluctance to accept the unpleasant truth that

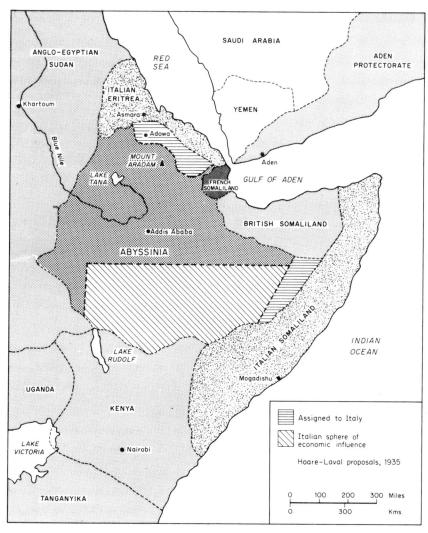

19   *The Abyssinian War: the Hoare-Laval Pact*

diplomacy ultimately relies upon the reality of military strength.

In August 1923 Mussolini provoked a crisis over Corfu. An Italian general, Tellini, and four staff officers, were ambushed and killed on Greek territory while they were surveying the new frontier between Greece and Albania. Mussolini demanded a public apology from Greece, as well as £500,000 compensation. When Greece declined to pay this sum the island of Corfu was bombarded, and occupied by Italian troops. Eventually the dispute was

referred to the great powers, and the crisis was resolved when the Conference of Ambassadors ordered Greece to pay the fine.

In 1924 Fiume was acquired from Yugoslavia, and treaties of friendship were signed with Yugoslavia, Rumania, Greece, Bulgaria, and Turkey. In the following year Italy was one of the signatories of the Locarno Pact (see Chapter 7). Italy also promoted friendly relations with Austria and Hungary, so that in 1934 when a Nazi attempt to seize power in Austria followed the assassination of Chancellor

Dollfuss, Mussolini in a show of strength despatched troops to the Austrian frontier, and Hitler backed down (see Chapter 20). In the spring of 1935 Italy supported France and Britain in their denunciation of German rearmament and joined the Stresa Front (see Chapter 20).

In October 1935 Italy attacked Abyssinia (Ethiopia). The origins of the war went back to the battle of Adowa (1896), when Italy's military reputation had been tarnished by a defeat at the hands of the Abyssinians.

Abyssinia, lying between the Italian colonies of Eritrea and Italian Somaliland, was very vulnerable to an invasion. The excuse for this came in December 1934, when a border clash occurred at Wal-wal, an oasis claimed by Italy, although it lay fifty miles inside Abyssinia's vaguely defined frontiers. Over the next few months tension grew. Mussolini let it be known that he was determined to annex Abyssinia, and he assembled troops and supplies in readiness for an invasion. He interpreted the silence of the French and British governments on the subject to mean approval. Mussolini was further encouraged by the League's failure to make any real effort to solve the dispute.

Abyssinia was completely unprepared to resist an attack. Tribesmen using ancient rifles were no match for troops using mustard gas, machine-guns and bombers. Their only advantage was the difficulty of communication in an undeveloped country, which meant that the Italians had to build roads before they could advance into the interior.

General Badoglio, who replaced the original commander, the aged Emilio de Bono, defeated the Abyssinians at Mount Aradam, but it was several months before Italian forces captured Addis Ababa, the capital. Shortly afterwards, General Graziano's army, advancing from Italian Somaliland, linked up with Badoglio's and resistance came to an end.

The Abyssinian campaign led to a complete reorientation of Italy's foreign policy. The League of Nations had reacted promptly to the Emperor Haile Selassie's appeal for help by branding Italy as the aggressor and applying economic sanctions (though they were totally ineffective). In December 1935, in an effort to pacify Mussolini, Sir Samuel Hoare, the British Foreign Secretary, and Pierre Laval, the French Prime Minister, concluded an agreement whereby Italy was awarded the greater part of Abyssinia, leaving one third independent. This pact evoked a storm of protest in both countries and Hoare resigned. The fact that both France and Britain had recoiled from a confrontation with Italy was not lost upon Mussolini, who went over to Hitler's side soon afterwards.

The estrangement between Italy and Germany had been rapidly healed when the latter refused to join with other countries in applying economic sanctions to Italy. A pact of friendship between the two countries was signed in October 1936. Mussolini declared that the close relationship between the two fascist powers would be an axis around which European affairs would revolve. Thereafter Germany and Italy were referred to as the Axis Powers. Along with Germany Italy became deeply involved in supporting General Franco's fascist forces in the Spanish Civil War. In 1937 Italy joined Germany and Japan in the Anti-Comintern Pact, although Italy had no quarrel with Russia, and no designs upon her territory.

For a brief, glittering moment in history Mussolini basked in the limelight of European affairs, being courted by the German Chancellor, Hitler, and by Britain's Prime Minister, Neville Chamberlain. When Hitler annexed Austria in March 1938 Mussolini this time made no move to oppose him and, in grateful recognition of Mussolini's good offices, Hitler visited Rome in May, where the cordial relationship between the two dictators was displayed to the world. In April 1938 Britain's Foreign Secretary, Halifax, visited Rome and signed an agreement whereby the British and Italian governments agreed to maintain the *status quo* in the Mediterranean, and to exchange naval information. Six months later, when the Sudetenland crisis erupted (see Chapter 20), Chamberlain asked Mussolini to act as a mediator.

Members of the Grand Fascist Assembly leaving the Ministry at Rome after the capture of Addis Ababa

Hitler's success in obtaining the Sudetenland territory encouraged Mussolini to talk of Italy's own 'natural aspirations', which included Tunisia, Corsica and Nice. When in March 1939 Germany occupied the rest of Czechoslovakia, Mussolini was provoked into ordering the Italian invasion of Albania (April 1939), where for the past twenty years Italy had been steadily building up an economic stake in the country. In June 1939 the friendly relationship between Germany and Italy was cemented into a formal alliance, although Italy did not enter the Second World War until 1940, when Mussolini believed it was virtually over.

Even Hitler was dismayed by the rashness of his ally. Italian forces were defeated by the Greeks when Mussolini attacked them in 1940, and by the British in North Africa. Ignominious defeat was only averted with German help. When the Italians eventually turned against their own government in 1943, German forces overran their own ally, and the Allied invasion of Italy became a war of liberation. Mussolini himself did not live to see the end of the war. He was captured and shot by his own countrymen. Dead, hanging upside down in a Milan square, reviled and spat upon by his erstwhile supporters, Mussolini made his final and most dramatic public appearance.

The death and destruction caused by the First World War convinced many people on both sides of the Atlantic that some way of resolving disputes between nations other than by resorting to war had to be found. Support for some kind of international organisation to keep world peace was strongest in the United States, but unofficial backing for a League of Nations had been widespread in Britain during the latter months of the war.

The League was an asociation of independent states which promised to cooperate with each other in preserving international peace and security. Its organisation and aims were set out in the twenty-six Articles of the Covenant, which formed the first part of each peace treaty drawn up after the war. Hence the League began its life on 10 January 1920 when the Treaty of Versailles came into force.

The machinery of the League consisted of an

The first session of the League of Nations, held in the Salle de la Reform, at The Hague, in 1920

Assembly, the Council, a Secretariat, and the Court of International Justice. The Assembly met at stated intervals, or whenever considered necessary. Each member state was allowed three representatives, but only one vote, so that the great powers could not dominate the Assembly. Although the Assembly could discuss any matters affecting international peace, its decisions had to be unanimous. Moreover, it could only recommend, not implement, action. Apart from voting the League's budget, therefore, the Assembly was important chiefly as a debating chamber, where world public opinion could be expressed.

It was originally intended that the Council should consist of five Permanent members (the United States, France, Great Britain, Italy and Japan), and four Non-permanent members elected by the Assembly. Thus the important role of the great powers was clearly recognised. Unfortunately, the United States' refusal to join the League made the number of Permanent and Non-permanent members equal, so that the intention of enabling the great powers to outvote the Non-permanent members of the Council was thwarted. Although Germany became a Permanent member in 1926, and Russia in 1934, the number of Non-permanent members rose by stages to nine. Furthermore, on most important matters the Council's decisions had to be unanimous, which proved to be a serious drawback.

The Secretariat conducted the day-to-day business of the League. It prepared information on matters and problems under consideration by the League, and kept the individual governments informed of the League's recommendations, becoming in effect a permanent international civil service. Its headquarters were in Geneva, and its first Secretary-General was Sir Eric Drummond. Closely associated with the Secretariat were the Court of International Justice and the various committees appointed by the Assembly to deal with particular problems such as mandates (see below), minorities and conditions of labour.

Established in 1921, the Court of International Justice was the successor to the World Court set up at The Hague in 1899. Its fifteen salaried judges were elected by the Assembly and Council, and held office for nine years. States were not bound to submit their disputes to the Court's arbitration. Indeed, few states, and no great powers, proved willing to risk what they considered to be their vital national interests to the Court's ruling, even though the Court had no means of enforcing its decisions.

Signatories of the peace treaties automatically became members of the League, but any independent state could join provided it promised to abide by the Covenant and its admission was approved by a two-thirds majority in the Assembly. The member states promised to respect each other's territorial integrity and political independence. Any dispute likely to lead to war was to be submitted either to arbitration, or to the Court of International Justice, or to the Council. Their findings were final, provided that the Council's decision, apart from one of the disputing parties, was unanimous. If arbitration failed to resolve the dispute a nation should give three months' notice of its intention to go to war. This would provide a 'cooling off' period, as well as time for other states to attempt to find a peaceful solution.

If any state ignored its obligations under the Covenant and resorted to war, it was considered to have committed aggression upon all the other League members. Economic sanctions, i.e. the severance of all trade and financial relations between the offending state and the League members, would automatically take place. Secondly, the Council would recommend whatever military action seemed necessary for ending the war. This was the principle of collective security.

The remaining provisions of the Covenant attempted to remove the causes of war. Secret alliances were outlawed, since all treaties were invalid until they were registered by the Secretariat, which would publish them as soon as possible. Unfair treaties would be revised as their inequalities became apparent. The nations agreed to disarm so that the danger of a future arms race would recede. The interests of national minorities and refugees were safeguarded by special commissions. Colonial rivalry would become a thing of the past as the mandates system developed. Member nations promised to 'secure and maintain fair and humane conditions of labour for men, women and children, both in their own countries, and in all countries to which their commercial and industrial relations extend'. Concerted action to abolish the traffic in women and children, drugs, and armaments, and to prevent or control the spread of dangerous diseases, was to be taken by individual governments.

The League was largely ineffective during the period of world depression and aggression (1929–41), but in the 1920s there was optimism that the League would succeed in persuading nations to regulate their conduct by respect for international law and order. On several occasions it certainly either averted open warfare or brought about an end to fighting.

The League's successes

The Aaland Islands

The first dispute referred to the League concerned the ownership of the Aaland Islands in the Gulf of Finland. The islands were formerly part of the Grand Duchy of Finland, which had been incorporated into the Russian empire. When Finland announced its independence in 1917 it claimed possession of the islands. The inhabitants, however, who were Swedish in language and racial affiliation, asked to be united with Sweden. In 1920 the League ruled that Finland's claim should be accepted, on the grounds that to permit a minority to secede from one state to join another could only be justified by serious and prolonged mistreatment.

Mosul, 1923–4

Mosul had belonged to Turkey for centuries before it was captured by British troops in 1918. The district was included in Iraq by the Treaty of Sèvres (1923), but the Turks refused to accept the treaty. Fortunately, neither the Turks, nor the British, who had been awarded Iraq as a mandated territory, relished the prospect of war over Mosul. In August 1924 both governments agreed to accept the League's arbitration. The Commission set up to investigate the problem reported that the predominantly Kurdish population of the area disliked both the Turks and the British, and wanted independence. Failing that, there was a slight preference for union with Iraq. Accordingly, the League awarded the greater part of Mosul to Iraq, and agreed to modify the terms of the mandate so that the Iraqis could be granted their independence before the 25-year mandate had expired. The League's decision was a sensible solution to a complicated problem.

The dispute between Greece and Bulgaria, 1925

In October 1925, following an incident on the frontier between Greece and Bulgaria, Greek forces invaded Bulgaria, which appealed to the League. The League responded promptly, and ordered both sides to cease hostilities, whereupon Greece withdrew her troops. A commission of enquiry reported that the Greeks had been largely to blame, and Greece was ordered to pay Bulgaria reparations.

Peru v. Colombia, 1932

The League also successfully intervened in a South American dispute, after a band of Peruvians had seized a strip of Colombian territory. Colombia appealed to the League, which ordered the Peruvian government to withdraw its nationals from the disputed area. A commission was despatched to the area to supervise the ceasefire.

Plebiscites

After the First World War, in accordance with the principle of national self-determination, plebiscites were held in a number of areas to ascertain the wishes of the inhabitants. In 1920 the East Prussian districts of Allenstein and Marienwerder voted overwhelmingly for union with Germany instead of being ceded to Poland. In March 1921 most of Upper Silesia was assigned to Germany after its population had voted in favour of retaining German citizenship. In 1935 the League's administration of the Saar ended, as laid down in the Treaty of Versailles. In the referendum over 90 per cent of the population voted for union with Germany.

The financial reconstruction of Austria

In September 1922 the Commissioner General of the League of Nations at Vienna reported that Austria was on the verge of total collapse. 'Austria could neither feed her people with bread nor her industries with raw materials without large purchases from abroad, and for these purchases she had no financial reserves. She had lived for three years largely on external loans, and no further loans could be obtained; the foreign seller could no longer be expected to accept her demoralised currency in payment for his goods.' A team of financial experts was sent to Austria to advise the government on measures to reform the currency and promote prosperity. By 1924 the Austrian

Turkey and Greece exchange populations: the first Muslims arrive at Aivalih, in October 1923

budget had been balanced, and the commission could report that Austria was able to take her place among the world's trading nations.

Mandates

The peace settlements had assigned Germany's colonies and the Arab provinces of the Ottoman Empire to mandatory powers, on the understanding that the 'well-being and development of such peoples formed a sacred trust of civilisation'. The League exercised its responsibility of supervising the mandatory powers by requiring them to give an annual account of their stewardship, and issuing reports on the progress made in the mandates towards self-government. While such work was unspectacular it did have some influence on responsible opinion in the countries concerned.

The problem of refugees and minorities

In 1920 Dr Nansen, a Swedish explorer and statesman who spent the latter part of his life helping the many hundreds of thousands of people who had been driven from their homes by war, organised a fleet of steamships to repatriate 400,000 prisoners-of-war. After the Graeco-Turkish War the League helped to raise a loan of £10 million for resettling over one million Greek refugees who had fled from the advance of Turkish troops in Asia Minor.

The League also concerned itself with the difficult problem of minorities. Over thirty million people formed minorities in post-war countries. Although this number was much smaller than the pre-war total, those states with alien groups in their midst resented any outside interference in their domestic affairs. The League's achievement in this field was, therefore, very limited, but the fact that it was interested in the plight of minorities served as some kind of restraint upon governments that were unsympathetic in their handling of this problem.

Control of drugs, diseases and slavery

The League took steps to reduce illicit traffic in dangerous drugs, such as opium, and the sale of women and children, particularly from areas affected by fighting. In 1921 the League succeeded in recovering many women captured during the war in the Middle East and sold as slaves. Rehabilitation camps were set up in Constantinople. Health commissions visited countries suffering from an epidemic to advise on methods of combating the spread of the disease.

The International Labour Organisation (ILO)

The aim of the ILO was to secure fair and humane conditions of labour for men, women, and children everywhere. It endeavoured to fix a maximum working day, to secure the payment of adequate wages and old age pensions, and to reduce unemployment. It defended the right of workers to belong to trade unions. All members of the League were automatically members of the ILO, while states that were not members could join, as the United States did in 1934. The ILO's publication of statistical reports on labour matters kept all governments informed of its progress and difficulties. So important, indeed, was its contribution on economic affairs, that the ILO survived the League to become one of the specialised agencies of the United Nations after 1946.

The failure of the League

If the League made a sound but unspectacular contribution towards the development of a better world society, its failures were glaring and dramatic. In 1931 when Japanese forces invaded Manchuria (see Chapter 16), the League did not condemn aggression, contenting itself with a report which largely exonerated Japan. It is not surprising that Mussolini was irritated by the League's decision to impose economic sanctions upon Italy following the Italian invasion of Abyssinia in October 1935. Even though the sanctions were ineffectual (for vital war materials, such as oil, were exempted from the embargo, so that Italy was able to conquer Abyssinia with little difficulty), Italy left the League in protest. Thus the League proved powerless to defend a small state aginst the aggression of a larger one.

There were many reasons for the League's failure. From the very beginning the League was plagued by abstentions and withdrawals. It never included more than five of the seven great powers. The United States never joined, for the Senate failed to ratify the Treaty of Versailles. Germany was admitted to the League in 1926, when the world outlook was optimistic, but withdrew in 1933 when Hitler wanted an excuse to rearm Germany. The Soviet Union was admitted in 1934, only to be expelled five years later, following its attack upon Finland. Meanwhile, Japan left the League in 1933, and Italy followed suit in 1937. Of the great powers, therefore, only Britain and France belonged all the time, and inevitably their influence attracted criticism that the League was little more than an Anglo-French mutual benefit society.

Certainly the League's impartiality was open to doubt. It was accused of bias against those states that had been defeated in the 1914–18 War. Neither Germany nor Russia was immediately welcomed into the League. In the eyes of the German people the League never lost its association with the hated *Diktat* of Versailles, for its founders were the same delegates who had framed the Versailles Treaty, in which Germany had been allowed no voice. Lenin described the League as a 'robbers' den'. The Japanese, too, felt aggrieved by the refusal of the peacemakers in 1919 to recognise racial equality. Austria, despite its severe economic difficulties, was forbidden to develop a customs union with Germany, since that might con-stitute a first step along the road to political union with Germany, or *Anschluss,* which had been forbidden by the Versailles Treaty. In 1920 Poland was allowed to keep the town and district of Vilna, which it had seized

from Lithuania. France actively supported Poland's claim to Vilna, since a strong Poland would be a useful counterweight in Eastern Europe to a revived Germany.

The League was seriously discredited in 1923 over its handling of the disputed ownership of Memel, and the Corfu incident. Memel, a German port with 70,000 German inhabitants, but with a Lithuanian hinterland, had been placed under Allied administration after the war. Lithuania, having lost Vilna to Poland, wished to pre-empt Polish and French plans to make Memel a Free City, like Danzig. In January 1923 Lithuanian troops occupied Memel, and refused to evacuate it. Eventually, a commission of representatives from neutral countries awarded Lithuania the port of Memel, which was therefore separated from Germany by force.

Much more serious, however, was the League's handling of the Corfu affair. When the Italian navy bombarded the Greek island of Corfu in retaliation for the murder of the Italian members of the commission surveying the frontier between Albania and Greece, the League allowed itself to be reduced to the role of adviser to the Conference of Ambassadors (Britain, France and Italy), and Italy's action went unpunished.

Perhaps the crucial test of the League's competence as an effective organisation for the maintenance of peace was its handling of the disarmament issue. By 1926 a League com-mission was able to report that Germany was effectively disarmed. Thus the way was now clear for the other nations to disarm. There was a wide measure of agreement that the arms race had been the greatest single factor in bringing about the First World War. The League constantly deplored the continued high level of armaments among the nations, and proposals for disarmament were on the agenda of every session of the Assembly from 1922 to 1933. Yet apart from the pious-sounding Kellogg–Briand Pact (1928), signed by a majority of the nations, all of whose govern-ments expressed their detestation of war, little was achieved in limiting armaments. Why was this?

Membership of the League and acceptance of the Covenant implied that each nation ceased to be the sole judge of what armaments it required for its safety. Yet most countries fiercely justified their right to decide their own level of war-preparedness. Those states which felt secure from attack were ready to accept a fixed percentage reduction of armaments by all nations, thereby retaining their advantage. Those states, such as Belgium, Poland, and France, which felt insecure, argued that disarmament could not alter the fact that countries such as Germany and Russia had far superior industrial potential, so that unless the League could offer convincing guarantees of protection their acceptance of disarmament would put their security at risk. Thus France maintained the largest army in Europe, and was not criticised by the League. When the Nazis won power in 1933 it was clear that Hitler would set out to rearm Germany. It was equally clear that Germany's neighbours which had been awarded German territory after the war dared not disarm.

After 1936, its utter weakness exposed by the Italian campaign in Abyssinia, the League as a means of ensuring collective security became a dead letter. It offered no opposition to the remilitarisation of the Rhineland in 1936, nor to the *Anschluss* in 1938, both of which violated the Versailles Settlement. It failed to prevent thousands of communist and fascist volunteers fighting in the Spanish Civil War, and it merely watched events as Czechoslovakia was dismembered in 1938–9, and Poland was overrun in 1939. Its expulsion of Russia in 1939, therefore, was a meaningless gesture.

Yet in the final analysis it could be said that it was not the League which failed, but the nations that collectively and individually made up the League. The League had no means of enforcing its decisions other than persuading its members to fulfil their obligations. It possessed no armed forces of its own. For its budget it relied upon the voluntary contributions of member nations. Its strength was derived from public opinion, which was often confused or apathetic. It was only too easy for governments and electorates to disclaim any responsibility for becoming involved in events which were taking place hundreds or thousands of miles away, especially during the years of the Great Depression (1929–39), when most governments were preoccupied with their faltering national economies. So long as the odds were heavily in favour of an aggressor state achieving its ambitions by resorting to war, international peace was fragile. Only the certainty of a superior opposing power could act as an effective deterrent. Therein lay the dilemma of nations. For which nation, or group of nations, should undertake the role of peace-keeping, and on what terms?

In 1890 Russia was a great power, but it was also, in many respects, a backward country. Eighty per cent of its population were peasants who, until as recently as 1861, had been serfs. Over one-third of the peasants were landless. Those who possessed land had to pay high rents and taxes, which often amounted to half the crop. Primitive methods of cultivation and communal ownership of land meant that productivity was low. Rural over-population in many areas added to the volume of discontent.

Industrialisation was at an infant stage compared with most western countries; iron and steel output, for example, was only one-tenth that of the United States. Russia also lacked chemical and machine-tool industries, which were vitally important to a country's development. Industrial backwardness meant military weakness.

Nevertheless, Russia was developing its industries very rapidly, particularly after 1892 when Sergius Witte became Minister of Finance. With the assistance of foreign capital the railway network was considerably expanded, notably by the construction of the Trans-Siberian Railway. Mining and heavy industries in the Urals and South Russia were developed. Production of oil, centred upon Baku in the Caucasus, was greatly increased. Moscow and St Petersburg became important centres of the textile industry, with factories containing thousands of workers. By 1914 Russia ranked fifth in order of production of the industrial nations, and its population contained three million factory workers.

Such a fast rate of economic growth caused severe social problems. Many of the factory workers were peasants, with obligations which forced them to return to their village communes after a period of time. Wages were low, and the laws regulating factory hours and conditions of work were often evaded by employers. Strikes were frequent. After 1880 the industrial proletariat (working class) began to turn to the socialist doctrines of Karl Marx.

Marxism

Karl Marx (1818–83) was the son of a German lawyer. After the failure of the 1848–9 revolution in Germany he fled to Paris, and from there to London, where he lived for the rest of his life. He collaborated with Friedrich Engels (1820–95) in writing the *Communist Manifesto* (1848). Marx's most important work, however, was *Das Kapital (Capital)*, which he published in 1867.

Marx argued that the ruling class in any society was the one which controlled the production and distribution of wealth. The source of wealth might be slaves, land, or industry and commerce, according to the stage of development of any particular society. As the basis of wealth altered, so conflict grew between the old and rising ruling classes. Thus in western countries feudalism had been replaced by capitalism, and the middle classes had forced the aristocracy to surrender most of its privileges. In a capitalist system the bourgeoisie, the property-owning class, dominated society through its control of industry and commerce, and general acceptance of the profit motive.

Since all wealth was the product of labour, the capitalist cheated his workers by paying them less than the full value of their labour, taking the 'surplus' as his profit. Class warfare between the proletariat and the bourgeoisie was, therefore, according to Marx, inevitable in a developed industrial society. Ultimately, he believed, the capitalist system would collapse, either as a result of its own defects, or through a violent working-class revolution. The proletariat would seize control of the machinery of state, and the means of production and distribution. Private property would be abolished. A classless, communist society would be formed, based on the principle of 'from each according to his ability, to each according to his need'.

The growth of revolutionary parties

Marx's book was translated into Russian, and from 1889 onwards groups of factory workers were organised by Gregory Plekhanov to study Marxism, and to spread socialist ideas. In 1898 delegates from these socialist groups met at a congress in South Russia, and founded the Social Democratic Workmen's Party. One of its leading members was Vladimir Ulyanov, better known as Lenin, who became a revolutionary after his brother was hanged for his part in a plot to assassinate Tsar Alexander III. In 1900 Lenin was released after three years' exile in Siberia for his revolutionary activities. He went to live in Switzerland in order to escape the attentions of the Tsarist secret police. There he edited a socialist newspaper *Iskra (The Spark)*, copies of which were smuggled into Russia.

From the beginning, however, the Social Democrats were divided between those who wished to bring about improvements in the condition of the working class, and those who aimed at overthrowing the Tsar's government by force. In 1903, at its second party congress in London, the Social Democrat Party split over the issue of its organisation. Plekhanov and his followers wanted a broadly based party similar to socialist parties in Western Europe.

Lenin argued that membership of the party should be restricted to active revolutionaries. Lenin's view won a majority of votes, and henceforth Lenin and his supporters were known as Bolsheviks, or 'majority men', as opposed to the Mensheviks, 'minority men', led by Plekhanov.

The Social Democrats aimed at winning the support of the industrial proletariat. Their

The assassination of the Grand Duke Sergius: when the shattered remains of the carriage had been cleared away, people searched the ground for mementoes of the dead Grand Duke

rival, the Socialist Revolutionary Party, founded between 1900 and 1902, appealed to the peasants. It was a loosely organised party which stood for the nationalisation of the land. An extremist wing of the Socialist Revolutionaries inherited the terrorist tradition of Bakunin's anarchist party of the 1870s and 1880s. Its chief weapon was political assassination, and prominent victims included

Plehve, the Minister of the Interior, assassinated in 1904, and the Tsar's brother, the Grand Duke Sergius, killed in 1906.

Political parties, however, were allowed little scope for sharing in the government of Russia, except at local level. Alexander II (1855–81) had created a system of local elected councils *(zemstva)*, which dealt with the administration of roads, education, and public welfare in general. Even this limited role was restricted by his successor, Alexander III.

Nicholas II (1894–1917), the last of the Tsars, believed that he had been appointed by God to rule with unlimited power. A charming but obstinate man, he rejected proposals for constitutional reform as 'senseless dreams', and thought that anyone who questioned his authority was necessarily wrong. In governing his vast empire he was assisted by a large, unwieldy bureaucracy, and by a Council of Ministers, whom he chose and dismissed at will. They were directly responsible to him, and he was responsible to God alone. Such was the autocratic system of government which was challenged in 1905.

The 1905 revolution

In 1905 the shock of defeat in the Russo-Japanese War (see Chapter 1), combined with the Tsar's refusal to grant constitutional reforms, brought about revolution. On Sunday 22 January a peaceful crowd of over 100,000 workers and their families, led by a priest, Father Gapon, tried to present a petition for reform to the Tsar at his Winter Palace in St Petersburg. The demonstrators were fired upon by troops, and hundreds were killed.

Bloody Sunday marked the first major confrontation between the Tsar and his people in the twentieth century. As news of what had happened spread, strikes broke out in every major industrial area, and in many parts of the country the peasants looted landowners' estates. In June the crew of the battleship *Potemkin* mutinied, a grim reminder to the Tsar that even his armed forces might not always remain loyal to the monarchy.

Nevertheless, the Tsar refused to grant concessions until a general strike in October paralysed the economy. In St Petersburg a Soviet, or Council of Workers' Deputies, headed by Leon Trotsky, was formed; because it organised all essential public services, it effectively controlled the capital. Throughout Russia hundreds of similar soviets were established in villages and towns. A revolutionary organisation had been created, through which the Bolsheviks would one day enforce their will.

Nicholas II now faced the choice of using the army to crush the revolution, at the risk of civil war, or granting political reforms. He chose the latter. The October Manifesto promised the summoning of a Duma, or parliament, elected by every male over the age of twenty-five. Overnight Russia became a constitutional monarchy, and in the sudden mood of public rejoicing the soviets lost their popular support. In December the government had no difficulty in arresting the 300 members of the St Petersburg Soviet, and suppressing an armed revolt organised by the Moscow Soviet. The 1905 revolution, the dress rehearsal for 1917, was over.

The Dumas

The first Duma met in May 1906. The Social Democrats and the Socialist Revolutionaries boycotted the elections, and the largest party was the Liberals, or Constitutional Democrats (Cadets), with 184 seats. Of the Duma's 500 members, 200 were peasants.

The Duma's proposals for reforms, however, were completely unacceptable to the Tsar, and it was dissolved in July. A similar fate awaited the second Duma. The third was chosen under a new electoral law which was heavily weighted in favour of the landowners. Consequently this Duma, and its successor, were docile bodies. The majority of members were willing to accept the very restricted role assigned to them by the Tsar.

Despite their limited powers the Dumas achieved a considerable degree of success.

Stolypin, Prime Minister from 1906 until his assassination in 1911, endeavoured to make the peasants a bulwark against revolution by enabling them to own the land they farmed. Plans were drawn up to abolish the ancient system of land tenure, whereby the peasant's holding was scattered throughout the village. Peasant Bank loans enabled peasants to extend their farms. Internal colonisation was encouraged as a means of easing the land shortage. When war broke out in 1914 half the peasant farms in European Russia were privately owned.

Given sufficient time, the experiment in parliamentary democracy might have saved the Russian monarchy, but the problems caused by Russia's size, and the ingrained habits of centuries of autocratic rule, could not be overcome in a single decade. In 1917, under the twin strains of a series of disastrous defeats in the First World War, and economic collapse, Russian society was engulfed by revolution.

Background to the Russian Revolution

The days of Tsarism are numbered. Revolution is now inevitable; it is only waiting for a favourable opportunity. Such an opportunity will come with some military defeat, a famine in the provinces, a strike in Petrograd,* a riot in Moscow, some scandal or tragedy at the Palace. It doesn't matter how!

A revolution may be of great benefit to a nation if it can reconstruct another political system for the one it has destroyed by violence. But with us the revolution can only be destructive, because the educated class is only a tiny minority, without political experience, or contact with the masses. That is the greatest crime of Tsarism; it will not tolerate any centre of political life and activity outside its own bureaucracy. . . . No doubt it will be the bourgeois, intellectuals, who give the signal

for revolution, thinking they're saving Russia. But from the bourgeois revolution we shall at once descend to the working class revolution, and soon after to the peasant revolution. And then will begin the most frightful anarchy.

These words, spoken by a Russian industrialist to the French ambassador in 1915, proved even more prophetic than the speaker could have realised.

As early as the summer of 1915 the patriotism of the Russian people had been largely replaced by feelings of frustration with the government's conduct of the war. As military disasters followed each other with monotonous regularity, the appalling casualty lists mounted. Manpower alone was not enough to overcome the shortages of munitions, and poor leadership. The transport problems which created chaos at the front line led to a scarcity of foodstuffs at home. Prices rose sharply, while incomes lagged behind. As popular discontent grew, the Liberals in the Duma called for the formation of a government based on public confidence. Its plea was rejected.

Rasputin

The Tsar's bureaucratic system of government now came increasingly under attack. Many people believed that Nicholas II and his wife, the Tsarina Alexandra, were under the spell of Rasputin, a self-styled monk who claimed to have miraculous powers. Rasputin had always opposed the war, and was regarded as pro-German. He was equally opposed to constitutional reform. His scandalous private life and his influence over the appointment and dismissal of ministers were notorious. In December 1916, in a desperate effort to rid Russia of his evil influence, a group of army officers murdered Rasputin at a party. His death, however, failed to bring about the necessary political changes, for government and society were now completely divided. Thus a discredited autocracy, a powerless Duma, and a resentful people form the background to the events of 1917.

*St Petersburg was renamed Petrograd at the beginning of the First World War.

The March Revolution

At the beginning of March 1917 strikes followed bread riots in Petrograd, and thousands of workers came on to the streets, agitating for an end to the Tsar's autocracy. After three days of growing disturbances Nicholas II ordered the commander of the Petrograd garrison to disperse the strikers by force, but the soldiers fraternised with the crowds. Very soon the entire garrison had mutinied, and General Khabalov telegraphed the Tsar, informing him that he was unable to restore order in the capital. Troops summoned from the front line now remained the government's only hope of recovering its authority. When they were prevented from reaching the city by a railwaymen's strike the Tsar's ministers, now completely isolated and powerless, were arrested.

The leaders of the Duma, who had long been urging Nicholas II to form a more representative government, were alarmed by the prospect of a breakdown of law and order. They formed a Provisional Government with Prince Lvov as Prime Minister, and Alexander Kerensky, a Socialist Revolutionary, as Minister of Justice. When Nicholas II learned that most of his generals had agreed to support the new ministry, he abdicated in favour of his brother, the Grand Duke Michael. Prince Lvov informed the Grand Duke that his safety could not be guaranteed if he accepted, and he agreed to leave the choice of a future head of state, and therefore the form of government, to a Constituent Assembly.

The formation of the Petrograd Soviet

In the meantime, the strike committees and the regiments in the capital had elected delegates to the Petrograd Soviet, or Council of Workers' and Soldiers' Deputies, which was a rival to the Provisional Government. The great majority of its delegates, however, were Mensheviks and Socialist Revolutionaries, who believed that any attempt to seize power in the name of the working class would be

A Bolshevik demonstration outside the Winter Palace in Petrograd

ВЕЛИКИЙ ВОЖДЬ
ПРОЛЕТАРИАТА
В. И. ЛЕНИН

Lenin

premature and disastrous. Not even the Bolshevik leaders, most of whom were in exile, realised that the revolution, which they had been planning for many years, was actually taking place.

The struggle for power

The Petrograd Soviet promised conditional support of the Provisional Government, even though this meant cooperation with the bourgeois Cadets, representing property interests, until a duly elected Assembly met to decide on a new system of government for Russia. But from the start an uneasy relationship existed between the Soviet and the Provisional Government.

The Soviet had the support of the mass of industrial workers in the city, whose views it closely represented, for the delegates could be replaced by a simple majority vote. The delegates were in direct contact with the workers, who could therefore be easily mobilised against the Provisional Government. The Soviet also claimed the loyalty of the Petrograd garrison. In its famous Order No. 1 it had instructed the regiments to elect revolutionary committees, and to refuse to

carry out orders unless they were countersigned by the Soviet leadership. Thus the Soviet's potential for revolutionary activity was immense.

The Provisional Government was, therefore, in a difficult situation. It could hardly claim to be representative of the people, for the Duma had been chosen on the basis of the electoral law of 1907 which favoured the landowners. It commanded no armed forces. Moreover, as the Duma had technically been dismissed by the Tsar in March, the Provisional Government could not even claim a legal basis for its authority. It could function only with the consent of the Soviet. Effectively power still lay where, in Trotsky's vivid words, it had fallen – in the streets. Neither the Provisional Government nor the Soviet was at this time capable of seizing it.

In the provinces local government was left to its own devices, and hundreds of soviets replaced the *zemstva*. As the familiar patterns of authority broke down, the peasants encroached upon the landowners' rights, at first in such matters as grazing cattle on their pastures, then by attacking their mansions, and finally occupying their lands. As news of this spread to the front, the soldiers started to desert in order to return home and obtain their share of land.

Lenin's return to Russia

Lenin was taken by surprise by the events in Russia. His eagerness to return to Russia was matched by the willingness of the German government to help him, in the hope that the Bolsheviks would undermine the Russian war effort. Lenin and several of his associates were transported from Switzerland across Germany in a sealed railway carriage to Finland, whence they made their way to Petrograd in April. Lenin immediately set out to capture the support of the masses by demanding peace, and 'all power to the soviets'.

Lenin was widely regarded as a German agent, and the disastrous failure of Russia's July offensive was blamed on Bolshevik peace propaganda. A Bolshevik attempt to seize power in Petrograd was easily crushed by the Provisional Government, which outlawed the Bolsheviks. Many leading Bolsheviks, including Trotsky, were arrested, and Lenin fled to Finland.

Kerensky, however, who had virtually replaced Lvov as head of the Provisional Government, had been greatly discredited by the failure of the July offensive, and General Kornilov, the commander-in-chief, saw a chance to destroy Bolshevik influence altogether, and to replace Kerensky's administration with a right-wing government of his own. He ordered his army to march on Petrograd. The attempted *coup* failed when Kerensky called upon the Bolsheviks for assistance.

The November Revolution

The Bolshevik slogan 'Peace, Land and Bread' had immense popular appeal. By the end of October army discipline had collapsed, and the peasants were seizing land on a large scale. In both the Petrograd and Moscow soviets the Bolsheviks had secured majorities, while from exile in Finland, Lenin urged that the time had come to oust Kerensky from power.

Kerensky's proposal to move the capital from Petrograd to Moscow aroused fears that he was planning to surrender Petrograd to the Germans, thereby ridding himself of the problem of the Petrograd Soviet. The Bolsheviks therefore formed a Revolutionary Military Committee to defend the city. When certain battleships and regiments known to be under Bolshevik control were instructed to leave the capital, the Revolutionary Military Committee countermanded the order.

On the following day Kerensky ordered the Bolshevik newspaper offices to be closed down. Trotsky now acted. Bolshevik forces seized the bridges and chief buildings in the city, and stormed the Winter Palace. Kerensky fled, and the Bolsheviks declared that his administration had been replaced by a Council of People's Commissars, headed by Lenin. Trotsky was appointed Commissar for Foreign Affairs, and Stalin was made Commissar for Nationalities.

The Bolsheviks immediately set out to consolidate their power. By his famous Land Decree Lenin ensured that millions of peasants had a stake in ensuring the permanence of the revolution. The decree stated:

The right of private ownership is abolished forever. All lands pass to the nation and are turned over for the use of those who till them. The land is to be divided among the toilers according to needs or labour capacity, depending on local conditions. Each community is to decide for itself how its land is to be apportioned, whether it is to be held collectively, or as homesteads.

Other decrees established workers' control of industry, abolished legal titles and class privileges, separated Church and State, and replaced the police and the law courts by a workers' militia and revolutionary tribunals. The *Cheka* (secret police) was organised to seek out opposition to the government. When the Constituent Assembly was finally elected with an overwhelming anti-Bolshevik majority, Lenin ordered its immediate dismissal; the Bolsheviks had no intention of sharing power.

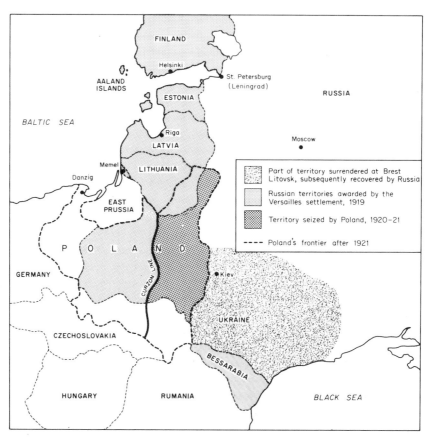

20   *Russia's losses after the First World War*

The Treaty of Brest Litovsk, 1918

Lenin realised that the success of the revolution depended upon making peace with Germany. This he was prepared to do, whatever the cost, since he was convinced that the governments of Western Europe would soon be overwhelmed by socialist revolution. With the creation of communist societies any injustices in the peace settlement, Lenin assumed, would be swiftly rectified.

Lenin appealed to the governments involved in the war to conclude peace based upon the principle of 'no annexations, no indemnities'. The German government gratefully responded, taking the opportunity to negotiate in December 1917 an armistice which deprived the Entente Powers of Russia's military help.

But Germany proved to be a hard taskmaster when it came to arranging actual peace terms. Trotsky, appalled by their severity, walked out of the peace conference, declaring that the Russians would neither fight the Germans nor make peace with them. This simple formula merely enabled the German armies to advance unopposed into Russian territory, until the Bolsheviks were compelled to accept Germany's terms for a peace settlement. Russia agreed to surrender the Baltic provinces, Finland, Poland, the Ukraine and the Caucasus, and to pay a huge indemnity. Lenin had therefore succeeded in preserving the revolution, but at a terrible cost – a million square kilometres of land and a third of Russia's population. Lenin had bought time with territory and people.

The Russian Revolution was at first welcomed by the Allies, who hoped that the replacement of the Tsar's hated personal rule by a popularly supported coalition government would revive the Russian war effort. This mood of cautious optimism turned to active hostility towards the Bolsheviks after November 1917.

Allied intervention in Russia

The reasons for Allied intervention were confused. The Allies were concerned to protect stores of military equipment at Archangel and Murmansk from capture by nearby German armies. There were also vague hopes that the Bolsheviks might be persuaded by the presence of Allied troops to resume the war against Germany. This wishful thinking was mixed with bitter anger over the Bolsheviks' betrayal of the Allies by signing a separate peace, which had released hundreds of thousands of German troops for the fighting on the western front. After the war had finished, Allied motives ranged from a desire to overthrow the Soviet government, which had cancelled all Russia's foreign debts and preached world revolution, to wild schemes for partitioning Russia.

The start of the Civil War

The Civil War began when the Czech Legion turned against the Bolsheviks. The Czech Legion had been formed by Kerensky in 1917 from Czech and Slovak prisoners-of-war, who changed sides in order to fight for an independent Czech state. When the Treaty of Brest Litovsk was signed, Lenin agreed to an Allied proposal that the Czech army should be evacuated via Vladivostok and transported half-way round the world to the trenches in France. Clashes occurred between the Bolsheviks and the Czechs, who feared that they were about to be interned, as a result of which the Czechs seized a number of towns along the Trans-Siberian Railway. They were joined by 'White' forces commanded by Admiral Kolchak.

The 'Whites' were anti-Bolsheviks, but they did not want to restore the Tsar. They were chiefly Mensheviks and Socialist Revolutionaries, who objected to the Bolsheviks' insistence on one-party rule. In the Ukraine, separatists proclaimed the existence of an independent republic, which was supported by German troops who had occupied the region. In Finland there was fighting between the 'Whites' and the 'Reds' (Bolsheviks).

In the meantime, British troops landed at Murmansk and Archangel in North Russia, and at Baku in the Caucasus. French troops arrived in the Crimea, and Japanese and American forces at Vladivostok. Although the Allied forces (with the exception of the Japanese) were to play a passive role in the Civil War, merely guarding military installations until they were eventually withdrawn when a Bolshevik victory became certain, there is no doubt that their presence in Russia encouraged the anti-Bolshevik factions to attack the newly formed Soviet government. The Russian people found it difficult to forgive or forget western military intervention at the birth of the Soviet state.

The course of the Civil War, 1918–21

When the Civil War began, the Soviet government had lost effective control of three-quarters of Russia. It faced enemies on all sides. In Siberia Admiral Kolchak proclaimed himself Supreme Ruler of Russia. Generals Yudenich in North Russia, Denikin in the Caucasus, and

In March 1918 Kolchak's army began its advance from Siberia into the region of the river Volga. The capture of Kazan, east of Moscow, in August, threatened the Russian capital itself. At this critical juncture Moscow was saved by the Red Army, hastily conscripted by Trotsky, who had been appointed Commissar for War. By September 1918 Bolshevik forces had regained Kazan.

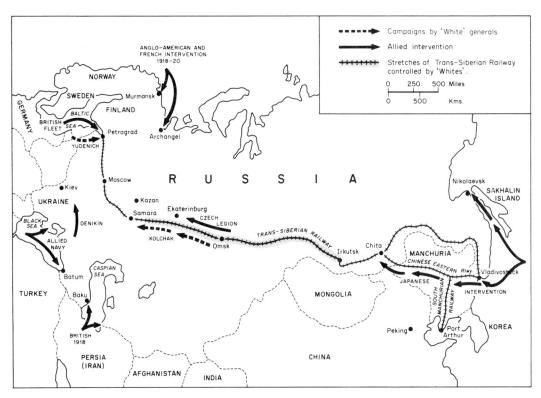

21   *The Civil War Campaigns in Russia, 1918–20*

Wrangel in the Crimea, led revolts. The Ukrainian nationalists were to be helped first by the Germans, and then by the Poles. Hostile foreign troops were stationed on Russian territory. Yet by the end of 1921 the situation had been transformed. Apart from the Japanese troops who stayed on in Siberia until 1922, all foreign troops had been withdrawn, and the Bolsheviks were in firm control of the country.

In early 1919 Kolchak resumed his advance, crossed the Urals, and threatened to link up with 'White' forces operating near Archangel. But Kolchak's offensive did not coincide with Denikin's advance from South Russia, and his army was eventually routed. His Czech allies, who had lost heart for the struggle, turned against Kolchak, and handed him over to the Bolsheviks. In February 1920 he was shot.

Bodies of massacred peasants exhumed from three pits which the victims had been forced to dig before being shot by the Bolsheviks

In September 1919 most Allied troops were evacuated. In a last desperate attempt to win the war, Yudenich advanced to within a few miles of Petrograd, while 'White' armies led by Denikin captured the Ukraine, and occupied much of the Don Cossack territory lying between the Black Sea and Moscow. By early 1920, however, their armies had been eliminated as fighting forces.

At this stage the Russo-Polish War broke out. Hitherto, the Poles, who hoped to acquire parts of the Ukraine, had bided their time. They captured Kiev in May 1920, but were then driven back by the Red Army, which reached the suburbs of Warsaw. There they were halted by General Pilsudski, who forced the Russians to retreat in haste. The Bolsheviks could now concentrate upon their last remaining foe, Wrangel's army in the Crimea. With its defeat in November 1920 the Civil War was virtually over. The Russo-Polish War was finally concluded by the Treaty of Riga in March 1921.

Reasons for the Bolshevik victory

There were many reasons for the Bolshevik victory. Their strength lay in European Russia, which included the great industrial regions around Petrograd and Moscow. The Bolsheviks represented historic Russia, and could draw upon the people's patriotism, while their opponents were associated with foreign invaders. The Bolsheviks also appeared less hostile than the 'Whites' to the claims of the various nationalities. Above all, they had the support of the peasants, who would have lost their newly-acquired lands if the 'Whites' had won.

The 'Whites', on the other hand, were divided not only by the facts of geography, but also by their competing aims. They did not plan combined offensives. At times they fought each other as well as the Bolsheviks. Trotsky was therefore able to use the advantages of internal lines of communication, and to deploy the Red Army to defeat the various 'White' armies one at a time. The 'Whites' received little help from the foreign troops, apart from some military stores.

War Communism

'War Communism' is the term applied to the economic policies followed by the Bolsheviks during the Civil War. When Lenin seized power Russia was on the verge of economic

more than five people were nationalised in December 1920. Private trading was abolished and a system of barter operated. Food was rationed according to the nature of each individual's work, so that manual labourers received three times the amount allocated to those in the professions.

In order to feed the army and the industrial workers, the peasants were ordered to sell their grain at low, fixed prices. With no consumer goods available for purchase, and with money

Worse-fated than Louis XVI: Nicholas II and his children on the roof of their prison, at Tobolsk, for a breath of fresh air. They, and the Empress, who was ill when this photograph was taken, were shot on 17 July 1918, though there is some controversy over whether the Grand Duchess Anastasia, seated to the left of Nicholas II, may have survived

collapse. Less than one-third of the railway system was in good working order. Much of the rolling stock was worn out, or simply 'lost'. There were chronic shortages of essential raw materials and foodstuffs, since the means of production and distribution had almost totally broken down. All these problems were made worse by three years of civil war.

Faced with these difficulties, Lenin introduced sweeping state controls, known as 'War Communism'. Mines and factories were to be operated by committees of workers and managers. When this system failed to work well, all factories and industrial plant employing

becoming valueless, the peasants hoarded their grain. The Bolsheviks organised brigades of town workers who invaded the countryside and confiscated grain stocks at gun-point. The peasants reacted by growing only enough food for themselves and their families.

The New Economic Policy (NEP)

When the Civil War ended Russia was in economic ruins. Industrial production was only 13 per cent of the pre-1914 total. Food production had declined by more than half.

Discontent was widespread. The peasants, on whose support the Bolsheviks ultimately relied, since they made up 80 per cent of the population, were no longer prepared to tolerate War Communism. Evidence of this was supplied when a serious mutiny of the Kronstadt garrison took place in March 1921; among other things, the mutineers demanded that the peasants should be given full control over their land and produce.

Although the Kronstadt mutiny was crushed, Lenin was convinced that further insistence on War Communism was a recipe for disaster. The transition to a purely socialist society could not be accomplished in one step. Accordingly, he persuaded the party to agree to abandon War Communism for the time being, and to permit a considerable degree of private enterprise. This change of direction was called the New Economic Policy (NEP).

The peasants were allowed to hire labour, and to cultivate as much land as they wished, though the state remained the legal owner of the land. Instead of having their crop surplus confiscated by the government, the peasants were taxed on what they produced, and left free to sell their crops on the open market. The state retained control of the major industries, but small-scale businesses were revived by returning them to private ownership. Lenin justified this retreat from communism by arguing that private incentives could not be avoided if economic growth was to be achieved.

The leadership contest

In May 1922 Lenin suffered the first of four strokes. He died in January 1924, after being almost totally paralysed for ten months. Lenin had no obvious successor, such was his authority in the Communist party, so that when illness made it impossible for him to control the government, a struggle for power developed within the communist hierarchy. The four chief contenders were Zinoviev and Kamenev, chairman of the party organisations in Leningrad (formerly Petrograd) and Moscow respectively, Trotsky, and Stalin.

Leon Trotsky (1879–1940) was a middle-class intellectual, who had visions of world-wide revolution in his own lifetime. As Commissar for War and the creator of the Red Army he had been the architect of the Bolshevik victory in the Civil War. A brilliant orator, he was also sensitive and highly critical. Lenin's last will and political testament supported Trotsky as the ablest of his lieutenants. But Trotsky was isolated and, an idealist devoted to the Communist party, he refused to exploit the power he commanded by his control of the armed forces.

Joseph Stalin (1879–1953) was, by contrast, of peasant stock. Secretive and cautious, he was greatly under-estimated by his rivals. Intelligent, ruthless and cunning, Stalin was an organisation man who understood the nature of political power. Like Trotsky, he was a member of the five-man *Politburo* (later increased to nine), which decided Communist party policy. Stalin therefore had access to the inner secrets of the party. As General Secretary of the Communist party since April 1922, he controlled key appointments. This, and knowledge of what was happening in all branches of government, gave Stalin considerable power, which he used with great skill to eliminate his rivals.

Stalin knew that any attempt to make himself leader would be resented by his colleagues, who expected that Russia after Lenin's death would be ruled by a committee. Stalin therefore worked closely with Zinoviev and Kamenev, who were also anxious to check Trotsky's influence.

The feud between Stalin and Trotsky was permanent, bitter, and based on a clash not merely of personalities but also of principles. They hated each other, and differed fundamentally in their policies. Trotsky wanted to encourage world-wide revolution without which, he argued, Russia would never be safe from hostile foreign powers, and an end to Lenin's New Economic Policy. Stalin maintained that the chief need was to consolidate the revolution in Russia. His policy of 'Socialism in One Country' had greater appeal at the time than Trotsky's 'permanent revolution'.

Trotsky, outnumbered in the *Politburo*, soon found his position untenable, and in January 1925 he resigned his office as Commissar for War. Stalin then brought into the *Politburo* three new members who supported him. They included Marshal Voroshilov, and Molotov, later to become the Soviet Union's foreign minister.

Zinoviev and Kamenev were now out-manoeuvred. In 1926 Zinoviev, the head of the Comintern,* was blamed for the failure of the General Strike in England, and dismissed. Zinoviev, Kamenev, and Trotsky now combined to check Stalin's growing influence, but it was too late. Stalin's position in the party was too powerful, and in November 1927 Zinoviev and Trotsky were expelled from the party. Zinoviev recanted his errors, but Trotsky was first exiled to Central Asia and then, in 1929, was expelled from the Soviet Union. He eventually went to Mexico, where he surrounded himself with armed guards in his fortified ranch-house. In 1940 one of his guards, an agent of Stalin, killed him with an axe.

'Socialism in One Country'

By 1925 it was clear to Stalin that there would be no communist revolution in Europe. He argued that less emphasis should be placed upon the Comintern's role of encouraging revolution in other countries, which merely aroused resentment in Western Europe, and more on consolidating the achievements of the revolution in the Soviet Union. With one-sixth of the earth's land surface, the Soviet Union could become self-sufficient and strong against its enemies.

The New Economic Policy had served its purpose of reviving the nation's economic life from its low point of 1919. But industrial output was growing very slowly, and 1913

*The abbreviation for the 'Communist International', whose function was to spread communism in other countries.

levels of production were only reached in 1927, despite an eight million increase in population. Moreover, by allowing private ownership, the NEP encouraged the growth of a large class of wealthy peasant farmers, called *kulaks*. Stalin suspected that the food shortages of 1927 in the towns could be partly explained by the reluctance of the peasants to sell their grain, in the hope of forcing up prices. This was one of the reasons for Stalin's decision to introduce collective farming.

Collectivisation

Russia's agriculture was very backward compared with most European countries. In 1928 there were 25 million small-holdings, with an average size of 200 acres, for one result of the 1917 Revolution had been the break-up of the great landed estates, which had been seized by the peasants. Over half the peasants harvested by hand, and only a minority owned horses or oxen to pull their ploughs.

The amalgamation of the peasants' individual plots of land into large units would be more efficient. Modern farm machinery could be introduced, and, by reducing the need for labour, surplus manpower would be released for employment in heavy industry. Finally, the abolition of private ownership of land would be a return to true socialism.

The campaign to persuade the peasants to enter collectives began in 1928, when party officials were sent into the country districts to organise the vast operation. The poorer peasants were readily persuaded, but the more prosperous peasants, and particularly the *kulaks*, resisted. Rather than surrender their cattle to the collective herd they slaughtered them, and sold the meat in the towns.

The consequences were alarming. Nearly half the country's horses and cattle, and two-thirds of its sheep, were killed by 1930, and for several years, until the herds could be replaced, there were severe shortages. Stalin called a temporary halt to the programme of collectivisation, but after a brief respite for the peasants the campaign was resumed. Life was made intolerable for the *kulaks*. They were forced to pay their hired labourers higher wages than those paid by less well-to-do farmers, and they were unable to obtain farm machinery, for the new collectives were given priority. Many thousands were arrested for hoarding or speculating, and deported to Siberia, where they worked in mines or labour camps.

By 1934 resistance had been overcome, and by 1938 98 per cent of Russia's farm land lay in collectives, which varied in size from 1,000 to 7,000 acres. Hundreds of tractor stations were built, providing technical advice and hiring out combine harvesters and other machinery to the collectives.

Each collective was run by a manager, on the lines of an agricultural factory. The peasants had to work up to 100 days on the collective. The rest of the time could be spent on their private holdings, for each family was permitted to own up to 2½ acres. After various deductions had been made, such as the cost of seed or hiring farm machinery, the state took 60 per cent of the collective's produce. The remainder was shared out among the peasants according to the importance of their work, or sold in the towns.

Stalin had won the campaign. Farming became more efficient. Output increased greatly by the outbreak of the Second World War, and surplus labour was made available for the heavy industries. Yet the cost had been heavy. There had been immense suffering in rural areas, where the *kulaks* as a class were liquidated. A crop failure in 1932–3, combined with the chaotic state of agriculture, led to a a terrible famine in the Ukraine, in which three million people are estimated to have died.

The Five Year Plans

The revolution in the countryside was accompanied by a staggering increase in industrial production, for the success of the collectivisation programme depended upon the ability of industry to produce sufficient farm machinery. In 1928 Stalin admitted that there were only 7,000 tractors in the whole of Russia. Furthermore, industrial expansion was a military necessity: the Soviet Union lagged fifty or a hundred years behind the advanced nations. Stalin aimed to close the gap in ten years. If he failed, Stalin told the party, the country would be crushed. Ten years after

Ukrainian peasants at work on their fields

Stalin delivered this warning, Germany attacked the Soviet Union.

The first Five Year Plan was introduced in October 1928. It set out to double industrial production, a target which was achieved in only four years. In the second Five Year Plan it was hoped to produce more consumer goods, but Hitler's rise to power in Germany, and Nazi ambitions in Eastern Europe, increased the threat of war, and the emphasis upon heavy industry remained. The third Five Year Plan was interrupted by the start of the Second World War.

The relentless progress towards industrialisation caused great hardship. Thousands of peasants were forced to migrate to the unfamiliar surroundings of industrial towns. Since foreign loans were difficult to obtain, industrial growth was financed by increased taxation, loans from the people, and exports of foodstuffs and manufactures. This meant that many basic necessities such as food, fuel, housing, and clothing were in short supply. Luxury goods were almost unobtainable. Private businesses were closed down by ruinous taxes. Slackers and absentees were fined, though there were special awards for those who exceeded their production quotas. Managers who failed to meet their targets were dismissed.

The Soviet Union's achievement during the period of the Five Year Plans was remarkable. By 1937 the output of coal had tripled, that of iron had quadrupled. Production of machinery, trucks, and metal goods increased fourteen-fold. Ninety new towns were developed, and a new class of technicians and industrial managers was created. Most of the new industrial centres were sited behind the Ural Mountains in Asia, where they were less vulnerable to foreign invasion. Within the space of ten years the Soviet Union became a major industrial power, displacing Britain in third rank in terms of gross national product.

The purges

Stalin's position in the Communist party was immensely strong by 1930, but some leading party members, such as Bukharin and Rykov, criticised the harsh treatment of the *kulaks*, and the rapidity of industrial growth, which was creating stresses in the Soviet economy. They believed that the persecution of the *kulaks* was an economic disaster and politically unsound. They called for a more moderate pace in the march towards a socialist state. To Stalin, however, criticism implied a threat not merely to his authority, but also to the unity of the party.

The purges followed the assassination of Sergei Kirov, one of Stalin's closest associates, in December 1934. Many years afterwards it was rumoured that Stalin himself had had a hand in the plot to kill Kirov, whose ability and popularity made him a rival for the party leadership. Whatever the truth of the matter may be, Kirov's death gave Stalin an opportunity to act against the dissidents.

Zinoviev and Kamenev, and a dozen leading supporters, were tried and sentenced to long terms of imprisonment. One year later Zinoviev and Kamenev were tried on more serious charges, found guilty, and shot. Several hundred officials of lesser rank were also purged. More treason trials took place during the next two years, when many important communists confessed publicly to crimes against the state, including sabotage and espionage. It has been estimated that during the period of the purges nearly one million people were executed, and a further seven million people imprisoned or sentenced to hard labour. Many years later Khrushchev revealed that over half the delegates to the Seventeenth Party Congress of 1934 were charged with treasonable offences.

Western journalists present at the Treason Trials were puzzled by the willingness of the accused to confess openly to crimes carrying the death penalty. Several explanations have been put forward. The accused may have been subjected to physical or psychological pressures, nowadays called 'brain-washing'. They may have hoped to save their lives, or protect their families. No doubt in the case of the generals and other high-ranking officers, the exchange of classified military information had been acceptable when military cooperation between Germany and the Soviet Union had been officially approved. In the light of the growing hostility between the two countries in the later 1930s, however, it could be regarded as a serious mistake. Loyalty to the Communist party may also have been a powerful consideration. By admitting their errors the accused would do the party a service by helping to strengthen party discipline.

Although the very large numbers involved rule out the possibility of a serious plot to overthrow Stalin, the purges coincided with the period when Germany's military power was growing rapidly, and its objectives were becoming clearer. Stalin may have taken the precaution of eliminating opponents lest they should seize the opportunity presented by a war with Germany to get rid of him.

The effects of the purges were widely misjudged by observers outside the Soviet Union. The removal of the larger part of the military High Command led Hitler to believe that the Red Army would be a disorganised and incompetently led fighting force. In the event, Hitler was to be proved wrong. Nor did Stalin, unlike Hitler, have to contend with wartime opposition from some of his generals. The sinister activities of the secret political police, then known as the NKVD, and the evidence of widespread discontent in Soviet Russia, did not herald Stalin's downfall. On the contrary, Stalin emerged from the period of the purges as the unquestioned dictator of a socialist state, to whose creation many of his victims had devoted all their lives.

The 1936 Constitution

In 1918 Russia was given a new constitution, and was declared a Soviet Federated Socialist Republic, renamed in 1923 the Union of Soviet Socialist Republics (USSR). Apart from all those who had been closely associated with the Tsarist regime, such as landlords, priests and officials, everyone over the age of eighteen was given the vote. Membership of the Communist party, however, was limited to a tiny percentage of the population. Those selected were dedicated communists, who placed themselves entirely at the service of the state.

The government was chosen by a system of indirect representation. The voters returned members to a local soviet, which selected delegates to a regional soviet. A national Congress of Soviets was elected by the regional soviets on the basis of one member for every 25,000 town dwellers, or 125,000 peasants. The Union Congress of Soviets, a large, unwieldy body of 1,000 members, chose a Central Executive Committee of 400. This in turn delegated most of its powers to a Politburo and a Council of Commissars, which constituted the real government of the country.

Under the 1936 Constitution the Congress of Soviets and the Central Executive Committee were abolished. They were replaced by the Supreme Soviet of the USSR. Elected directly by the voters, this consisted of two assemblies, a Council of the Union, and a Council of Nationalities. Each had equal law-making powers, and all bills had to be passed by majority votes in both assemblies before they became law. All citizens were guaranteed civil rights, such as the vote, freedom of the press, assembly and speech, though, as the purges taking place were to prove, it was wise to exercise these rights with caution.

Foreign policy, 1921–39

By 1921 the Soviet Union had recovered from the low point of 1919. The Bolsheviks had defeated foreign intervention and had won both the Civil War and the Polish War. In 1921, by the Treaty of Riga, Russia agreed its frontiers with Poland. It also signed treaties with Iran, Afghanistan and Turkey, and a trade agreement with Britain. Meanwhile, the Bolsheviks had recognised the independence of Finland, Estonia, Latvia and Lithuania, formerly parts of the Tsarist Empire.

Collaboration with Germany

Russia's isolation in world affairs was ended by the Treaty of Rapallo in 1922 (see Chapter 7). Although the basis of Russo-German cooperation was self-interest rather than genuine friendship, it was nevertheless real. When Germany signed the Locarno treaties in 1925, and joined the League of Nations in the following year, Stresemann carefully avoided any German commitment to take action against the Soviet Union.

After 1928 Russo-German collaboration gradually ceased. Stalin hoped that the capitalist system in Germany would be destroyed by the world recession in trade after 1929, and he instructed the German Communist party to cooperate with the Nazis in bringing about the downfall of the Weimar Republic. Cooperation finally ended when Hitler declined to guarantee the frontiers of the Baltic states and signed a Non-Aggression Pact with Poland in 1934. Stalin feared that Poland might be willing one day to return the Polish Corridor to Germany in exchange for territory in the Ukraine.

After 1929, therefore, the Soviet Union was increasingly isolated, despite its admission to the League in 1934. Internally, Stalin strengthened the Soviet Union by his Five Year Plans, and by the liquidation of anyone whose loyalty to the regime was suspect. Abroad he sought reconciliation with governments which opposed fascism.

Non-aggression pacts were signed with Poland, France, Finland, Estonia and Latvia in 1932 (Lithuania had already signed a treaty of friendship with the Soviet Union in 1926). Litvinov, Foreign Minister from 1930 to 1939, supported the League's doctrine of collective security, and made military alliances with France and Czechoslovakia (1935). The Comintern reversed its role of promoting revolution abroad and ordered communist parties everywhere to cooperate with all anti-fascist movements. Popular Fronts against fascism were established in France, Spain, and some Latin American countries.

Effective cooperation between the Soviet Union and the western powers, however, hardly existed. Lacking a common frontier with either of its allies, the Soviet Union could not come to their aid without breaking the neutrality of Poland or the Baltic states, or obtaining their permission for the passage of Soviet troops through their territory, which they were not willing to give. Likewise, France could not help Russia without infringing the Locarno settlement.

Stalin intervened against fascism in Spain, and he urged military cooperation against Germany during the Czechoslovak crisis of 1938–9. But the Soviet Union was not even consulted by Britain and France. The Munich settlement confirmed Stalin's suspicions that the two western powers were largely indifferent to German militarism provided it was directed against the Soviet Union.

The Popular Front strategy ended abruptly in August 1939, when the Nazi-Soviet Pact was concluded (see Chapter 20). Stalin thought a Polish-German war was inevitable. In that event the pact awarded eastern Poland to the Soviet Union. If, therefore, as he expected, Britain and France failed to assist Poland, the Soviet Union was guaranteed Polish territory which would act as a buffer zone between the new expanded Germany and Russia. If the two western powers did come to the rescue of Poland, then Stalin expected the result to be a long struggle. In either event, he hoped, the USSR would benefit.

Nevertheless, Stalin had no illusions about the nature of Nazism, nor about the peril which faced the Soviet Union. When war broke out he took steps to strengthen the USSR. The eastern slice of Poland was occupied, and the Baltic states were taken under Soviet protection. Finland's refusal to cooperate resulted in the Russo-Finnish War (November 1939 to March 1940). Eighteen months later, when Hitler ordered the invasion of Russia, the Great Patriotic War began, in which twenty million Russians lost their lives.

The First World War had revolutionary consequences for the Near East and Middle East.★ When Turkey allied itself with the Central Powers its defeat became a major objective of the Entente nations, and its empire was regarded as legitimate spoils of war. Britain immediately proclaimed protectorates over Egypt and Kuwait, and a series of wartime agreements concerning the Ottoman Empire envisaged its complete destruction.

By the Treaty of London (1915) Italy was promised part of Asia Minor in order to lure her into fighting alongside Britain, France, and Russia. At the end of the war Russia was to be allowed to keep Constantinople, and to control the Dardanelles. Britain and France awarded themselves large chunks of Arab territory by means of the secret Sykes–Picot Agreement of May 1916 (see Chapter 14). Arab hopes of winning independence from Turkish overlordship were encouraged. Negotiations between the British and Hussein, ruler of the Hejaz and leader of the Arab nationalists, which went on from January 1915 until March 1916, resulted in an Arab revolt against Turkey. Led by an English officer, Colonel T. E. Lawrence, Arab forces helped the British army by harassing Turkey's lines of com-munication. In December 1917 General Allenby captured Jerusalem, and in October 1918 Damascus fell. In the following month Allied troops occupied Constantinople, and the task of reconciling the conflicting claims and promises of the victorious powers began.

As a result of its defeat Russia had forfeited any right to participate in the peace settlement. Thus Britain and France were left in a paramount position in the Near and Middle East. Britain, however, had become dis-enchanted with French ambitions in the Near East, and the traditional rivalry between the two countries had reasserted itself. To the British it seemed that Commonwealth and British troops had borne the brunt of the fighting there, yet France still expected an equal share of the spoils. Once the defeat of Turkey became certain, the British gave as much encouragement as possible to the Arabs. After Faisal, the third son of Hussein, had captured Akaba, he was given the title of Commander of the Northern Arab Army, and his troops were allowed to make a ceremonial entry into Damascus. This town was in a French sphere of influence, but by technical right of conquest, and aided by the presence of British troops, Faisal was able to claim Syria as his kingdom.

King Faisal defied the French until July 1920. Lloyd George, the British Prime Minister, persuaded the French to give up their interests in Palestine and Mosul, but he was unable to persuade Georges Clemenceau, his French counterpart, to surrender any more. After several months of deadlock British forces evacuated Syria and Lebanon in November 1919, and Faisal was left to fend for himself. Eventually, on the anniversary of the storming

★Until the Second World War the term 'Near East' referred to that part of the Orient (East) nearest Europe, i.e. the lands bordering the eastern shores of the Mediterranean, while the 'Middle East' comprised those lands lying between the Persian Gulf and South-east Asia. Nowadays, the term 'Middle East' covers the countries of North Africa, the eastern Mediterranean states, the Arabian peninsula, Iran (Persia) and, occasionally, Afghanistan. The term 'Near East' is, therefore, seldom used.

of the Bastille, French troops under General Gourand marched upon Damascus and seized it. Faisal fled, to be offered by the British the kingdom of Iraq, which he accepted.

Meanwhile, Italian and Greek forces were asserting their countries' claims to Turkish territory, thereby further delaying a peace settlement. In April 1919 Italian troops landed

occupation of eastern Thrace and the town of Smyrna. In May 1919 Greek forces, protected by the guns of Allied warships, landed at Smyrna (Izmir), and advanced inland as the demoralised Turks fell back in disorder.

At this critical juncture in his country's affairs, the Sultan, Mehmed VI, appointed Mustafa Kemal, a Turkish general who had

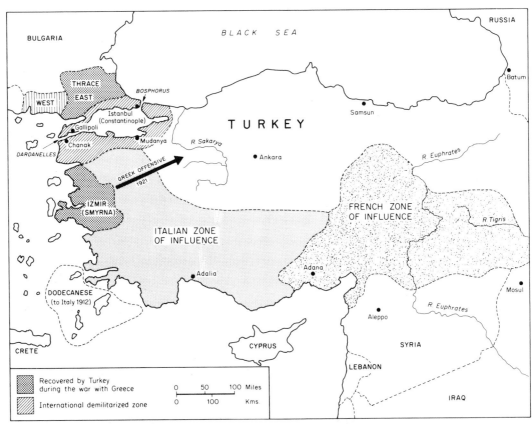

22   *The partition of Turkey, 1919–23*

in Adalia. But the chief threat to Turkey's integrity came from Greece. Asia Minor had been Greek in the days of the Byzantine Empire, until the Turks captured Constantinople in 1453. Greek claims to Turkish territory were sympathetically viewed by the Western European countries, and at the Paris peace conference Venizelos, the Greek Prime Minister, secured agreement to a Greek

distinguished himself during the war, to supervise the disarming of Turkish troops in northern Anatolia, according to the terms prescribed by the Armistice of Mudros (30 October 1918). Kemal (1881–1938) realised that the war had proved the bankruptcy of the Ottoman administration. Moreover, Mehmed VI, with his capital occupied by foreign troops, seemed powerless, or unwilling, to save Turkey from piecemeal destruction by the western nations. When Kemal arrived at Samsun, on the Black Sea coast, he took command of the Turkish army stationed there, and began to organise resistance to the Greek invasion. At the same time he put pressure on the Sultan's government to resist Allied demands.

During the final stages of the war local defence associations had been set up with the aim of preserving Turkey's independence and way of life. A National Congress of representatives from the defence associations met in 1919. It blamed the Sultan's ministers for Turkey's misfortunes, and declared that if the government in Constantinople failed to carry out its national duty Congress would establish itself as the effective national government. The Sultan ordered elections to a new parliament, but when it met in January 1920 many of its nationalist leaders were arrested by the British and deported to Malta. In March the parliament dissolved itself, and Kemal arranged for the election of a Grand National Assembly. This met at Ankara in April 1920, as a rival to the Sultan's government.

Mehmed VI, faced simultaneously with Greek victories and a gathering revolt by Kemal's nationalist party, decided that he had no choice but to seek the best terms he could obtain from the Allies. He outlawed Kemal and the nationalists, calling upon his loyal subjects to kill them as a religious duty. Secondly, he agreed to the terms of the Treaty of Sèvres (August 1920).

Turkey ceded to Greece eastern Thrace and most of the Aegean islands. The district of Smyrna in western Anatolia was also to be administered by the Greeks for five years, when its future would be decided by a plebiscite. Turkey agreed to dismantle its fortifications along the Straits, which became an international waterway controlled by a ten-power Commission established by the League of Nations. Armenia and the Arabian peninsula were granted independence. Palestine and Mesopotamia were awarded as mandates to Britain; Syria and Lebanon to France. Turkey itself was fortunate to survive as an area of

300,000 square miles with a population of 31 million.

Nevertheless, these conditions were intolerable for Turk nationalists, led by Kemal. Large numbers of Turkish soldiers deserted in order to join Kemal, who in January 1920 had been made dictator by the Grand National Assembly, in opposition to the Sultan's government. Kemal was given responsibility for defeating Turkey's foes, and for reforming the country's administration.

The Sultan's forces were overcome in January 1921 by Ismet, Kemal's ablest general, at the battle of Inönü. Two months later Kemal concluded a treaty with Soviet Russia, ceding the port of Batum in return for agreement on Turkey's eastern frontier. Nationalist troops then proceeded to occupy Armenia. Meanwhile, in western Turkey, the war against the Greeks was going well for the Turks, and in September, after a two-week battle at the river Sakarya, the Greek forces retreated.

These nationalist successes were convincing proof that any attempt to enforce the Treaty of Sèvres would be foolhardy, and the French prudently withdrew their forces from Asia Minor. (The Italians had already done so in June.) One year later the Turks recaptured Smyrna, where they slaughtered every Greek they could find.

The Chanak crisis, 1922

Although the Greeks had now been driven from the Turkish mainland, Kemal was determined to evict them from eastern Thrace, which meant Turk forces crossing the Straits. Lloyd George, who was strongly pro-Greek, ordered the British garrison at Chanak to resist any Turkish attempt to seize the Straits. The British bluff was called by Kemal, and the British government, finding itself completely isolated over the Chanak affair, was relieved to resolve the crisis by negotiation. By the Armistice of Mudanya (October 1922) Turkey's sovereignty over the Straits and eastern Thrace was recognised.

The destruction of Smyrna, September 1922

The Lausanne Conference, 1923

The final settlement of Turkey's frontiers was reached at Lausanne, in July 1923. Much of the Treaty of Sèvres was abandoned, and of the defeated powers Turkey was the only one not required to pay reparations. Turkey's frontier with Europe was virtually restored to what it had been in 1914. The problem of the Straits was settled by a separate convention. Both shores were to remain demilitarised, but Turkey was permitted to fortify Istanbul, as Constantinople was renamed. In time of war the passage of warships through the Straits was to be unhindered, provided Turkey was neutral; if Turkey was a belligerent this condition applied only to the warships of neutral countries. This arrangement remained in force until it was replaced in 1936 by the Montreux Convention, which virtually restored Turkish sovereignty over the Straits. The demilitarised zones were abolished, thus allowing Turkey to guard the Straits.

The modernisation of Turkey

Meanwhile, Kemal had set out to transform Turkey. In November 1922 the Grand National Assembly had abolished the Sultanate, leaving Mehmed VI only with the religious title and office of Caliph. When he fled into exile on board a British warship, Turkey became a republic, with Kemal as its first President.

Elections held in 1923 confirmed Kemal's popularity as the saviour of Turkey, for the majority of his opponents failed to secure re-election. The defence associations were converted into the People's Republican Party, and Ankara replaced Istanbul as Turkey's capital. Ismet, who had taken the name of Inönü after his famous victory, became Prime Minister. Although Islam remained the state religion the office of Caliph was abolished, and both education and justice were brought under state control.

Western social customs were encouraged. The *fez*, a symbol of traditional Turkey,

Mustapha Kemal inspecting troops, August 1922

was abolished, and western dress was introduced. Women were discouraged from wearing the veil and gradually became more emancipated. In 1928 the complicated Arabic script was replaced by a simpler language, which would facilitate the spread of literacy and new ideas. In 1935 a surname law ended the confusion created by a system in which all were known by their forenames. Kemal took the surname Ataturk, or 'father of the Turks', to add to his title *Ghazi* ('fighter in a religious war') which he had been given to commemorate the defeat of the Greeks in 1921.

By the late 1920s, however, political life in Turkey was stagnating, and Kemal tried to revive the spirit of reform by creating an official opposition party, in accordance with Western European political tradition. But the unexpected popular support it received convinced many Republican leaders that the experiment was too dangerous. They convinced Kemal of the need to ban it, on the grounds that it aimed at restoring many old-fashioned traditions and customs. Thus Kemal's attempt to establish a democratic system in Turkey was short-lived, and was only revived in 1946 after the Second World War.

Turkey's entry into the First World War brought about the destruction of the Ottoman Empire. Arab nationalists were persuaded that if they helped Britain and France by revolting against their Turkish overlords they would be rewarded by the creation of independent Arab kingdoms out of the ruins of the Ottoman Empire. Unfortunately, the circumstances of war led the great powers to enter into contradictory commitments to Arabs, Jews, and each other. Consequently, Arab hopes of self-government following closely upon the defeat of Turkey were cruelly disappointed. The only Arab state established was the kingdom of Hejaz in western Arabia, whose vague frontiers contained the holy cities of Mecca and Medina. The most important result of the war was the extension of British and French imperial interests in the Middle East, at the expense of the Arab peoples.

The strength of Arab nationalism was never fully appreciated in Western Europe. Although Britain and France in November 1918 spoke of 'the complete and final liberation of the peoples who have for so long been oppressed by the Turk', nothing of the kind occurred. The lesson of the Balkans – that an empire in the process of collapsing is best replaced by individual nation states – was learned too late by the allies, even after Turkey, alone of the defeated nations, successfully resisted the peace settlement imposed by the Treaty of Sèvres (1920). The principle of national self-determination, which was applied to the East European territories lost by Germany, Austria-Hungary, and Russia, was almost entirely ignored in the settlement of the Middle East. Instead, in 1920, large portions of the Ottoman Empire were acquired by

Britain and France in the form of mandates. Little wonder that Arabs referred to 1920 as *am an-nakba,* or the year of disaster. Many of the problems created then have still to be resolved, for the passage of time has made solutions more difficult to achieve.

The origins of the Arab–Jew conflict

A nation state has two chief components: a recognisable race of people and a territory which belongs to it. The misfortune of the Jewish race was that since biblical times it has been scattered over the face of the earth. The plight of the Jews was vividly described in 1936 by Chaim Weizmann (1874–1952), who later became the first President of Israel. Giving evidence before a Royal Commission on Palestine he declared:

. . . when one speaks of the Jewish people, one speaks of a people which is a minority everywhere. . . . It is a disembodied ghost of a race, without a body, and it therefore inspires suspicion, and suspicion breeds hatred. There should be one place in God's wide world where we could live and express ourselves in accordance with our character, and make our contribution towards the civilised world. We would not have to be always on the defensive, or on the contrary, become too aggressive, as always happens with a minority forced to be constantly on the defensive.

For centuries Jews in many countries had been treated as an alien race, tolerated most of the time, but regarded always with suspicion, and frequently with bitter hostility. Towards the end of the nineteenth century anti-semitism

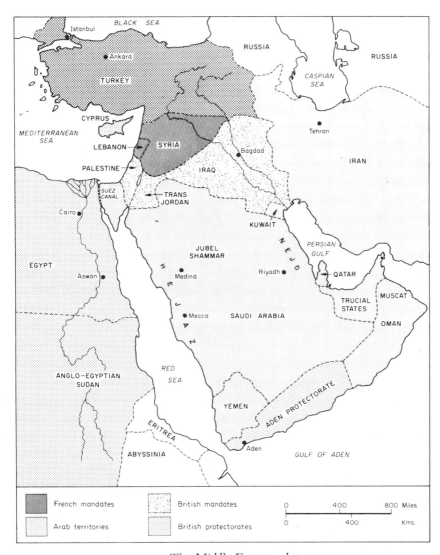

23   *The Middle East mandates*

(or persecution of Jews) became widespread in Europe. After 1879 Bismarck, Chancellor of the newly created Germany, successfully exploited the underlying dislike of Jews by associating the Liberals, whom he detested, with the Jews, in order to discredit the Liberal party. In Russia the Jews were blamed for the assassination of Tsar Alexander II in 1881. It brought down upon them the vengeance of the government, and there followed a series of *pogroms* (massacres), when many thousands of Jews lost their lives or their property. In France the *Affaire Dreyfus* aroused a storm of anti-semitism. Dreyfus, a Jew and a French army officer, was found guilty in 1894 of selling military secrets to Germany, and was sentenced to life imprisonment on Devil's Island. Evidence subsequently proving his innocence was concealed by the government in the interests of national security. It was only after a ten-year struggle to prove his innocence that Dreyfus was granted a presidential pardon.

In the meantime the *Affaire* divided the French nation by forcing all political parties to take sides on the issues involved.

Anti-semitism drove many Jews to settle in Palestine, or Zion (the Hebrew name for the Holy Hill of Jerusalem). Before 1897 Jewish emigration to Palestine had been mainly a small-scale Eastern European movement, but in that year Theodor Herzl, an Austrian journalist, convened a congress of Jews at Basle, in Switzerland, to discuss the founding of a Jewish state. Herzl had been assigned to Paris by his newspaper to report on the Dreyfus trial. He was appalled by the hostility displayed towards Jews, and became convinced that Jews could never be secure until they had their own land as a refuge when conditions became intolerable for them. In his book *The Jewish State* Herzl publicised the demand for a Jewish national home in Palestine which, he declared, would form a 'portion of the rampart of Europe against Asia, an outpost of civilisation as opposed to barbarism'. This statement reflected the attitude of many Europeans towards Turkey, whose treatment of religious minorities was sometimes horrifying in its brutality.

Palestine was a small country of 10,000 square miles, few parts of which were more than thirty miles from the sea. Jews (or Hebrews) had lived there since the days of Abraham, but they had been overrrun on several occasions by other peoples, including the Romans, Muslim Arabs, and Ottoman Turks. Over the centuries many Jews had left Palestine, but their descendants still regarded Palestine as the 'Promised Land', as Moses had described it to the survivors of the Flight from Egypt. Jews and Arabs had lived peacefully in Palestine, but this was only because in 1914 Jews still constituted less than 10 per cent of the population, and therefore did not threaten the interests of the Arab majority. This balance was to be upset by Jewish emigration which, as we have seen, began at the end of the nineteenth century.

The first Jewish emigrants to the Holy Land arrived in 1882, when two groups of Rumanian Jews founded communities at Samarin and Rosh Pina. The Turkish government opposed Jewish settlement, for it had no wish to disturb the Arab population, and laws prohibiting land purchase by Europeans were passed in 1882 and 1891. Nevertheless, settlers succeeded, by subterfuge

Jewish emigrants from eastern Europe arriving to settle in Palestine

and bribery, in persuading absentee Arab landowners to sell, and by 1914 12,000 Jewish immigrants had acquired over 100,000 acres of land. In addition, many Jews lived in the towns, where their energy and business initiative promoted commerce and industry. But while Jews could claim good relations with the Arab community, anti-Zionism was very strong among politically-minded Arabs.

The birth of Zionism coincided with the emergence of Arab nationalism, which dreamed of an independent Arab empire covering the entire Arabian peninsula. Arab nationalists were reluctant, however, to fight their co-religionists, the Muslim Turks. They also realised that Britain and France, with their imperial interests in the Middle East, and their military power, could become a serious obstacle to the development of free Arab states in the area. Their quandary was resolved by the pressures of war.

Both sides tried to enlist Arab support. Germany hoped to persuade the Sultan to proclaim a *Jihad*, or Holy War, against the infidels, which would greatly embarrass Britain, which ruled millions of Muslims in Egypt and India. Britain intrigued to stir up an Arab revolt against Turkey. The key to this situation was Hussein, sharif of Mecca and head of the Hashemite tribe of the Hejaz. His support was vital for either scheme to have any chance of success.

In January 1915 Hussein learned that many Arab nationalists expected him to lead a revolt against Turkey. He began secret negotiations with Sir Henry McMahon, the British High Commissioner in Cairo. Between July 1915 and March 1916 a series of ten letters passed between the two men. Hussein was finally convinced that he had obtained Britain's agreement to the creation of an Arab kingdom whose approximate boundaries were post-war Turkey and Iran, and the Mediterranean Sea, with the exception of modern Lebanon and the coastal region of Syria. McMahon claimed later that Palestine had also been excluded from the area assigned to Hussein, and that since France had interests in the region, detailed agreement could only be reached by discussion

after the war. There is little doubt that matters were left deliberately vague in order to gain Hussein's support.

Hussein's mind was made up for him by the Turks, who unearthed evidence of an Arab revolt and hanged several nationalists in Damascus and Beirut. On 5 June 1916 Hussein proclaimed himself King of the Arabs, and raised the standard of revolt against Turkey. Bedouin forces led by his son Faisal, and an English officer, T. E. Lawrence, attacked Turkey's lines of communication. In the final campaign Arab forces cooperated with General Allenby, and it was Faisal's army which made a ceremonial entry into Damascus in September 1918.

Faisal formed a provisional government in Damascus, but the Arab advance towards self-government had come to an abrupt stop. Apart from the understanding Hussein and McMahon had reached, two more agreements concerning the disposal of Turkey's possessions had been made during the war. In the secret Sykes–Picot Agreement of 1916, Syria was allotted to France as a sphere of special interest, while Palestine was to come under an international administration. The details of this agreement, to which Russia became a party, on the understanding that she was to receive part of Armenia, were released by the Bolsheviks after the 1917 Russian Revolution.

In November 1917 Chaim Weizmann, the leader of the Zionists in Britain, persuaded the British Cabinet to commit itself to the principle of establishing a Jewish national home in Palestine. Weizmann convinced the government that a statement of goodwill towards the Zionist cause would win the support of Jews everywhere to the Allied cause, particularly in the United States, which had declared war on Germany in the previous April. This was the background to the publication of a letter from Lord Balfour, the British Secretary of State for Foreign Affairs, to Lord Rothschild, a prominent Zionist. The Balfour Declaration stated:

His Majesty's Government view with favour the establishment in Palestine of a National Home for the Jewish people, and will use their best endeavours to facilitate the achievement of this objective, it being clearly understood that nothing shall be done which may prejudice the civil and religious rights of existing non-Jewish communities in Palestine, or the rights and political status enjoyed by Jews in any other country.

Thus ambiguous wartime diplomacy sowed the seeds of the tragic conflict between Jews and Arabs, which grew steadily between the First and Second World Wars, and blossomed into open warfare in 1948. During the same period Arab discontent with the mandates imposed upon them by the League of Nations became more and more bitter, until many Arabs came to believe that war with the Western European countries would be necessary before the Arab peoples could achieve their full economic and political independence.

Palestine

Nowhere was Arab bitterness more intense than in Palestine, where Britain faced an impossible task in trying to reconcile the contradictory promises made to Arabs and Jews. At the end of the war, however, both sides were optimistic that their hopes were about to be realised. Thus when Weizmann met Faisal in the summer of 1918 their talks were cordial enough on the surface. Faisal, whose rule in Syria was precariously dependent upon British goodwill and support against the French, was anxious to seem reasonable in his attitude towards Zionism, which appeared to have British sympathy, and a written agreement between the two leaders was signed in 1919. Faisal, who had no mandate to speak or act on behalf of the Arab peoples, endorsed the Balfour Declaration, and accepted the prospect of Jewish emigration to Palestine. Weizmann promised consideration for the rights of Arab tenant farmers, and economic aid for the Arab state which at that time the Arabs still hoped would be established. Faisal, however, added a proviso that if any changes were made the agreement would become null and void.

The treaty became a dead letter almost immediately. There was never any likelihood that the promised Arab state would be created, and in July 1920 Faisal was thrown out of Syria. His installation by the British as ruler of Iraq was an inadequate consolation prize for humiliating failure and a succession of broken promises.

Meanwhile, Zionists naturally hoped that a national home in Palestine would soon be established. Pressure was mounting upon Jews as a result of anti-semitic policies pursued in the highly nationalistic new states created by the Versailles Settlement out of the wreckage of the Austro-Hungarian, German and Russian empires. During the period 1920–4 over 40,000 Jews emigrated to Palestine from Eastern Europe.

Arab hostility towards this invasion of their homeland exploded into communal riots in 1920 and 1921. These so alarmed Sir Herbert Samuel, the High Commissioner for Palestine, that the British government took immediate steps to calm the situation. The White Paper issued in 1922 by the Colonial Secretary, Winston Churchill, reinterpreted the Balfour Declaration. It assured the Arabs:

Unauthorized statements have been made to the effect that the purpose in view is to create a wholly Jewish Palestine. Phrases have been used such as that Palestine is to become 'as Jewish as England is English'. H.M.'s Government regard any such expectation as impracticable and have no such aim in view. . . . They would draw attention to the fact that the terms of the Declaration referred to do not contemplate that Palestine as a whole should be converted into a Jewish National Home, but that such a Home should be founded in Palestine.

The Jews accepted this interpretation firstly because the British government warned them that, if they did not, it would refuse to implement the terms of the League of Nations mandate (which included Balfour's guarantee), and secondly, because they hoped to become eventually a majority of the population of Palestine. The Arabs had nothing to gain by agreeing to the White Paper, and they flatly rejected it.

The Arabs did not see why they should be treated as a minority race when they constituted 90 per cent of the population. Nor did they see why Arabs should make way for Jewish settlement. Zionism, they claimed, was imperialism in disguise, and, furthermore, violated one of Wilson's Fourteen Points, which promised the Arab peoples national self-determination. They refused to recognise the mandate, and demanded self-government in Palestine based upon majority rule.

The Zionists, on the other hand, accused the British government of breaking pledges and of surrendering to Arab extremism, thereby giving encouragement to the Arab policy of non-cooperation.

By 1936 Britain's policy of maintaining equal obligations to both sides – by refusing both the Arab demand for majority rule, and the Zionist demand for official recognition of a Jewish national home – had reached an impasse. In some desperation, therefore, the Peel Commission was set up to investigate and recommend a solution. In its report, issued in 1937, the Commission concluded:

The problem cannot be solved by giving either the Arabs or the Jews all they want. The answer to the question 'Which of them will in the end govern Palestine?' must surely be 'Neither'. We do not think, now that the hope of harmony between the races has proved untenable, that Britain ought to hand over to Arab rule 400,000 Jews, whose entry into Palestine has been for the most part facilitated by the British government and approved by the League of Nations; or that, if the Jews should become a majority, a million or so Arabs should be handed over to their rule. But, while neither race can justly rule all Palestine, we see no reason why each race should not rule part of it.

It therefore recommended the partition of Palestine. In this way the Arabs would achieve self-government, and the Jews would secure a national home.

The Arab reaction to the findings of the Royal Commission was open rebellion. Both sides resorted to murder and sabotage as the Jews met terror with terror. The Stern Gang and the Irgun Gang were both formed by the Zionists during this period, while the Jewish Defence Force, the Hagannah, was also organised. The guerrilla warfare threatened the complete breakdown of law and order in Palestine, and in 1938 martial law was introduced. By 1939, 20,000 British troops had succeeded in restoring order.

In an effort to provide a breathing-space in which both Arabs and Jews could progress towards a peaceful solution of their predicament, Britain announced that Jewish immigration was to be restricted to 15,000 a year for the next five years, with an additional 25,000 Jews allowed in from Nazi Germany. At the end of this five-year period Jewish settlement would only be permitted with Arab consent. In this way Britain hoped to allay Arab fears that they would be swamped by Jewish immigration.

A storm of Jewish protest greeted Britain's decision. The Jews living in Germany had lost all their civil rights, while those living in Poland faced the terrifying prospect of war. The 225,000 Jews who had emigrated to Palestine during the previous eight years now considered themselves the fortunate ones. For the duration of the Second World War the gates of most European countries were closed to Jews.

Saudi Arabia

During the First World War the British tried to persuade the ruler of the Nejd, Abdul Aziz ibn Saud, to support an Arab uprising against the Turks. Ibn Saud, who had become ruler of the Nejd in 1901 when he captured its capital, Riyadh, with fifteen men, was sympathetic, but did not respond. His powerful neighbour, the pro-Turk Emir of the Jubal Shammar to his north, was too strong for him to dare to risk it. Secondly, Ibn Saud was leader of the fanatical branch of Sunni Muslims* known as the Wahabi. To have

---

*The Sunni Muslims, who have their own versions of the traditions of Muhammad (AD 570–632), form the overwhelming majority of the world's Muslim population.

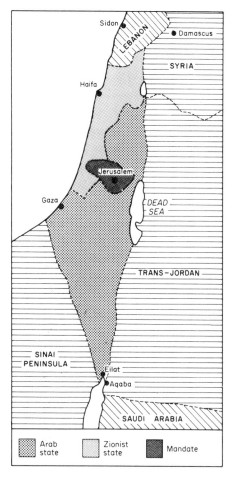

24   *Palestine: Royal Commission
     partition plan, 1937*

this office, Ibn Saud invaded the Hejaz. Indeed, only British disapproval had prevented him from taking this step in 1919, after Hussein's son, Abdullah, had raided the Nejd. By 1926, however, Hussein, who had lost the sympathy of the British, whom he declared had broken their promises to him, was forced to abdicate, and Ibn Saud was proclaimed ruler of the Hejaz in his place.

By the Treaty of Jidda (1927) Britain recognised Ibn Saud as ruler of the Hejaz, Nejd, and its dependencies, which in 1932 became the kingdom of Saudi Arabia. Friendly relations between the two countries followed, and Ibn Saud adopted a 'good neighbour' policy towards the kingdoms of Iraq and Transjordan, ruled by Hussein's two sons, Faisal and Abdullah. After the discovery of vast oil fields Saudi Arabia became a major oil-producing nation, and one of the richest states in the Middle East.

Iraq

In 1918 Mesopotamia (which was renamed Iraq in 1921) lay under the control of a British military administration. Originally the country was to have been divided into British and French spheres of influence, but at the end of the war France surrendered its claim to the district around Mosul, and Britain assumed responsibility for the whole country. This was not an easy task. The tribal character of the population, combined with the lack of efficient communications, made government peculiarly difficult. Moreover, the existence of Faisal's Arab administration in Syria led the nationalists to expect the early grant of self-government as promised by the Hussein–McMahon Correspondence.

The decision of the San Remo Conference in March 1920 to award Mesopotamia as a mandate to Britain shocked the two rival nationalist groups into uniting in opposition to British rule, and in June a serious revolt erupted in the Middle Euphrates region. This was crushed at a cost of £20 million and the lives of 400 Indian and British troops, but it

assisted the British in their designs would have meant an alliance with Hussein, sharif of the Hejaz, whose lands included Mecca and Medina, regarded by his followers as centres of idolatry. Moreover, Ibn Saud and Hussein had a personal hatred for each other, and Ibn Saud was further alienated when Hussein took the title of King of the Arabs in 1916.

Nevertheless, Ibn Saud maintained an attitude of friendly neutrality towards the British, and after Turkey's collapse he took the opportunity to expand his territories northwards by annexing the Jubal Shammar in 1921. Three years later, when Hussein alienated many Muslims by taking the title of Caliph after Kemal had stripped the sultan of convinced the British Cabinet that the mandate in its present form was unworkable. Many officials, uncomfortably aware that their government was breaking the spirit, if not the letter, of promises of self-government made to the Arabs during the war, sympathised with the nationalists. Furthermore, there was always the danger that a failure to reach a compromise agreement might result in the nationalists turning for support to Kemal's government in Turkey, which was steadily gaining prestige for its successful resistance to the Greeks.

At the Cairo Conference, convened by the Colonial Secretary, Winston Churchill, it was decided to make the country a kingdom, and to offer the crown to Faisal, who had been driven out of Syria the previous year by the French. This decision was in accordance with Article XXII of the Covenant of the League of Nations which declared that 'certain communities formerly belonging to the Turkish Empire have reached the stage of development where their existence as independent nations can be provisionally recognised subject to the rendering of administrative advice and assistance by the Mandatory until such time as they are able to stand alone'. The new kingdom was called Iraq, an Arabic term intended to revive memories of Islam's glorious past, for Mesopotamia, called Iraq by the Arabs who conquered it in the seventh century AD, became in the Middle Ages the centre of Islamic culture.

Britain's retention of various treaty rights, and the granting of a constitution in 1924, stimulated the growth of Iraqi nationalism. In June 1930 Britain agreed to the formal abolition of the mandate, and recognised Iraq's complete independence. In turn Iraq promised to pursue a friendly foreign policy and to provide facilities for bases in wartime. In 1932 Iraq joined the League of Nations, the first of the mandated territories to do so. When Faisal died in 1933 he was succeeded by his son Ghazi. His reign, which lasted for six years until he was killed in an accident, was ineffectual, for he devoted more of his time and attention to motor racing than to ruling his country.

Transjordan

In 1918 Transjordan, as part of the great Arab kingdom Hussein expected to be established after the war, was administered from Damascus by Faisal's provisional government. Shortly after Faisal's expulsion from Syria in July 1920, Britain announced its intention to grant self-government to its mandate, Transjordan. But before an administration could be set up Faisal's brother, Abdullah, announced his plan to lead a revolt against French rule in Syria. The British, who were anxious to obtain Arab goodwill, allowed him to occupy Amman, the capital of Transjordan, and to establish a government there. At the Cairo Conference (1922) Abdullah was recognised by Britain as the ruler of Transjordan, provided he abandoned his opposition to French rule in Syria and accepted British assistance. The Arab Legion, founded in 1921 and trained by British officers, was for many years an important factor in support of Britain's interests in the Middle East. It was Abdullah's friendly relationship with Britain which finally resulted in his assassination in 1951 by Arab nationalists.

Syria and Lebanon

The Sykes–Picot Agreement of 1916 secretly arranged for Syria to become a French sphere of influence after the war. The French, however, did little to encourage an Arab rebellion against the Turks, being conscious that their North African possessions were vulnerable to nationalist agitation among the largely Muslim population. Nor did French troops play any significant part in the campaigns in the Middle East. Even before the end of the war, therefore, the traditional rivalry between Britain and France in the Middle East was reasserting itself. Many British officers resented the fact that France was to acquire large tracts of Arab territory for little apparent effort, and were very sympathetic to Arab aspirations. When Damascus fell to General Allenby's army in October 1918, Faisal's troops were allowed

*Arrival of a refugee ship at Haifa: crowds eagerly wait to meet
relatives outside the dock gates*

a ceremonial entry into the city, thus giving the
Arabs possession by technical right of conquest.
In March 1920 Faisal was proclaimed ruler of
the kingdom of Greater Syria, Lebanon, and
Palestine.

One month later France was given Syria and
Lebanon as mandates, although the King–
Crane Commission (1919) set up by the Paris
Peace Conference to investigate the situation
in Syria reported that there was widespread
resentment against the imposition of French
rule. For another three months Faisal claimed
the right to administer Syria, in defiance of
France's legal responsibility for the territory.
But without the presence of British troops to
act as a restraint upon French policy, Faisal was
in an unenviable position. After several
clashes between French and Arab troops the
French commander, General Gouraud,
delivered an ultimatum to Faisal, and on the
anniversary of the Fall of the Bastille, French
troops occupied Damascus. Faisal fled, and his
government collapsed.

The French imposed military rule upon Syria,
exploiting its religious divisions in order to
strengthen their hold on the country. Syria was
divided into four areas, and Lebanon was
expanded by the inclusion of the towns of
Beirut, Tripoli and Sidon, and territory down
to the Palestine frontier. Nevertheless, Arab
resentment burst into revolt in 1925, which
the French authorities dealt with ruthlessly
and efficiently by a three-day bombardment
of Damascus, a measure which had to be
repeated the following year.

The rebellion convinced the French that it
was impossible to govern their mandated
territories along military lines indefinitely, and
efforts were made to reach a negotiated settlement with the nationalist groups. Lebanon
was declared a republic in 1926 and, after
much delay, granted a constitution in 1933.
Syria became a republic in 1930, and was
given a constitution in 1932. Plans to grant
Syria and Lebanon their independence in 1939
came to naught when the French Assembly
refused to ratify the treaties drawn up in 1936.
By the time the Second World War broke
out, Arab discontent was threatening the
collapse of the French mandates.

CHAPTER FIFTEEN
Revolution and Civil War in China

By the beginning of the twentieth century popular support for the Manchu dynasty was dwindling rapidly. China's humiliation by Japan, technically a vassal state, in 1894–5, and by the European great powers in 1900 (see Chapter 1), convinced many Chinese of the urgent need to modernise their country.

The Manchu dynasty's chances of survival, however, were reduced by the influence of the aged Empress Dowager (1835–1908). The Chinese respect for age often conferred great authority on members of the older generation, so that the Emperor was not necessarily the

effective head of the government. For the last ten years of his life the Emperor Kuang-hsu (1871–1908) was made a virtual prisoner in his own court by his mother, the Empress Dowager, who ruled in his place. She was powerfully supported by Yuan Shih-k'ai, commander of the imperial army and Governor General at Tientsin. She opposed reform, and only agreed against her will to the modernisation of the army by Yuan, and to the introduction of a constitution based on western models in 1908. When both the Emperor and the Empress Dowager died in the

A Chinese official, escorted by troops, makes his escape from Tientsin

same year, Pu-yi, the infant son of the Emperor's brother, succeeded, with his father, Prince Ch'un, as Regent. He immediately dismissed Yuan, thereby making a powerful enemy of him.

Japan's seizure of Korea in 1910 demonstrated once again the dynasty's inability to defend its

The 1911 revolution

In May 1911 the government announced its terms for nationalising the Szechwan railway. It was only willing to pay shareholders the current market price of the company's stock, which was low in view of mismanagement of

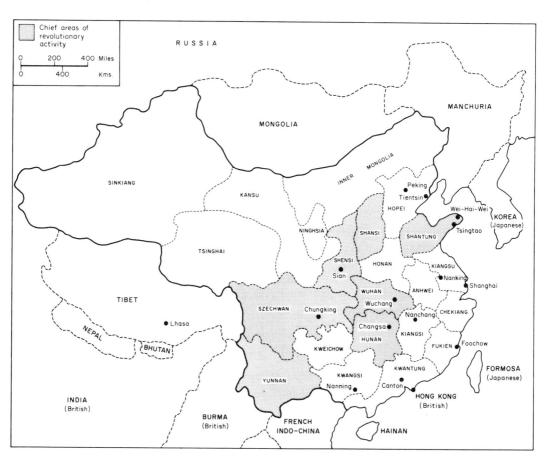

25   *The Chinese Revolution, 1911*

territories. The provincial assemblies elected in 1909 demanded further reforms, and took advantage of the Peking government's weakness to extend their own authority. Thus the Manchu decision in 1911 to nationalise China's main railway lines was likely to arouse fierce opposition. The government's proposal to take over the Szechwan railway proved to be the origin of the 1911 revolution.

the company's affairs. Riots and strikes developed as dissatisfaction with the government's offer blended with other discontents. Open rebellion began when a revolutionary uprising took place in Wuchang, the capital of Szechwan province, on 10 October (the Double Tenth, so called because it succeeded, whereas ten previous attempts at revolution had failed).

The Chinese revolutionary movement was led by Dr Sun Yat-sen (1867–1925). Educated at a village school in Hawaii and at Hong Kong University, where he qualified as a doctor of medicine, Sun believed his mission was to lead the Chinese Revolution. As early as 1895 he organised a conspiracy to seize Canton. In 1905 he founded in Tokyo the Alliance League, whose aim was the overthrow of the Manchu dynasty. Since then there had been five uprisings, but all had failed through poor organisation and lack of money and arms.

The Wuchang uprising occurred when explosives stored in premises belonging to members of the Alliance League were accidentally detonated. Government troops searched the place and discovered a list of the conspirators' names. The revolutionaries were therefore forced to act, the alternatives being to do nothing and risk arrest, or flee. The rebellion quickly spread to many parts of China.

By the end of 1911 a revolutionary government had been established at Nanking, and Sun Yat-sen, who was touring Europe in order to raise funds, was declared President of the Chinese Republic. In the meantime, the Prince Regent had recalled Yuan Shih-k'ai, and appointed him Prime Minister, with the task of saving the Manchu dynasty. Yuan soon realised that this was impossible.

Yuan negotiated with Sun, who agreed to resign as Provisional President and allow Yuan to take his place, if the latter forced the Emperor to abdicate, and established a republican form of government. The Manchu dynasty was helpless, and on 12 February 1912 China became a republic. In March Yuan was duly elected first President of the Chinese Republic.

The dictatorship of Yuan Shih-k'ai

Sun failed to persuade Yuan to move the government from Peking to Nanking. Yuan's dislike of parliamentary government soon became clear, and a struggle for power between the two developed after Sun formed an open political party called the Kuomintang (Country-People-Party), an amalgamation of the Alliance League and the other revolutionary groups. Sun based the party on the Three Principles of Nationalism, Socialism, and Democracy. Its members were called Nationalists, after the adoption of nationalism as the first principle. In the 1913 elections to a new parliament the Kuomintang won a majority of the seats. Thereupon Yuan outlawed the party and dismissed the parliament. Sun and his supporters fled to southern China, and Yuan by stages made himself dictator.

Yuan had shown great political skill in avoiding civil war and foreign intervention. By 1914 all China except Kwangsi and Sinkiang was under his control. He had the financial backing of the European powers, who welcomed him as a strong ruler capable of maintaining China's unity. The start of the First World War, however, left China isolated and powerless in 1915 to refuse Japan's Twenty-One Demands for privileges and concessions in China, which gave the Japanese considerable influence on the Chinese mainland. Yuan's attempt to consolidate his regime by making himself emperor was a failure. He was opposed by the Nationalists and by the Manchu supporters, and he quickly abandoned his plans, allowing himself to become a figurehead. He died shortly afterwards in June 1916.

Warlord rule, 1916–26

After Yuan's death China was ruled by warlords. Peking still represented China, but in the struggles for power no individual warlord was able to control Peking for long, let alone govern the whole country. Some warlords were little better than bandits, whose personal armies ravaged the countryside in the battles against rival warlords. Others, such as Chang Tso-lin in Manchuria, and Yen Hsi-shan, governor of Shansi, were benevolent, efficient rulers of the territory they controlled. None of them, however, harnessed the power of Chinese nationalism in the way that Sun was able to do. They were all too dependent upon foreign powers for loans and military supplies, and they lacked Sun's vision of a united China.

The beginnings of Chinese communism

Chinese resentment of western influence in their affairs had been strengthened by European indifference to Wilson's Fourteen Points so far as they applied to China, and by Japan's claims on the Chinese mainland. On 4 May 1919 Peking students organised a boycott of Japanese goods, and led mass demonstrations against China's treatment at the Versailles Conference. The Fourth May Movement, as this campaign was called, stimulated Chinese nationalism.

The Soviet government from the very start took a keen interest in the Chinese revolutionary movements, especially when Lenin's expectations of revolution in Europe failed to materialise. Lenin hoped to exploit anti-western feeling in China in order to embarrass the capitalist western nations. While the latter clung on to their rights and privileges in China, the Soviet Union, by the Karakhan Declaration of July 1919, surrendered the concessions made by China to Tsarist Russia, which admittedly it was in no position to enforce. In 1920 Comintern agents were sent to China to organise the Chinese Communist party and, at the same time, establish close links with the Kuomintang.

The Chinese communist movement was started by two professors at Peking University, Ch'en Tu-hsui, and Li Ta-chao. Ch'en formed marxist study groups in 1918 and, in May 1920, moved to Shanghai, where he organised communist cells in different parts of China. Li Ta-chao was the founder of the Fourth May Movement.

The official foundation of the Chinese Communist party, however, dates from July 1921 when twelve delegates and a Russian observer attended the First Party Congress, which appointed Ch'en Tu-hsui as chairman. In 1922 delegates from both the Kuomintang

and the Communist party attended the First Congress of the Toilers of the Far East, held in Leningrad.

The Kuomintang–Communist alliance

The Kuomintang and the Communist party had much in common. Both were strongly nationalist and anti-warlord. Both parties were revolutionary in their aim of uniting China under a strong government. To the Soviet Union, which could see little difference between the two parties, an alliance between the two movements was sound tactics. The Kuomintang was a large organisation with a membership of 150,000. It has already succeeded in establishing a government at Canton, and it was the only organisation in China capable of sustaining a campaign against the warlords. The Communist party, on the other hand, was in its infancy, and could not expect to resist the Kuomintang. By joining it, however, the communists would not only greatly increase their influence, and so recruit more members, but could also hope eventually to win control of the Kuomintang organisation.

At first Sun could see little benefit to be gained from an alliance with the communists, but in 1922 the Kuomintang government was driven out of Canton by the Kwantung warlord. Sun fled to Shanghai, where he accepted an offer of Soviet military aid from Adolph Joffe, a Comintern agent, in early 1923. The Comintern agreed that the Three Principles should be the basis of the Kuomintang–Communist alliance, while Sun agreed that communists could join the Kuomintang without renouncing their party membership. Chiang Kai-shek, Sun's most trusted follower, visited the Soviet Union to study military organisation, and Mikhail Borodin was sent to reorganise the Kuomintang. He drafted a new constitution for the party, in which communists held several important posts. Meanwhile, Sun's government had been re-established in Canton.

Chiang Kai-shek returned to China, and

opened an officer cadet training school at Whampoa, near Canton, in January 1923. There his task was to create an army completely loyal to the Kuomintang. The cadets from Whampoa played an important part in the Kuomintang's conquest of Kwantung province in 1925.

Communist influence grew rapidly as a result of the alliance with the Kuomintang. At the the hands of Wang Ching-wei and Chiang Kai-shek, who controlled the Kuomintang army. In December 1925 a number of right-wing members, who believed that communist infiltration of the Kuomintang had reached a dangerous stage, demanded the expulsion of the communists, only to be overruled by a National Congress, and themselves expelled. At this stage Chiang Kai-shek's attitude to the

Nationalist cavalry patrol riding through Canton, November 1925

beginning of 1923 Communist party membership stood at 300. By 1927 membership had increased to 50,000, and the communists claimed to control over two million industrial workers, as well as several million peasants. Sun never fully trusted his communist allies, but he believed that his views would prevail in any debate over the Kuomintang's role. This was probably true, such was his great prestige, but in 1925, at the age of 58, Sun died of cancer of the liver.

The Kuomintang leadership now passed into communists was not clear, but in March 1926, claiming that he was acting to foil a plot to overthrow him, Chiang arrested the Soviet advisers and many communists.

They were released shortly afterwards, and the Kuomintang–Communist alliance was maintained, but communist influence in it was greatly reduced. No communist could be head of an organisation, or government department. Communists were not allowed to have more than one-third of the seats on any committee, and all political indoctrination in the

Kuomintang was to be based on Sun's Three Principles.

Thus the communists seemed to have lost their chance of taking control of the Kuomintang. They accepted the new terms, however, because they were not yet strong enough to win a struggle against the Kuomintang.

The Northern Expedition and the Shanghai Massacres

In the summer of 1926 Chiang Kai-shek began a military campaign to overthrow the warlords in central and northern China. Aided by communist-inspired peasant uprisings, Kuomintang forces advanced as far as Hankow and Hanyang by September, and captured Kiangsu and Fukien by the end of the year. In March 1927 Nanking and the communist stronghold, Shanghai, were captured.

The communist leadership was in a dilemma. Its encouragement of a peasant revolution could no longer be reconciled with support of the Kuomintang, which seemed to be on the point of achieving victory. Nevertheless, the armed workers of Shanghai were ordered not to oppose Chiang Kai-shek's army.

In April 1927, however, Chiang Kai-shek broke the Nationalist alliance with the communists. He denounced the existing Kuomintang government which had moved from Canton to Hankow, and established his own Kuomintang government in Nanking. At the same time Nationalist troops killed thousands of communists in Shanghai. Similar massacres took place in all the cities controlled by the Kuomintang.

The Autumn Harvest uprising and the start of the civil war

After the Shanghai Massacres, and the failure of the communist attempts to seize Nanchang and Canton, most of the communist leaders went into hiding. Mao Tse-tung (1893–1976) who was to become Chairman of the People's Republic of China from 1949 until he died, realised that the communists would have to act quickly or they would lose their support in the towns and villages as the Kuomintang strengthened its hold on occupied territory. He gathered together four small armies and captured Changsha, the provincial capital of Hunan. Almost immediately, however, the communist armies were defeated, and Mao himself was captured.

Mao had the good fortune not to be recognised by his captors, and he was allowed to buy his freedom. He led the remnants of the communist armies into the remote, mountainous interior of the province. There he set up the first Chinese communist state, the Kiangsi–Hunan Soviet, which survived for six years.

Mao was elected chairman of the communist government based at Juichin. In April 1932 he declared war on the Japanese, who had invaded Manchuria in 1931 (see Chapter 16). Although it was physically impossible for the communists to fight the Japanese, Mao's declaration of war was a valuable propaganda weapon against Chiang Kai-shek's government, which controlled nearly all China.

Between 1931 and 1934 Chiang Kai-shek launched several campaigns aimed at destroying the Kiangsi–Hunan soviet. The first three were failures. The communists, who were lightly armed and able to use peasants as local guides, were aided by the lack of roads, which hampered the movement of Kuomintang troops. Furthermore, Chiang was forced to reserve his best troops to guard against the possibility of a Japanese attack on the Chinese mainland. The second-rate troops he employed were easily discouraged, and were defeated piecemeal by communist guerrilla bands, who operated with the support of the peasant population.

It was during this period that Mao developed the strategy on which the final communist victory was based. Pitched battles were to be avoided unless the communists were certain of victory, for they depended on capturing the enemy's military equipment and supplies. Mao's guerrilla tactics may best be summed up in his own words: 'The enemy advances, we retreat; the enemy camps, we harass; the enemy tires, we attack; the enemy retreats, we pursue'.

Communist policy was to win the support of the peasants, whom Mao once likened to the sea, in which the fishes (the communists) could safely swim. The Chinese Red Army treated the peasant population with consideration, as people to be liberated, not conquered. Lands belonging to the large landowners were confiscated, and redistributed among the peasants.

The end of the Kiangsi–Hunan Soviet and the Long March, 1934–5

In 1933 Chiang Kai-shek concentrated a large army against the communists. Roads were built, and the Kiangsi–Hunan Soviet was encircled and blockaded by a system of small forts, or blockhouses. Deprived of supplies, the communists were forced to retreat to the interior, where their situation gradually became impossible.

In October 1934 Mao Tse-tung decided to break through the enemy blockade and lead his army to the relative safety of Shensi province in northern China. There, he told his commanders, they would be able to fight the hated Japanese. Kuomintang control of the Yangtze valley forced the communists to make a long and dangerous detour to the south. Eventually, after fourteen months of fighting and forced marches, in which the communists travelled 6,000 miles across mountain ranges, deserts, rivers, and swamps, 20,000 survivors reached safety. Yenan became the capital of the Shensi Soviet, and remained the seat of the communist government until its victory in 1949.

The Long March was both a defeat and a triumph. In the first place it was a retreat. Only one-fifth of the original army which set out survived, for losses due to incessant fighting, disease and desertion were heavy. But the communist movement survived and

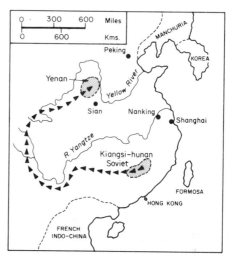

26   *The Long March, 1934–5*

established a secure base, while Mao Tse-tung was confirmed as the leader of the Chinese Communist party.

The Sian incident and the united front against Japan

In 1936 the communists announced their readiness to cooperate with the Nationalists against the Japanese, who were strengthening their position in northern China. A number of left-wing members of the Kuomintang secretly sympathised, feeling that the Japanese, not the communists, were China's real enemies. Meanwhile, communist forces moved from their base into the neighbouring province of Shansi, which served the double purpose of enlarging the area under their control, and enabling them to fight the Japanese at the same time.

The Kuomintang commander in northern China was Chang Hsueh-liang, formerly warlord of Manchuria until his expulsion by the Japanese. Many of his troops were infected with communist propaganda, and Chang himself would have preferred to fight the Japanese. Consequently, Kuomintang operations against the communists degenerated into an unofficial truce.

In December 1936 Chiang Kai-shek flew to Sian in order to remonstrate with Chang over his refusal to fight the communists. A few days after his arrival Chiang Kai-shek's bodyguard was overpowered, and Chiang Kai-shek himself was kidnapped. Chou En-lai, a leading communist, was flown from Yenan to Sian to negotiate terms for a new Kuomintang–Communist alliance. It seems likely that a vague agreement was reached, for the communists relaxed their policy of land confiscations, and the civil war was not resumed. Meanwhile, Chang Hsueh-liang returned with Chiang Kai-shek to Nanking, where he was arrested and imprisoned for thirty years.

Kuomintang–Communist relations during the Chinese–Japanese War

In view of growing Chinese unity, the Japanese government speeded up its preparations for the conquest of China. War broke out in July 1937 following a skirmish between Chinese and Japanese soldiers at the Marco Polo Bridge, near Peking. Japanese armies swiftly gained the ascendancy on the Chinese mainland, and captured the coastal cities. After the fall of Hankow in October 1938 the Nationalists retreated to the isolated, mountainous region around Chungking.

The united front against Japan soon crumbled. The communists avoided pitched battles by moving into another area, tactics which aroused Nationalist suspicions that they merely intended to take control of it. As clashes between the Nationalists and communists developed, the Kuomintang refused to supply the communists with arms, lest they should be used against Nationalist troops. Communist suspicions that the Kuomintang leadership was considering coming to terms with the Japanese were deepened when Wang Ching-wei, Chiang Kai-shek's deputy, fled from Chungking, and negotiated a settlement with the Japanese, who appointed him head of a puppet government at Nanking in March 1940.

The resumption of civil war and the establishment of the People's Republic of China

When Japan surrendered in August 1945 the Second World War ended, and Nationalist forces, with American help, were reinstated in the coastal cities, while communist guerrillas controlled the countryside. Civil war broke out again in earnest in 1947. Despite American support, the Kuomintang collapsed and, in April 1949, the Nationalists retreated to the offshore islands of Formosa (Taiwan), Quemoy, and Matsu. Chairman Mao Tse-tung proclaimed the People's Republic of China in October 1949, with its capital in Peking.

China, Japan, and the First World War

The outbreak of war in August 1914 directly involved the Far East, since four of the European combatants – Britain, France, Russia, and Germany – had major interests in mainland China and the Pacific island territories. Thus the efforts of the Chinese and American governments to maintain peace in the Far East failed.

Britain was reluctant to invoke the Anglo-Japanese alliance, for Japan's involvement in the war would not please American public opinion. Furthermore, Japan's claims to German colonies in the north Pacific were unpopular with the Dominions, particularly Australia and New Zealand. In the hope of restricting Japan to a subsidiary naval role, Britain merely requested the help of the Japanese navy in destroying German warships in the Pacific. But Japan was not to be denied the opportunity to add to her overseas territories. Independently, she declared war on Germany.

In November 1914 Japanese troops captured the German port of Tsingtao, in Kiaochow, and the Caroline Islands. The proposed transfer of the islands to an Australian force aroused such a storm of protest in Tokyo that Britain agreed that their future should be settled at the end of the war.

The Twenty-one Demands, 1915

Japan's ambitions soon became clear. China's request that Japanese troops should be withdrawn from the Shantung peninsula was refused. Instead, in January 1915, the Japanese government presented a list of Twenty-one Demands to Yuan Shih-k'ai. They included the transfer of Germany's rights in Shantung to Japan, with permission to build another railway in the province, and recognition of Japanese interests in southern Manchuria. China was forbidden to surrender or lease any part of its coastline to another power. Japanese military and financial experts were to advise the Chinese government. So extensive were the Demands that, had they been accepted in full, China would have been converted into a dependency of Japan.

China leaked news of the Demands to foreign governments, which urged moderation upon Japan. Eventually, Japanese demands were limited to those concerning Shantung and southern Manchuria, to which the Chinese government, under the threat of war, agreed.

Great-power recognition of Japanese gains in the Far East

Aware that peace might bring renewed pressure to restrict her gains, Japan sought international recognition of her stake in China. By a secret Russo-Japanese treaty of July 1916 each country promised cooperation to prevent a third power, hostile to them both, exercising political influence in China. This agreement, aimed against the United States, was cancelled by the Bolshevik government less than two years later.

In November 1917, by the Lansing–Ishii Agreement, the United States admitted that China was an area of special importance to Japan. In return the latter promised to respect

China's independence, and to support America's 'Open Door' policy.

The Versailles Settlement confirmed Japanese possession of the Shantung peninsula, and awarded Japan mandates over Germany's colonies north of the Equator, the Caroline, Marshall and Mariana Islands. Japan was also given a seat on the League Council as one of the five Permanent Members. China refused to sign the treaty, but was too weak to resist Japan.

The Japanese government, however, received a setback over its request that a clause guaranteeing racial equality should be inserted in the Covenant of the League of Nations. This was important not only for prestige reasons, but also for its application to the migration issue. Opposition from Australia and the United States, where California had passed anti-Japanese legislation, resulted in its rejection. The Japanese bitterly resented this open avowal of white supremacy.

Japanese intervention in Siberia, 1918–22

Meanwhile, Russia's defeat and the Bolshevik Revolution (1917) had led to disturbances in Siberia, where 50,000 Czechoslovakian prisoners-of-war had seized sections of the Trans-Siberian Railway in their bid to escape from Russia. On the pretext that the disorders might spread, thereby threatening Japanese interests in Manchuria, Japanese troops invaded parts of Siberia, where they soon outnumbered the combined forces sent by the United States, Britain and France. They remained in eastern Siberia until November 1922, long after the latter had been withdrawn, and did not evacuate the northern half of Sakhalin Island until 1925.

The Washington Naval Conference, 1921–2

International tension in the Far East was complicated by the existence of the Anglo-Japanese alliance. Britain was concerned over the ill-feeling between the United States and Japan, and alarmed at the possibility of being involved in any future war between these two Pacific powers. The Dominion governments, particularly those of Canada and Australia, were also anxious that the alliance, due to expire in July 1921, should not be renewed.

Thus Canada's suggestion, at the Commonwealth Conference in London in 1921, that the great powers should meet to discuss Pacific affairs and naval disarmament, was generally welcomed. The exception was Japan, which correctly suspected that Britain wished to drop the alliance with her.

Nine governments with interests in the Pacific (China, Japan, the United States, Belgium, Britain, France, Italy, the Netherlands, and Portugal) took part in the Washington Conference. High in the order of priorities was naval disarmament. The United States, Britain, and Japan agreed to a 'naval holiday', when no new capital warships would be built, and to restrict the size of their navies in the proportion of 5:5:3 respectively. France and Italy each accepted a lower ratio of 1.75. The Japanese government, however, insisted that no new naval bases and fortifications should be constructed in the Pacific. This virtually guaranteed Japan's immunity from a naval attack.

The Anglo-Japanese alliance was replaced by a Four Power Treaty (the United States, Japan, Britain and France). The signatories promised to respect each other's rights in the Pacific, and to consult each other on any Pacific problem.

The powers promised to respect China's sovereignty. Japan agreed to restore Shantung to China, on the understanding that China would purchase the railways which had been built, and would respect Japanese mining interests in the peninsula. Britain restored Wei-hai-wei to China. But Japan insisted that its rights regarding the South Manchurian Railway and in Kwangtung (Liaotung) should remain unaltered.

Manchuria

Most Japanese believed that the integration of the Manchurian and Japanese economies was essential. They differed only on the means whereby this could be achieved. Some wished to develop genuine cooperation with China. Others were prepared to leave substantial powers to the Manchurian government, provided Japanese interests were adequately

Japanese extremists began a campaign of violence and terror in an effort to force the government to annex Manchuria. When the Prime Minister, Hamaguchu, tried to restrain the Kwangtung Army generals, he was assassinated. Several other public figures suffered the same fate. Many moderate politicians were too frightened to criticise those who were advocating military measures. Moreover, Japan, like other industrialised

Japanese soldiers march into Chinese territory

protected. A growing proportion, who believed that a war with the United States was inevitable, wanted complete control. The Kwangtung Army was determined to bring Manchuria into the Japanese Empire, if necessary by provoking China into war. Only then, the Army considered, would Manchuria be a secure base for future expansion, either in Siberia or on the mainland of China.

In June 1928 the Kwangtung Army High Command plotted the assassination of Chang Tso-lin, the warlord ruler of Manchuria, hoping to create a breakdown of law and order which would justify military intervention. The plot misfired. Chang was peacefully succeeded by Chang Hsueh-liang, who proceeded to come to terms with Chiang Kai-shek, the leader of the Chinese Nationalist government in Nanking.

countries, was suffering from the growing world trade recession which began in 1929, and an aggressive and successful foreign policy might distract attention from the country's economic ills. Thus it became increasingly difficult for the civilian government to control the Kwangtung Army.

On 18 September 1931 two explosions occurred near the track of the South Manchurian Railway at Mukden. No damage was done. Chinese saboteurs, however, were blamed, though none were caught. The incident was clearly staged by the Army, for within hours Japanese troops had occupied Mukden.

Chiang Kai-shek instructed the Manchurian government not to resist. He did not wish to provoke the Japanese, and he relied upon the League of Nations to halt the aggression. The Kwangtung Army proceeded to occupy the

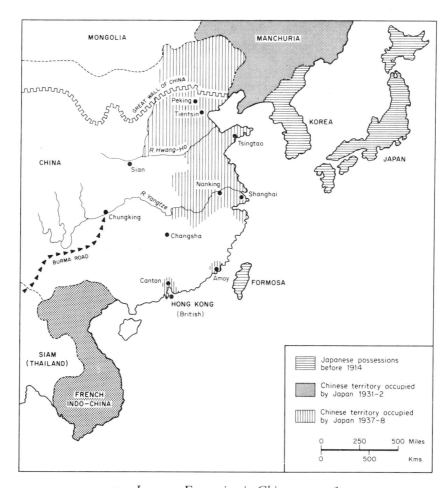

27   *Japanese Expansion in China, 1914–38*

whole of Manchuria, disobeying its own government. In March 1932 the Japanese proclaimed the creation of the independent state of Manchukuo. The last Manchu emperor, Pu Yi, was installed as a puppet ruler.

In 1933 the League of Nations Commission, headed by Lord Lytton, presented its report. It branded Japan as a technical aggressor, but meekly added that Japan was a civilising power which would bring order and efficiency to Manchuria's affairs. No action was taken against Japan. The United States was not prepared to intervene, and the other Far Eastern power, the Soviet Union, did not belong to the League. Nevertheless, Japan withdrew from the League in protest. In its first serious confrontation with a major power

the League had failed disastrously.

Two months after the publication of the Lytton Report, China resigned itself to the loss of Manchuria, and the Truce of T'ang-ku (May 1933) created a demilitarised zone between Peking and the Great Wall.

China and Japan at war

In July 1937 an exchange of shots between Japanese and Chinese soldiers at the Marco Polo Bridge, near Peking, developed into a full-scale war. Japanese forces captured Peking and Tientsin, and by the end of the year were also in possession of Shanghai and Nanking. By midsummer of 1938 Japan controlled the ports and major cities of northern China, together with its railway network.

China, relying on foreign aid, and on its vast size and unlimited manpower, refused to surrender, but Japan was greatly assisted by the civil war between the communists and the Nationalists, which had been almost continuous since 1927. Both sides competed not only for control of Japanese-occupied territory, but also for territory held by their opponents.

By 1939 Japan had developed a stranglehold upon China. In 1940, confident of ultimate victory, the Japanese government proclaimed a 'Greater East Asia Co-Prosperity Sphere', consisting of Japan, China, Manchuria and Korea, to correspond with Hitler's 'New Order' in Europe. Japan's naval supremacy in the China seas was undisputed. Diplomatically, it seemed, Japan had little to fear. Public opinion in the United States, though opposed to Japanese aggression in China, was strongly isolationist. In 1936, by joining the Anti-Comintern Pact, Japan had secured the diplomatic support of Germany. In 1937 this pact was strengthened by the addition of Italy. News of the Nazi-Soviet Pact of Neutrality (August 1939), though a shock to the Japanese government, made little practical difference so far as its military strategy was concerned. Although serious clashes between Russian and Japanese troops took place in 1939 along the borders of Manchuria and Mongolia, as each side tested the other's strength, neither country was intent upon war, and an uneasy peace was preserved.

The outbreak of the Second World War further assisted Japan. After Germany had defeated France in 1940, Britain ceased to send aid to China along the Burma Road, for fear of provoking Japan into war. The weakness of the Vichy government in France, which was utterly dependent upon German goodwill, enabled Japan to secure control of Tongking in September 1940, thereby cutting off another supply route to China, as well as obtaining three airfields from which China's cities and communications could be bombed. When

Germany attacked the Soviet Union in June 1941, supplies of Russian munitions and aircraft to China, which had followed the signing of the Russo-Chinese Non-Aggression Pact in August 1937, also ceased.

Hitler hoped that Japan would declare war upon the Soviet Union. Instead, in July 1941, Japan extended its control to the whole of Indochina, thus securing bases from which it could attack British Malaya and the Dutch East Indies. American intelligence had broken the Japanese diplomatic code, and the United States government knew that Japan wished to end the war with China in order to be free to attack the British, French, and Dutch possessions in South-east Asia. The United States, therefore, increased its flow of aid to the Chinese Nationalists, in the hope that revived resistance would force the Japanese to postpone their attack. President Roosevelt also banned exports of oil to Japan, and Britain and Holland followed suit.

Deprived of essential oil supplies, two grim choices presented themselves to the Japanese government. The first was to surrender to American pressure by ending the war with China, and casting aside its ambitions for empire and supremacy in South-east Asia. The second was to seize the whole of South-east Asia, and obtain access to its vast wealth in oil, raw materials and foodstuffs, before Japan's stocks of oil ran out in six months' time. The first choice was totally unacceptable. Japan therefore attacked the American fleet at Pearl Harbour on 7 December 1941, for by destroying America's naval power in the Pacific Ocean Japan hoped to win undisputed control of South-east Asia.

This was achieved with brilliant success, but Japan was doomed to defeat. Eventually overwhelmed by the military power of the United States, Japan lost all its overseas possessions less than four years later, at the end of the Second World War. Peace did not come to China itself, however, until the communists achieved victory over Chiang Kai-shek's Nationalist armies in 1949.

Soon after the Civil War ended in 1865 the United States entered a period of phenomenal economic growth. In 1869 the Pacific and Atlantic oceans were linked by railroad when the Union Pacific and Central Pacific lines met at Promontory Point, in Utah. The Frontier, which marked the steady advance of population westward, finally disappeared after the Apache rebellion ended in 1886 and the Indians were compelled to live in reservations. Montana, North and South Dakota, and Washington joined the Union in 1889, Idaho and Wyoming in 1890, and Utah in 1896. Meanwhile the flow of immigrants from Europe provided an abundant labour force and swelled the population of the towns. Output of industry and agriculture, aided by new machinery, soared, and the country's wealth grew very rapidly, so that by the turn of the century the United States had become one of the world's leading industrial nations. Confident of their future prosperity, the American people felt that their country's influence in international affairs should reflect its economic strength. It was in this expansionist mood that the United States joined the ranks of the world powers when it declared war on Spain in April 1898.

The Spanish American War, 1898

In 1895 Cuba revolted against Spanish rule. Many Americans, who wanted to see an end to European colonial influence in the Caribbean, sympathised with the Cuban rebels, and relations with the Spanish government deteriorated. In February 1898 the battleship USS *Maine*, on a visit to Cuba, was

28   *The United States of America (showing dates when States joined
the Union)*

mysteriously blown up in Havana harbour, and 260 American sailors were killed. The Spanish government apologised, but refused to grant Cuba its independence, and war broke out between Spain and the United States. Within a few weeks, in one of the briefest wars in modern history, American forces captured Cuba and Puerto Rico, while Commodore Dewey's squadron destroyed the Spanish fleet at Manila, in the Philippines, without losing a single casualty.

By the Treaty of Paris (December 1898) the United States obtained Guam, Puerto Rico, and the Philippines, which Spain was forced to sell for 20 million dollars. Although the Filipinos had no more desire to be ruled by the Americans than by the Spanish, and rebelled against Yankee imperialism, their resistance was soon overcome, and the Philippines became an American possession. In the meantime, in July 1898, Hawaii had been annexed, to become later the site of a great naval base, Pearl Harbour.

Cuba became a virtual protectorate of the United States in 1903, when it allowed the American government to establish naval bases on its territory, and to supervise its internal affairs. Puerto Rico was granted limited self-government in 1900, and its inhabitants became American citizens in 1917.

Latin America

In 1901 the Panama Canal project was revived when the French and British governments were persuaded to surrender their treaty rights in it. American businessmen in the eastern seaboard states had been campaigning for several years for a canal link between the Pacific and Atlantic oceans, which would promote their Far Eastern trade. The American Admiralty, too, greatly influenced by Mahan's book on sea power, was also aware of the strategic value of a canal across the isthmus of Panama, which would enable the Pacific and Atlantic fleets to reinforce each other without the need for a long and arduous voyage around Cape Horn.

When the Colombian government blocked plans for the construction of the canal in 1903, the disappointed Panamanians revolted. The United States gave the rebels unofficial support and encouragement. President Theodore Roosevelt at once recognised the existence of an independent Panama Republic, and American warships prevented the landing of Colombian troops to suppress the rebellion. At the same time the United States purchased from Panama for $10 million the Canal Zone, a strip of territory ten miles wide, through which the canal was to be built. The Panama Canal, which cost $375 million, was opened in August 1914.

Roosevelt's success in persuading the European governments to surrender their interests in Panama was only the first evidence of his determination to make American influence dominant in the Caribbean and throughout the western hemisphere. On several occasions he invoked and extended the Monroe Doctrine. First announced by President Monroe in 1823, this doctrine declared that the United States would continue to recognise existing European colonies in the New World, but would regard any attempt to enlarge European influence as a sufficient cause for war.

Roosevelt argued that the United States had a moral duty to ensure that the Latin American countries gave no cause for foreign powers to intervene in their affairs. The United States, therefore, had to assume responsibility for the maintenance of stable, financially sound governments in Latin America.

Thus in 1902, when Venezuela was blockaded by Germany, Britain and Italy in an effort to force the Venezuelan government to redeem its debts, Roosevelt not only compelled Venezuela to accept arbitration by the International Court of Justice at The Hague, but also obtained the agreement of the three powers to accept the verdict. The American government also intervened in Dominica, where it assumed control of that country's finances so that foreign creditors would be paid.

Under Roosevelt's successor, William Howard Taft (1909–13), there was a deliberate attempt by American bankers to replace

Europeans as the creditors of the South American countries. 'Dollar diplomacy', however, as it was called, aroused much resentment in Latin America, where hitherto the United States had been regarded as a protector against the European powers. It also involved the United States in a civil war in Nicaragua, where a reactionary government was kept in office. By 1915 Haiti, the Dominican Republic, Cuba, Nicaragua and Panama were American protectorates, while during the civil war in Mexico (1911–17) American marines landed at Vera Cruz to protect United States interests.

Roosevelt's attitude towards Far Eastern and European affairs

The United States wished to protect its growing Far Eastern trade and in 1899 John Hay, the American Secretary of State, declared his country's support of the 'Open Door' policy towards China. Roosevelt, however, realised that American policy depended upon British naval power, especially after the formation of the Anglo-Japanese alliance in 1902, and he was only prepared to use diplomatic influence in maintaining China's integrity.

When the Russo-Japanese War broke out in 1904 America's sympathies lay with Japan, for Russia was regarded as the greater threat to China. But Japan's runaway victory caused anxiety lest Japan should be tempted to exploit its military supremacy in the Far East by extending its hold on the Chinese mainland. Roosevelt therefore offered to mediate in a settlement which would guarantee Japan's special interests in China, and at the same time create a balance of power in the Far East by maintaining Russia's foothold in Asia. The United States encouraged Japan to agree moderate terms with Russia. (For details of the Treaty of Portsmouth (1905), see Chapter 1).

Constructing the Panama Canal: dredgers at work in the Culebra Cut 1913. Apart from diseases such as malaria and yellow fever, one of the major problems was the removal of millions of tons of rock and earth

Between 1906 and 1908 California's anti-immigration laws caused much Japanese resentment. Roosevelt was conciliatory, but in 1908, in order to impress Japan with America's naval strength, he despatched the Pacific fleet on a world tour. This had the desired effect on Japanese policy, and in 1908 the American and Japanese governments agreed to respect each other's possessions and to guarantee the Open Door policy. Roosevelt's action was yet another illustration of his favourite maxim, 'Speak softly and carry a big stick'.

Roosevelt was equally concerned about maintaining a balance of power in Europe, for he realised that the domination of Europe by Germany would bring dangers for the United States. In 1906, at the Algeciras Conference, convened to resolve the first Moroccan crisis, the United States supported Britain and France. Nevertheless, in spite of Roosevelt's success in ensuring that the other great powers gave full recognition to America's views on world problems, he failed to persuade the American people to abandon isolationism.

The United States and the First World War

When war broke out in Europe President Wilson, a Democrat, announced his determination to keep America out of it. This accurately reflected the mood of the American people, many of whom were recent immigrants from Central European countries. The vast majority of the population had no desire to become involved in Europe's troubles, and wanted to make the great American dream of prosperity a reality. Since the United States was neutral, American businessmen were able to supply goods and war materials to the belligerents on a 'fetch and carry' basis, and industry boomed.

America's chief customer was Britain, since Germany lacked a merchant fleet and the naval strength to maintain direct trade links with the United States. Consequently, Germany resorted to unrestricted submarine warfare in 1915, as a result of which a number of American ships were torpedoed. American opinion was inflamed, and Wilson warned the German government that unless it abandoned unrestricted submarine warfare it risked war with the United States. Wilson also began to prepare America's defences. Haiti and Nicaragua were taken under America's protection. In 1916, in order to avoid the possibility that the Virgin Islands might be obtained by Germany for use as a submarine base, the United States government purchased them from Denmark at a cost of $25 million.

Despite Wilson's pledge to maintain neutrality, which was the basis of his Presidential victory in the 1916 elections, America was at war with Germany in April 1917. German-inspired sabotage in American armaments factories angered public opinion. Superior British propaganda had also convinced many Americans that Austria-Hungary and Germany were to blame for the war. But the chief reasons for the United States' entry into the war were the publication of the Zimmerman Telegram (see Chapter 4) and Germany's resumption of unrestricted submarine warfare in February 1917.

The United States organised for war with speed and efficiency. A National War Labour Board was set up to prevent loss of production through strikes. Agricultural and industrial output were greatly expanded. The railways were taken over by the government, taxes were increased, and men were conscripted into the armed forces. The U-boat menace was quickly overcome with the help of the American navy and the development of the convoy system.

By the beginning of 1918 there were 150,000 American troops in France, under the command of General Pershing, and for the next five months an average of 10,000 landed daily in France. The intervention of the United States was decisive, for it came at a time when Germany had achieved superiority of numbers on the western front. In this sense there is no doubt that it prevented a German victory.

The United States rejects membership of the League

President Wilson led the American delegation at the Paris peace conference. Although he had already compromised his Fourteen Points by allowing American troops to take part in Allied intervention in Soviet Russia, he succeeded in gaining general acceptance of them (see Chapter 5). He was forced to agree that Germany should be made to pay astronomical reparations, but he foiled the other Allied leaders in their plans to dismember Germany in the west, and he made sure that the Covenant of the League was incorporated in all the peace treaties. Wilson returned to America confident that the League would rectify any injustices in the peace settlement.

But by 1920 the Americans had lost much of their idealism, and disenchantment over America's role in Europe's affairs was growing. Wilson's tactical mistake in not taking with him to Paris any prominent Republicans, who might have persuaded the rest of the party to support his concept of the League, now became painfully obvious. A Senate Foreign Relations Committee, packed with Republicans, had already tabled reservations to the Covenant which, if accepted, would have reduced the League's effectiveness. Wilson advised the Democrats not to accept the amended version of the League, in the vain hope that popular support for the League would bring pressure to bear upon Congress. Eventually, in March 1920, the Senate voted 49 to 35 in favour of accepting the Versailles Treaty, but this did not produce the two-thirds majority needed to ratify the treaty. The United States did not join the League, and eighteen months later it signed a separate peace with Germany.

The return to 'normalcy'

The landslide Republican victory in 1920, when Warren Harding became President, signified the American people's wish to return to 'normalcy', which in foreign affairs meant isolationism. This did not, however, prevent the United States from attempting to promote world disarmament. The Washington Naval Conference (1921–2) ended the unhealthy naval rivalry which was developing in the Far East by guaranteeing Japan naval supremacy in the Pacific. At the same time Britain was persuaded to end its alliance with Japan when the great powers agreed to respect the *status quo* in the Far East.

Although isolationism was strengthened by the breakdown of the Geneva talks on further naval disarmament in 1927 – both France and Italy declined to attend, and Britain insisted on its need for a large number of cruisers – the United States persisted in its efforts to promote peaceful world development. In 1928 over sixty countries agreed to avoid war in settling disputes by signing the Kellogg–Briand Pact, a meaningless treaty since future aggressors such as Italy, Germany, Russia and Japan, all subscribed to it. International peace could not be guaranteed by pious talk.

Pan-American politics

The United States claimed the right to intervene in Latin America if its vital interests were threatened, and it exercised this right frequently during the 1920s. With the exception of Mexico, all the Central American republics were protectorates, and American marines did not finally leave Nicaragua until 1932. Until 1927 there was considerable tension between the United States and Mexico, which was regarded by the former as a source of communist propaganda.

In 1923 the United States persuaded the Fifth Pan-American Conference to agree that none of its members would recognise a government set up by a revolution. The Gondra Treaty provided a commission to investigate disputes between South American states, which promised to give six months' notice of any declaration of war. This would provide a 'cooling off' period, during which conciliation could take place.

The 'Good Neighbour' policy

By 1928 Latin American resentment against the political and economic influence of the United States in their affairs was so strong that it galvanised the American government into a determined effort to improve its relations with the twenty Latin American republics. The Seventh Pan-American Conference at Montevideo declared that no state had the right to intervene in the internal affairs of another. Although Franklin Roosevelt, who became President in 1933, interpreted this to mean armed intervention, he adopted a conciliatory policy towards the Latin American countries, which became known as the 'Good Neighbour' policy.

In 1934 Roosevelt cancelled the Platt Amendment, which had given the United States special rights in Cuba. After 1934 more liberal trade agreements were signed with eleven Latin American states, which had been badly hit by the Depression. In 1936 Roosevelt proposed that all the American countries should consult each other if their peace was threatened. Administrative machinery for implementing this agreement was set up at the Lima Conference in 1938. Pan-American cooperation was strengthened further by the outbreak of the Second World War, when the Latin American states declared their intention to stay neutral.

The Neutrality Acts

Throughout the 1930s Congress was strongly isolationist. When Italy attacked Abyssinia in 1935 Congress passed the first of a series of Neutrality Acts. Their intention was to prevent the United States becoming involved in any future war by forbidding the export of armaments, or the advance of loans, to any country at war.

Roosevelt was concerned that the Neutrality Acts made no distinction between aggressor states and the victims of aggression, but he could not persuade Congress to alter its policy. In October 1937 his proposal that aggressor states should be placed in quarantine, when other countries would refuse to trade with them, had no response. When the Japanese, who had invaded northern China, sank the American gunboat *Panay* in the Yangtze river in December 1937, Congress accepted the Japanese government's apology.

Neutrality comes to an end

When the Second World War began in September 1939 Roosevelt, in one of his 'fireside chats', promised Americans that 'this country will remain neutral'. Equally significantly, he added, 'but I cannot ask that every American remain neutral in thought as well'. America was gradually turning away from isolationism. In November 1939 Roosevelt was able to force Congress to accept an amendment to its Neutrality legislation to enable countries at war to purchase American munitions on a 'cash and carry' basis. In practice this meant Britain and France. On the pretext of strengthening national security he traded fifty American destroyers to Britain in return for bases in the western hemisphere. Finally, in March 1941, the Lend-Lease scheme was introduced, whereby the United States would 'lend' Britain vast quantities of munitions.

Despite these breaches of strict neutrality, most Americans were still determined to keep out of the war if possible. War was forced upon the United States when Japan attacked the American Pacific Fleet at Pearl Harbour in December 1941. Congress declared war on Japan, though not on Germany. Roosevelt's dilemma was solved when Germany came to the support of its ally three days later and declared war on the United States.

In 1929 every industrial country plunged into the worst trade depression ever experienced. Ten years later economic recovery was still far from complete. The forces of stagnation remained stronger than those of long-term expansion. To a large extent it seemed that only selfish remedies, such as individual governments protecting their national economies at the expense of their neighbours' recovery, and particularly the drive towards rearmament, were effective. Economic nationalism, the growth of militarism, and the political upheavals which occurred as a result of the trade recession were the tragic pathways which led to the Second World War.

The causes of the World Depression were complex and deep-rooted. Its origins may be traced back to the economic difficulties created by the First World War. The industrial countries of Europe, forced to concentrate upon waging war, lost their supremacy in world markets. Many of their best pre-war customers, deprived of the manufactured goods they wanted, either turned to other sources of supply, notably to the United States of America and Japan, or developed their own manufacturing industries. This is clearly shown by the 10 per cent decline in Europe's share of increased world trade in the mid-1920s.

The pre-1914 economic structure of Central Europe was destroyed by the peace settlements which followed the military collapse of the three great continental empires. New states were created, and old states altered, in 1919. The new states erected tariffs to secure much-needed revenues, as well as to encourage the growth of their industries. The Danube valley, which had long been a vitally important trade route, became a region of tariff barriers. With the exception of Czechoslovakia, none of the Succession States which emerged from the ruins of the Habsburg Empire had balanced economies. There is a good deal of truth in the accusation that the peacemakers had little understanding of the economic consequences of the settlement they made.

There were other economic weaknesses of a permanent, or semi-permanent, nature. Germany was deprived of several vitally important industrial regions, and was saddled with huge debts. She could no longer stimulate the economies of her neighbours in the way that she had done before the war. The foundations of Austria's economic survival were shaky. Bolshevik Russia was isolated, and involved in a civil war until 1922. Britain had run down her overseas investments, and was too reliant on certain basic industries, such as coal, iron and steel, textiles, and engineering, in which there was severe competition in overseas markets.

Nearly all the countries involved in the war had accumulated huge debts. The only exceptions were the Soviet Union, which cancelled the foreign debts incurred by the Tsarist governments, and the United States. During the war the Allies borrowed seven billion dollars from the United States for the purchase of war materials, while Congress authorised a further three billion dollars' worth of aid for the post-war reconstruction of Europe.

The debtor nations found it very difficult to repay the money they had borrowed, and they therefore became very dependent on the United States. Europe's gold and dollar reserves had fallen during the war. Large amounts of gold had been shipped to the United States in exchange for munitions and raw materials. American industry thrived on the wartime orders it received and, after the war, protected by tariffs, experienced the unprecedented boom conditions known as the 'Roaring Twenties'. Far from needing to import manufactures from the debtor nations, thereby enabling them to earn dollars with which they could begin to

manufactures in lieu of cash, for this would create unemployment in their own countries, and without large-scale exports Germany could not pay reparations.

Moreover, reparations, which were intended to cripple Germany, had harmful effects

A symbol of America's prosperity and way of life: Model T Fords ('Tin Lizzies'), parked in the main street of Henderson, Texas, in 1927

repay their debts, American businessmen were only too keen to develop fresh markets in Europe for their mass-produced goods.

The problem of war debts was closely linked with reparations. In Britain and France, America's chief debtors, there was strong feeling that their indebtedness was due entirely to the war, for which they blamed Germany. They were willing to repay their debts out of the reparations they received from Germany. They were not willing, however, to accept

on other countries, for their prosperity largely depended upon that of Germany. British suggestions that war debts and reparations should be cancelled or reduced were turned down by the French, who feared Germany's recovery, and by the Americans, who argued that war debts and reparations were separate issues, and that the European governments should honour their debts. The attitudes of France and the United States were understandable, but unhelpful. The dilemma was resolved by American loans to Germany, and by the restructuring of reparations payments by the Dawes Plan in 1924. Europe's dependence upon the United States was dangerous. If the American economy slumped, there was no way European prosperity could be maintained.

Despite the relative prosperity of the period 1926–8, the first signs of a trade recession had already appeared with the falling world prices of foodstuffs and raw materials. With the post-war recovery of European farming, North American grain exports were no longer in such demand, and soon the prairie grain elevators were filled to overflowing. World grain stocks more than doubled in the period 1925–9. There were also drastic falls in the prices of other primary products, such as coffee, cocoa, sugar, rubber, and wool.

In the short term the industrialised countries benefited. Low prices for raw materials meant a reduction in manufacturing costs. With food plentiful and cheap, the pressure for higher wages was eased. In the longer term, however, low prices meant low demand from the primary producing countries for manufactured goods, since their low export prices meant they they lacked the income to make purchases from the industrial nations. The result was a shrinkage in the volume of world trade.

The effects of this process were first felt in the United States, which accounted for over 40 per cent of the world's output of manufactured goods. Factories cannot easily stockpile their products, if only because their price would be reduced when they were eventually released on to the market. Interest payments on loans taken out when industry was booming had to be met, and shareholders expected dividends. Both could only be earned from sales.

At first businessmen cut prices in order to gain a competitive advantage, but their rivals quickly followed suit. Lower prices meant smaller profits, which in turn meant that less money was available for wages, dividends, and loan repayments. It was this sudden realisation that caused the collapse in prices on the Wall Street Stock Exchange.

The Wall Street Crash

In the boom of the mid-1920s it seemed that the Americans had discovered the secret of perpetual prosperity. With mass production of consumer goods such as cars, radios, refrigerators, and washing machines, and easy hire purchase terms readily available, American industry flourished as never before. As firms' profits rose, so did share prices on the Stock Exchange. Between December 1928 and September 1929 share prices doubled.

Much of the money invested in the Stock Exchange had been borrowed in the hope of making a quick profit. In October 1929 there came an inevitable reaction when the financial institutions such as banks, insurance companies, and trusts, realised that share prices were too high. On 24 October, known as 'Black Thursday' in the history of the Wall Street Stock Exchange, panic selling developed as the rush to buy shares became a rush to sell them. In one week the value of American shares and securities dropped $40,000 million.

Many thousands of Americans who had brought shares when prices were high, or who had failed to sell in time, were ruined. Their inability to meet their hire purchase and mortgage commitments in turn affected banks and other credit institutions, whose loans could not be repaid. In the period 1930–32, 5,000 banks in America collapsed. At the same time the less efficient companies were going bankrupt, while the stronger companies survived only by reducing their work forces. By 1932 industrial production in the United States was only half that of 1929, and 13 million workers were unemployed.

The New Deal

President Hoover failed to convince the American people that the Republican Party could solve the nation's economic problems, and in 1932 Franklin D. Roosevelt became President. In his election campaign Roosevelt promised a 'New Deal' for the people, in which

Demonstration of unemployed, demanding the right to work, 1934

the government would take strong action to restore prosperity.

Roosevelt's first aim was to restore confidence. In his Presidential Address he declared: 'The only thing we have to fear is fear itself'. First, Roosevelt corrected the weaknesses in the banking system. An Emergency Banking Act gave the government powers to close banks and to allow only those in sound financial condition to re-open. Various measures were taken to reduce unemployment and create jobs, thereby increasing people's spending power, and 'setting the wheels of industry in motion again'.

As a result of an Agricultural Adjustment Act farmers were paid subsidies in order to produce less of certain basic crops in order to reduce surpluses. Eventually the prices of farm products began to rise, although it was not until 1941 that the farmers' incomes reached the 1929 levels. Farmers and businessmen were also helped to obtain credit, and mortgages on their property. A National Industrial Recovery Act fixed minimum wages and maximum hours of work. Trade unions were protected by the Wagner Act, and federal aid was made available to the elderly, handicapped, and unemployed. Over $3,000 million were spent on public works such as roads, slum clearance, and conservation.

The most spectacular public works project was the creation of the Tennessee Valley Authority to develop the industry and agriculture of seven states. Huge dams such as the Hoover and Fort Peck Dams were constructed to prevent the Mississippi and its tributary rivers from flooding the surrounding countryside, and to harness their energy to generate cheap electrical power on which the prosperity of the Tennessee Valley is based.

World-wide consequences of the Depression

Meanwhile, the effects of the Wall Street Crash had been felt in most parts of the world, and particularly in Europe, which depended upon American loans for its prosperity. As world trade slumped, so American banks called in the loans they had made to European countries, and severely restricted future lending. Europe was therefore starved of the cash which might have made economic recovery easier to achieve.

In May 1931 Austria's largest bank, the Kreditanstalt of Vienna, collapsed. The repercussions were immediately felt in Germany, where foreign capital was rapidly withdrawn, bringing the German economy to a state of virtual collapse. President Hoover suggested that all countries should postpone payment of their debts to one another for one year, in the hope that this would assist the recovery of world trade.

Nevertheless, world trade continued to shrink. Demand for goods fell as governments did their best to check imports in order to help their own ailing economies. Many countries devalued their currencies in order to make their exports cheaper. These policies of 'economic nationalism', by which individual countries tried to shield themselves against the worst effects of the Depression, only harmed the economies of their neighbours, who retaliated in a similar fashion. Ultimately the world-wide decline in purchasing power resulted in over 30 million workers becoming unemployed.

The Depression was a severe test for the democracies, where great bitterness was caused by the failure of governments to protect the people from circumstances over which they had no control. The contrast between rich and poor created social tensions and political instability, in which some governments based on rule with the consent of the people became casualties.

In Germany a period of government by emergency decrees was succeeded by Hitler's dictatorship. The success of fascism in a second great power (Italy being the first in 1922) encouraged the growth of fascist movements elsewhere. In Britain, where there were 3 million unemployed during the depth of the Depression, Oswald Mosley's fascist party received some popular support. In Belgium the Rexists, founded by Leon Degrelle, were supported by such diverse groups as land-owners, nationalists, and unemployed, who hoped that a strong government would impose solutions to the country's economic problems. In France a Popular Front was established to combat the growth of fascism, while in Spain political extremism led to the outbreak of civil war in 1936.

Spain's defeat by the United States in the war of 1898 was a bitter blow to national pride. The loss of nearly all its colonies, at a time when other European countries were adding to their overseas possessions, stripped Spain of the last relics of its former greatness. More importantly, defeat and disillusion exposed the Spanish government and society to severe criticism.

Three institutions occupied a privileged position in Spain. These were the monarchy, the army, and the Catholic Church. Originally they had all played their parts in uniting the country, but now they aroused envy and hostility.

In theory Spain was a democracy, but the parliament *(Cortes)* was unrepresentative of the people. Alfonso XIII, who was born after his father died in 1885, succeeded in 1902 at the age of sixteen. He cherished dreams of restoring the monarchy's power by abolishing the parliamentary constitution. Alfonso XIII ruled Spain until he abdicated in 1931.

The monarch's influence had been weakened by the army's role in Spanish politics. By tradition the army regarded itself as the protector of law and order, and on several occasions during the nineteenth century it had intervened in order to force its own choice of government upon the Spanish people. Its officers were recruited from the wealthy sections of the community, for whom a military career offered the attraction of social prestige.

The Catholic Church, like the monarchy and the army, was closely associated with the upper classes. Its conservative attitude and great wealth alienated it from the mass of the people. Resentment of the power of the Church was an important factor in the events leading up to the civil war.

Revolutionary forces

These institutions were threatened by anarchism and socialism, revolutionary movements which had developed during the latter part of the nineteenth century. Anarchism aimed to abolish the central government, and replace it by a system of self-governing groups, or corporations, representing townships, trades, or professions. In 1911 anarchists formed a workers' union, or *Confederacion Nacional de Trabajo* (CNT), which had a membership of half a million by 1918. By its very nature anarchism provoked stern government repression, and the anarchists resorted to terrorism, such as bombings and assassinations of leading politicians.

The socialist movement sought power by constitutional methods. In 1888 it founded a socialist trade union, the *Union General de Trabajo* (UGT), which by 1914 had managed to secure the election of several socialist deputies to the Cortes. After the First World War the socialist party split. Inspired by the success of the Bolsheviks in Russia, an extreme group broke away to form the Spanish Communist party in 1920. It joined the Communist International in 1922, but the party's influence was small until the outbreak of the civil war.

As discontent with falling wages and rising unemployment led to revolutionary strikes, the employers replied by forming their own unions of workers to fight the socialist unions. In 1909 a week's rioting in Barcelona was sparked off by a government call-up of troops to protect Spanish coastal possessions in Morocco. In 1919 rival unions employed professional gunmen *(pistoleros)* to eliminate leading opponents in an outburst of gang warfare.

The dictatorship of Primo de Rivera

Although the police and army crushed revolutionary socialism, the political violence and unrest of the period 1909–23 aroused a demand for strong government. Alfonso, who had supported his generals' plans for the military conquest of Morocco, was blamed for the massacre of Spanish troops at Anual in 1921. Two years later the army, convinced that the government had outlived its usefulness, forced Alfonso to appoint General Primo de Rivera as his chief minister.

Rivera was a great admirer of Mussolini, who had seized power after the March on Rome in 1922. A patriot, Rivera believed that his mission was to rescue Spain from its troubles, and make it strong and prosperous. His Civil Directory combined military-style government with a real concern for the welfare of the working classes. He suppressed the CNT, but introduced a programme of public works to reduce unemployment. In Morocco the Spanish army cooperated with the French in pacifying the protectorate. Helped by the general improvement in world trade during the mid-1920s, Spain enjoyed a period of relative prosperity.

After 1929 Rivera rapidly lost support. He failed to solve Spain's economic problems, which worsened after the onset of the world trade recession. His government's intervention in business affairs angered the industrialists. The Catalan nationalists opposed him because he had refused to grant them regional self-government, after having appeared sympathetic to their grievances. Alfonso, who feared that growing dissatisfaction with Rivera's policies would bring down the monarchy, dismissed him in January 1930, and replaced him with General Berenguer.

The Spanish Republic

Berenguer was even less successful than Rivera. In February 1931 he, too, was dismissed, and Alfonso restored the constitution. The elections to a new assembly in April, however, turned into an unofficial referendum on the monarchy, in which the republicans scored overwhelming successes. Rather than face the prospect of civil war, Alfonso abdicated. The Spanish Republic was proclaimed on 14 April.

The new constitution divided the country by its attack upon property and the Catholic Church. The state was given powers to nationalise the great landed estates. The Jesuit order was banned, and its members were commanded to leave the country. Divorce was made easier. Church schools were to be abolished. The links between Church and State were broken, and the Church was allowed to own only as much property as would enable it to fulfil its religious functions.

Support for the Church was rallied by Bishop Segura, who asked Catholics not to stand by idly while their religion was attacked. This infuriated the anti-clericals, and throughout Spain many churches were set on fire. The attacks upon Church property led Gil Robles to form a new political party, *Accion Popular*, whose aim was to defend the privileges of the Church and the wealthy classes. In the 1933 elections it won 110 seats in the Cortes.

In the meantime Azana's republican government aroused much opposition. Although it pleased the Catalans and the Basques by granting them limited self-government, its attempt to reduce the power of the army made it unpopular with the generals. One of them, General Sanjurjo, led a revolt against the government. It failed, but it was an ominous sign for the future.

Plans to redistribute the great landed estates in southern Spain made slow progress, partly because the government lacked sufficient funds to provide compensation for the owners, and partly because the socialists were unable to decide whether the lands should be allocated to individuals or to collective farms. Working-class discontent erupted in violent strikes. In January 1933 an uprising in Barcelona was ruthlessly crushed by government forces.

In the November 1933 elections the right-wing parties won a majority of seats. Church property was restored, and the Church schools allowed to continue. A communist revolt in the Asturias in October 1934 was overcome by troops imported from Morocco. The left-wing parties now tried to set aside their difficulties and to cooperate by presenting a united front against their opponents. In February 1936 the Popular Front won a narrow victory at the polls.

Moderation was now fast disappearing from Spanish political life. Largo Caballero, the socialist leader, urged revolution. José Primo de Rivera, son of the former dictator, formed an extreme nationalist organisation, the *Falange*, which fought communists in street battles in the major towns and cities. The Falange appealed to the army to intervene in order to prevent the establishment of a communist dictatorship.

The Civil War

The Civil War began on 17 July 1936, when three generals, Mola, Goded, and Franco, led a mutiny of the army in Spanish Morocco against the government. The revolt quickly spread to the mainland garrisons, and within a few days the rebels controlled one-third of Spain, chiefly in the more backward southern and western parts of the country. Three months later the rebels proclaimed a Government of National Defence, with Francisco Franco (1892–1976) as Head *(Caudillo)* of the Spanish state.

Franco's supporters were the army, the monarchists, landowners, and devout Catholics. They called themselves Nationalists. Their opponents, the Republicans, had the support of the Catalans and Basques, who wished to preserve their newly won local independence, and the left-wing parties, the anarchists, communists, and socialists. Republican strength was concentrated in the industrial area bounded by Madrid, Barcelona, and Valencia.

The Nationalists were supported by the two fascist powers, Italy and Germany. Mussolini sent thousands of troops, disguised as volunteers. Hitler followed Mussolini's lead by sending bombers and aircrews (the famous Condor

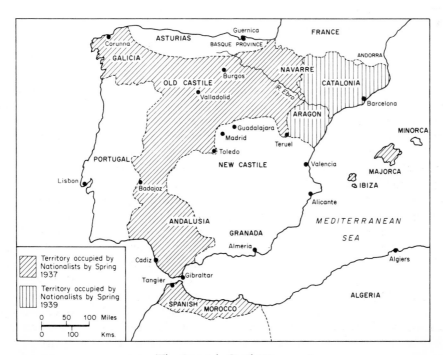

29   *The Spanish Civil War, 1936–9*

Legion), tanks, and artillery. The Republicans were assisted by the Soviet Union and the International Brigades. Stalin sent munitions, technical advisers, and political commissars. Since Russian aid was sent directly to the communists, their importance became much greater than their pre-war numbers warranted. The Comintern organised the International Brigades, bands of volunteers of various nationalities, who arrived in November 1936, just in time to defend Madrid from Franco's onslaught.

In France and Britain public opinion was deeply divided over the Spanish Civil War. In France the Popular Front government dared not openly support the Republicans lest it provoke a bitter class struggle. The British government urged other countries to adopt a policy of non-intervention. After Italian submarines had sunk a number of merchant ships, a conference of great powers met at the Swiss resort of Nyon in July 1937. They agreed that unidentified submarines in Spanish waters should be attacked on sight, and

assistance to the two sides in the Spanish Civil War should be restricted. Although submarine activity abruptly ceased, fascist aid to the Nationalists only ended when Franco's victory was assured in March 1939.

In the summer of 1938 Stalin abandoned his policy of intervention, realising that neither the British, nor the French, government was willing to cooperate. Stalin's disillusion with their failure to support the idea of collective security was increased by Britain and France's short-sighted attempt to pacify Hitler by handing over the Sudetenland to Germany in October 1938, thereby fatally weakening Czechoslovakia (see Chapter 20).

The withdrawal of Soviet aid to the Republicans enabled the Nationalists to push forward to victory. In December 1938 Franco's forces reached the Mediterranean Sea north of Valencia. In January 1939 Barcelona was captured. Madrid and Valencia held out until March, though the Republican cause was hopeless. With their fall Republican resistance finally came to an end.

Republicans, taken prisoner on the Somosierra front, September 1936

Bomb damage in Madrid caused by a Nationalist air raid: a foretaste of the destruction many other towns and cities throughout Europe were to suffer within the next few years

The Civil War in perspective

In a narrow sense the Spanish Civil War was a tragic class struggle, in which both sides committed terrible atrocities on civilians and prisoners. Probably 600,000 Spaniards lost their lives during the three years of fighting. In a broader context the Civil War was an unofficial dress rehearsal for the Second World War. Spain was a vast training area for the fascist armed forces. Relays of German aircrews gained valuable wartime experience at little risk to themselves. The destruction of Guernica in April 1937 was a clinical exercise in terrorising an urban population by an aerial bombardment.

Spain was a battleground for the competing ideologies of the democratic and fascist states, in which the latter showed much greater unity of purpose. Throughout the period of the Spanish Civil War the fascist leaders kept the initiative in Europe. Although Hitler and Mussolini failed to make Franco their ally, their aggressive policies in Spain, Abyssinia, the Rhineland, Austria, and Czechoslovakia finally led to war. Soon after the fighting ceased in Spain, most of Europe became embroiled in a far greater and more deadly conflict when the Second World War broke out.

Within eight years of becoming Chancellor, Hitler destroyed the Versailles Settlement and conquered much of Europe. He ignored the League of Nations, which by 1936 was little more than a feeble association of Britain and France and, by skilful diplomacy, out-manoeuvred his opponents, who simply wished to preserve peace. The western democracies were distracted by the problems of the World Depression, and by fascist successes in China, Abyssinia and Spain. Their fear and suspicion of the Soviet Union prevented any effective cooperation between the countries of Eastern and Western Europe, which were equally threatened by German militarism. At the same time the United States was determined to avoid any entanglement in Europe's affairs. It is against this background of international problems and disagreements that Hitler's diplomatic and military achievements during the period 1933–9 must be assessed.

German rearmament

During its brief existence the Weimar Republic laid the foundations of a rearmed Germany. The Treaty of Rapallo (1922) between Germany and the Soviet Union made arrangements for secret military cooperation between the two countries. The Locarno treaties, and Britain's desire to conciliate Germany, further weakened the restrictions imposed upon Germany by the Versailles Treaty. In 1930 allied troops evacuated the Rhineland, five years ahead of schedule.

Hitler was allowed to disregard the disarmament clauses of the Versailles Treaty,

upon which France's security rested. He began by appealing to the great powers to disarm. When they did not do so, he withdrew from the Disarmament Conference (1932–4) and from the League of Nations in October 1933, declaring that Germany had the moral right to rearm when the other nations refused to disarm.

Hitler skilfully allayed the fears of Germany's neighbours by making a Non-Aggression Pact with Poland in January 1934. The German government promised to resolve any disputes between the two countries by peaceful negotiation, and it renounced the use of force for a period of ten years. Poland, which placed little value on its alliance with France, welcomed the idea of friendship with Germany, which seemed to offer greater security against its powerful neighbour, Soviet Russia.

In March 1935 Hitler announced his intention of creating an army of 550,000 men by introducing conscription. He declared that an airforce already existed. The British, French, and Italian governments disapproved but took no effective action. Representatives of the three countries merely met at Stresa, where they promised to collaborate with each other in order to preserve the peace of Europe.

The collapse of the Stresa Front

The Stresa Front against German militarism was fragile and short-lived. In June 1935 the British government, which sympathised with Germany's right to rearm at a time when France maintained a large army, concluded a naval agreement with Germany. The latter was permitted to build up to 35 per cent of

Britain's surface warships, and 100 per cent of its submarine strength. Sir Samuel Hoare, the British Foreign Secretary, who negotiated the settlement with Ribbentrop, hoped to avoid a naval race between the two countries by conciliating Germany at the outset.

Britain's action was foolhardy. The French government felt it had been betrayed, and Italy was threatened by the growth of German naval power which Britain had sanctioned without consulting either of her partners. The Stresa Front was destroyed almost at its birth.

The remilitarisation of the Rhineland

In March 1936, while Britain and France were preoccupied with Italy's attack on Abyssinia, Hitler ordered a detachment of troops to enter the Rhineland, a demilitarised zone established by the Versailles Treaty and confirmed by the Locarno treaties. Hitler justified his action by claiming that the recently ratified Franco-Russian alliance threatened Germany's security and broke the spirit of the Locarno settlement.

Once again the British and French governments offered no resistance. They were more concerned with reaching a settlement with Italy over Abyssinia. Having annoyed Mussolini by imposing economic sanctions on Italy, they still hoped to retain his friendship. Nevertheless, they had lost an ally against Hitler. The British reaction to the remilitarisation of the Rhineland may be summed up in the saying, 'After all, they [the Germans] are only walking into their own back garden'.

A military parade, announcing the removal of the restrictions placed by the Allies on the German Army

France dared not act against Germany without Britain's support.

The Versailles Treaty regarded *any* violation of the demilitarisation clauses as a 'hostile act', to be automatically opposed by the guaranteeing powers, Britain and Italy. The Locarno treaties, however, made a distinction between flagrant and non-flagrant violation.

Secondly, Germany rapidly constructed powerful fortifications, the Siegfried Line, in the Rhineland, which transformed the military situation in Western Europe. Germany no longer lay open to invasion by France, which more than ever relied upon the false hope that the Maginot Line offered security against a German attack.

A detachment of German troops crossing the bridge at Mainz into the Rhineland

Britain was only committed to using military force in the event of flagrant violation, i.e. if war was a likely consequence. Since this was clearly not the case, the German troops were not compelled to withdraw, although negotiations on the subject continued for several months.

The remilitarisation of the Rhineland had far-reaching consequences. In conjunction with the League's failure to halt Italian aggression in East Africa, it proved beyond all doubt the League's inability to protect its members.

The strengthening of Germany's western frontier made French intervention against Germany even less likely than it had been in the past. This fact was not lost upon Germany's neighbours. Belgium obtained permission to opt out of the Locarno agreements, and returned to complete neutrality. Holland, Luxemburg, and the Scandinavian countries soon followed suit. Rumania anxiously sought more friendly relations with Germany, and Yugoslavia tried to clear up its differences with Hungary and Italy. But it was Austria and

Czechoslovakia that were most keenly affected by the transformation of Germany's military power. After 1936, Hitler was relatively free to turn his attention to securing his territorial objectives in Eastern Europe.

The enlargement of Hitler's Germany

By accomplishing the difficult task of rearming Germany without incurring the wrath of those countries which had most to lose from it, Hitler made possible the achievement of his other objectives in foreign policy. These were the recovery of German lands lost by the Versailles Treaty, and *Lebensraum* – 'living space' – in Eastern Europe. In these territories the Slav inhabitants would either be displaced by German settlers or forced to work for the benefit of Greater Germany. With the vast agricultural and industrial resources of Eastern Europe under its control, Germany would dominate the continent, and revenge for the humiliation of Versailles would be complete.

The Saar plebiscite, 1935

One objective had already been achieved. In 1919 the French had been authorised to occupy the Saar for the purpose of exploiting its coal resources for fifteen years, after which the future of the province would be decided by a plebiscite. In January 1935 the Saarlanders voted by an overwhelming majority for reunion with Germany. This result was hailed by the Nazis as a great diplomatic victory.

The Rome–Berlin Axis and the Anti-Comintern Pact

Although economic sanctions against Italy ceased in July 1936, the Abyssinian crisis had done much to align Italy with Germany. Mussolini was grateful for Germany's diplomatic support, and in October 1936 the two countries were joined in an alliance which became known as the Rome–Berlin Axis. Relations between the two fascist states became even closer as a result of their intervention in the Spanish Civil War.

In November 1936 Germany and Japan signed the Anti-Comintern Pact, when the two countries agreed to cooperate against communism. In the following year Hitler's diplomatic position was further strengthened when Italy joined the Anti-Comintern Pact in November and resigned from the League in December. Mussolini virtually abandoned his former allies, Britain and France.

Mussolini soon became the subordinate partner in the Rome–Berlin Axis, as Italy was weakened by the Abyssinian War and by its intervention in Spain. Mussolini, therefore, could hardly afford to antagonise his powerful ally, even if he wished to do so. This was to have fateful consequences so far as Austria was concerned. *Anschluss* (the union of Austria with Germany) was Hitler's next objective, and after the developments of 1936–7 the least he could expect was Mussolini's unenthusiastic acceptance of German policy.

The Anschluss, 1938

In July 1934 Hitler had miscalculated when he attempted to incorporate Austria into Germany following the murder of the Austrian Chancellor, Dollfuss, by Nazi assassins. Mussolini, who had no desire to see Germany's frontiers expand southwards, acted as the champion of Austria's independence. Italian troops were sent to the Brenner Pass, ready to block any German attempt to invade Austria. Hitler hurriedly disclaimed any intention to annex the country. Even though Germany had not yet rearmed, it is perhaps significant that Hitler retreated when opposed by a country prepared to use force in support of the Versailles arrangements.

In July 1936 the Austrian and German governments signed a 'gentleman's agreement' whereby the former promised to base its policies on the fact that Austria was a German state, while Hitler recognised its independence.

This agreement enabled Hitler to exert pressure upon the Austrian government whenever he wished.

In February 1938 Schussnigg, the Austrian Chancellor, was summoned to meet Hitler, who violently criticised him for the alleged ill-treatment of Austrian Nazis by the Austrian government. On Hitler's instructions Schussnigg appointed Seyss-Inquart, an Austrian Nazi, as Minister for the Interior, a strategically important post giving him control of the police.

On his return Schussnigg decided to risk Hitler's displeasure by arranging a plebiscite on the *Anschluss* question. When Hitler learned of the plan, he demanded its cancellation and Schussnigg's resignation. Seyss-Inquart took over as Chancellor, but the Austrian President's refusal to recognise his appointment led to a political crisis. As civil disorder grew, Seyss-Inquart requested German help, and Hitler, having learned that Mussolini would raise no objections, sent German troops over the Austrian frontier on 12 March. On the next day the union of Austria with Germany was proclaimed.

Although *Anschluss* had been strictly prohibited by the Versailles Treaty, it was accepted by Britain and France. Neville Chamberlain, the British Prime Minister, felt it was an application of the principle of national self-determination, although this was to conveniently overlook the fact that the Austrians were only German-speaking. Austria had not been part of Germany since 1867, when it had been deliberately excluded from the Second Reich by Bismarck. The truth of the matter is that neither Britain nor France was prepared to risk a showdown with Hitler over a lost cause, for the Austrians themselves, by a massive vote in favour, seemed to approve the change in their country's status. Hitler himself helped to divert opposition by declaring that his action had prevented the outbreak of civil war in Austria.

The annexation of Austria was a strategic disaster for Czechoslovakia, whose fortress system was now outflanked by German territory. It was obvious that the incorporation of the three million Germans living in the Sudetenland would be Hitler's next target.

The destruction of Czechoslovakia

Hitler detested the Czechs, whose existence as a nation symbolised the hated Versailles Treaty. As a leading member of the Little Entente, a series of defensive treaties signed by Czechoslovakia, Yugoslavia and Rumania in 1920–1 to restrain Germany's expansion eastwards, Czechoslovakia had attracted the special enmity of German nationalists. There can be little doubt that Hitler was determined to destroy the Czech state, whatever the cost.

Although Czechoslovakia was the most industrialised, and powerful, country on Germany's eastern frontier, with a large, well-equipped army of 35 divisions, and a natural defensive barrier in the Sudeten Mountains, it had serious weaknesses, which were soon to prove fatal.

Internally, Czechoslovakia was far from united. The existence of three million Germans violently opposed to Czech rule was a severe problem for the newly founded nation. The activities of a well-organised Nazi party led by Konrad Henlein, who was under Hitler's instructions to stir up disturbances in the Sudetenland, threatened to destroy Czech democracy. Henlein also had the short-sighted but fervent support of Slovaks, Ruthenes and Magyars, none of whom had any love for Czech supremacy. There was a real danger that Czechoslovakia would break up into its component parts under the pressure of their demands for self-government. In addition, both Poland and Hungary coveted Czech territory.

In the spring of 1938 Hitler warned the German army to be ready for war, and he told Henlein that he was determined to solve the Czech problem in the near future. Henlein was instructed to demand concessions which the Czech government would be unwilling to grant, in order to provide Hitler with the excuse he needed for acting against the Czechs.

As the crisis developed, Chamberlain made it clear to the French government that Britain would not become involved in a war against Germany over the Sudeten question. The British and the French governments put pressure on the Czech government to make concessions to Henlein. When these were rejected Lord Runciman flew to Prague, where he warned the Czechs that unless they reached an agreement with Henlein they would be left to their own devices by Britain. The Czechs therefore agreed to all Henlein's demands – only to discover that this was no longer enough.

At the Nazi party rally in Nuremberg on 12 September Hitler violently attacked the Czechs, and Nazi-instigated disorders broke out in the Sudetenland. The Czech government introduced emergency powers to deal with the situation, and outlawed Henlein's party. War seemed very close at hand.

Chamberlain was determined to preserve peace. On 15 September he flew to Germany, and met Hitler at Berchtesgaden. There it was agreed that those parts of the Sudetenland whose population was 50 per cent German-speaking should be transferred to Germany. Under extreme pressure the Czech President, Benes, agreed.

One week later Chamberlain met Hitler at Godesburg, where he was shocked by Hitler's statement that this was not enough. The German leader demanded that all Czech forces must be immediately evacuated from the Sudetenland, so that it could be occupied by German troops. Benes refused.

On 28 September Chamberlain proposed that Hitler, Mussolini, Daladier (the French Prime Minister), and himself should meet to resolve the problem. The Four Power Conference met at Munich the following day. There the four leaders agreed that the whole of the Sudetenland should be handed over to Germany, and that the evacuation of Czech troops from the area should be completed by 10 October. The Czechs were not involved in these discussions.

When Benes was informed of the outcome of the talks he had the stark choice of submission or fighting. If he chose the latter course he could expect no help from Britain or France, nor would any aid be forthcoming from Czechoslovakia's ally, the Soviet Union, which was prepared to act only if France took the initiative. Furthermore, both Poland and Hungary were likely to join in the war, whose probable outcome would have been the partition of Czechoslovakia. Benes therefore agreed to surrender the Sudetenland to Germany. Chamberlain returned to London, where he informed a relieved and joyful public that war had been avoided, and 'peace in our time' secured.

The Czech state now rapidly disintegrated. In October 1938 Poland seized the disputed area of Teschen, and in November, Hungary acquired a strip of territory along its border with Slovakia and Ruthenia. In early 1939 the Slovaks were encouraged by Germany to demand complete independence. When negotiations between the Czechs and the Slovaks broke down, the Slovaks proclaimed their independence. The Ruthenes immediately followed suit.

Czechoslovakia was now on the brink of total collapse. Hacha, the new President, was summoned to Berlin. There he was given the alternatives of requesting a German protectorate over what remained of Czechoslovakia, or a German invasion. Hacha chose to surrender peaceably, so that Germany's seizure of the rump of Czechoslovakia was given the cloak of legality. On 15 March Bohemia and Moravia became a German protectorate, while Hungarian troops occupied Ruthenia. Czechoslovakia no longer existed.

An assessment of the Munich settlement

The fate of Czechoslovakia finally discredited Chamberlain. Like many other people at the time, Chamberlain believed that Germany had been unjustly treated at Versailles. If Hitler's demands for the return of territories inhabited by Germans were granted, and Germany's right to defend itself was granted, then (it was assumed) Germany could be expected to become a satisfied, peaceful member of the European community of nations.

Chamberlain, therefore, was determined to avoid giving Hitler the idea that Britain was organising collective resistance to Germany, which would only make a settlement of Europe's problems more difficult. He was thus willing to negotiate with the Axis powers, and by making concessions to both, to reassure them

jectives and some regard for the sanctity of international agreements. Hitler's ambitions were neither limited nor reasonable. He could not, therefore, be appeased, and Munich was a shameful settlement. The morality of sacrificing another people's freedom for the sake of peace is at least a debatable issue. In the case of the Munich settlement war was merely delayed for six months.

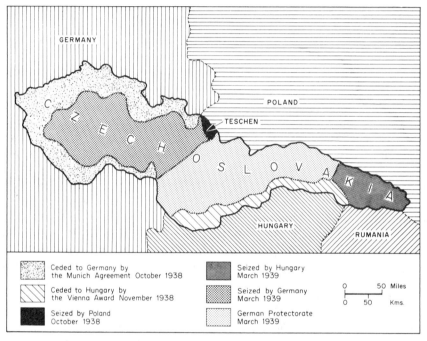

30   *The destruction of Czechoslovakia. After Czechoslovakia had been partitioned, Poland was to be Hitler's next victim*

of Britain's peaceful intentions. This was appeasement in action.

Chamberlain's motives were those of a peace-loving statesman. It is important to realize, too, that they reflected not only the wishes of the great majority of the British people who, like Chamberlain, hated the idea of war, but also the country's state of military preparedness. No government could dare to commit a country to war unless it had the united support of the people, and sufficient armed force to overcome its enemies.

Chamberlain's mistake was in treating Hitler as a reasonable politician, with limited ob-

Poland

After the destruction of Czechoslovakia Hitler's next demands were for Memel and Danzig. In March 1939 Memel was seized from Lithuania, but the problem of Danzig was greater than Hitler anticipated.

Hitler wished to recover Danzig and gain access to East Prussia through the Polish Corridor without making an enemy of Poland. He offered the Poles the prospect of compensation in the Ukraine, and invited Poland to join the Anti-Comintern Pact. The Polish government, unwisely over-confident in the ability of its armed forces to resist German aggression, declined to accept these proposals, fearing that Poland would become a mere satellite of Germany.

Meanwhile the British government introduced peacetime conscription at the end of March 1939. Chamberlain also announced that Britain would come to the aid of Poland if it was attacked by Germany, although the promise was meaningless, since there was no way to help Poland without the support of the Soviet Union or France. Hitler, however, was infuriated. He denounced the Anglo-German naval agreement of 1935 and the Non-Aggression Pact with Poland.

Mussolini was not prepared to stand idly by while Hitler expanded Germany's territory eastwards, and on Good Friday, 7 April, 100,000 Italian troops invaded Albania, which had been a virtual Italian protectorate since 1927. King Zog I fled to Greece, and five days later the Albanian crown was offered to Victor Emmanuel III of Italy. Further aggression by the two dictators seemed likely when Mussolini and Hitler signed the Pact of Steel in May 1939, when they promised to cooperate with each other in promoting the interests of their countries.

Meanwhile, alarmed by the prospect of the whole of Central Europe falling to fascist aggression, Britain and France offered guarantees of support to Rumania, Greece, and Turkey in an effort to strengthen the resolve of the Balkan states to withstand German pressure, and entered into negotiations with the Soviet Union for a defensive alliance.

Britain, however, was not willing to agree to Russia's request that the Baltic states as well as Poland should be guaranteed against both direct and indirect aggression, fearing that this would enable the Soviet Union to occupy the Baltic countries on the pretext of protecting them from German aggression. The negotiations eventually broke down in late August, when Stalin reached an agreement with Hitler! Although Hitler was convinced that Britain's promise to assist Poland was a bluff, he could

make doubly certain of victory in a war with Poland by securing the neutrality of the Soviet Union. This would avoid the danger of Germany having to fight a war on two fronts. Stalin was willing to agree terms, despite Hitler's frequent assertions of his determination to destroy communism. He believed that Britain and France wished to save themselves by encouraging German expansion in Eastern Europe. Russia's willingness to help Czechoslovakia in 1938–9 had been ignored. An agreement over Poland would buy time and territory, while, Stalin believed, involving the Western European countries in a long and costly war.

The Nazi-Soviet Pact was signed by Ribbentrop and Molotov on 24 August 1939. The Soviet Union and Germany each promised neutrality if either became involved in a war. The Baltic states, with the temporary exception of Lithuania, were to be regarded as lying within the Soviet Union's sphere of influence. In the event of a Polish-German war, Poland was to be divided between Germany and the Soviet Union.

Poland was doomed by the Nazi-Soviet Pact, although Mussolini urged Hitler to resolve his quarrel with Poland peaceably, declaring that Italy could not consider entering a war until 1942. Hitler, however, had already set the date for the invasion of Poland, and on 1 September 1939 Germany attacked Poland. Britain and France declared war on Germany on 3 September, the date which is generally accepted as the start of the Second World War.

Yet in a real sense the war had already begun, with Poland its fifth victim, Abyssinia, China, Czechoslovakia, and Albania being the other four. In another sense the war did not become world-wide until Japan attacked the United States at Pearl Harbour in December 1941. The one thing that cannot be debated is that none of the combatants had any inkling of the scale of destruction which was to be unleashed upon mankind in the next six years, nor of the stupendous technological 'revolution that would accompany the war.

INDEX